Lecture Notes
in Business Information Processing 23

T0237863

Klaus Fischer   Jörg P. Müller
James Odell   Arne Jørgen Berre (Eds.)

Agent-Based Technologies and Applications for Enterprise Interoperability

International Workshops
ATOP 2005, Utrecht, The Netherlands, July 25-26, 2005, and
ATOP 2008, Estoril, Portugal, May 12-13, 2008
Revised Selected Papers

 Springer

Volume Editors

Klaus Fischer
DFKI GmbH
Stuhlsatzenhausweg 3, 66123 Saarbrücken, Germany
E-mail: klaus.fischer@dfki.de

Jörg P. Müller
Technische Universität Clausthal, Institut für Informatik
Julius-Albert-Str. 4, 38678 Clausthal-Zellerfeld, Germany
E-mail: joerg.mueller@tu-clausthal.de

James Odell
CSC
3646 W. Huron River Drive, Ann Arbor, MI 48103, USA
E-mail: email@jamesodell.com

Arne Jørgen Berre
SINTEF
Forskningsveien 1, 0314 Oslo, Norway
E-mail: arne.j.berre@sintef.no

Library of Congress Control Number: Applied for

ACM Computing Classification (1998): J.1, H.3.5, I.2.11, D.2.12

ISSN	1865-1348
ISBN-10	3-642-01667-7 Springer Berlin Heidelberg New York
ISBN-13	978-3-642-01667-7 Springer Berlin Heidelberg New York

springer.com

© Springer-Verlag Berlin Heidelberg 2009
Printed in Germany

Typesetting: Camera-ready by author, data conversion by Scientific Publishing Services, Chennai, India
Printed on acid-free paper   SPIN: 12677122   06/3180   5 4 3 2 1 0

Preface

Today's enterprises operate in a dynamic environment that is characterized by global outsourcing, shrinking product life-cycles, and unstable demand. To prosper in this environment, enterprises face a growing need to share information and to collaborate with each other at all levels of the value chain. As organizations are gradually transforming into *networked organizations*, interoperability becomes the main challenge to realize the vision of seamless business interaction across organizational boundaries. Interoperability problems occur at different levels: at the business level (how organizations do business together, what needs to be described and how?), at the knowledge level (different formats, schemas, and ontologies), and at the level of the underlying information and communication technologies (ICT) and systems.

Agent technologies provide a cross-cutting approach promising to enable intelligent and proactive automation, adaptive planning and execution, decentralized coordination, and semantic interoperability. The Model Driven Architecture (MDA) is another promising approach for the support of interoperability due to its promise of providing consistent models at different abstraction layers with well-defined mappings in between these layers. As a third thread of activity, Service-Oriented Architectures (SOA) try to reach interoperability, focusing on, but not restricted to, the information and communication technology (ICT) level. The main contribution and goal of SOA is to achieve loose coupling among software entities representing business objects (processes, organizational units, etc.).

Agents, MDA, and SOA provide complementary solution components to parts of the enterprise interoperability problems. Agents enable dynamic collaboration and orchestration in changing and unpredictable situations; MDA provides mechanisms that generate artifacts for different platforms; SOA gives us late-binding interoperability between business process requirements and providers of service implementations. It is unlikely, then, that any of these approaches will succeed stand-alone in achieving the degree of interoperability that will be necessary to successfully construct, run, and optimize networked organizations. Rather, it is likely that a combination of these basic technologies will evolve in the next few years to provide an appropriate basis for interoperability. Therefore, the workshop aims at bringing together researchers and fostering interaction and collaboration to work jointly on solutions to achieve interoperability.

The ATOP workshop series focuses on technologies that support interoperability in networked organizations, on successful applications of these technologies, and on lessons learned. The main goal is to stimulate a discussion on how far agent technologies can support interoperability in this context and to compare current trends in the development of agent technologies with recent developments in service-oriented and model-driven system design, with respect to their ability to solve interoperability problems. Regarding model-driven system design, the presentation and discussion of metamodels of the underlying technologies, for example agent technologies and service-oriented architectures, is especially of interest.

To date, two ATOP (Agent-based Technologies and Applications for Enterprise Interoperability) workshops have been held in 2005 and 2008 with the AAMAS conferences in Utrecht (The Netherlands 2005) and Estoril (Portugal 2008). The articles in this book are extended versions of the most significant contributions to the workshops that were selected for inclusion.

March 2009   Klaus Fischer
                                                             Jörg P. Müller
                                                              James Odell
                                                         Arne Jørgen Berre

Organization

The ATOP 2005/2008 workshops on Agent-based Technologies and Applications for Enterprise Interoperability were held with the AAMAS conferences in Utrecht (The Netherlands 2005) and Estoril (Portugal 2008).

Organizing Committee

Arne Jørgen Berre	SINTEF, Norway
Klaus Fischer	DFKI, Germany
Joerg P. Mueller	Technische Universität Clausthal, Germany
James Odell	Oslo Software, USA

Program Committee

Sahin Albayrak	TU Berlin, Germany
Bernhard Bauer	University Augsburg, Germany
Amit Chopra	NC State University, USA
Michael Georgeff	Monash University, Australia
Dominic Greenwood	Whitestein Technologies, Switzerland
Axel Hahn	University Oldenburg, Germany
Christian Hahn	DFKI, Germany
Oystein Haugen	SINTEF, Norway
Timo Kahl	IWi, Germany
Stefan Kirn	Hohenheim University, Germany
Renato Levy	IAI, USA
Margaret Lyell	IAI, USA
Saber Mansour	Oslo Software, France
Michele Missikoff	LEKS; IASI-CNR, Italy
Eugenio Oliveira	University of Porto, Portugal
Herve Panetto	University Nancy, France
Omer Rana	Cardiff University, UK
Ralph Ronnquist	Intendico Pty. Ltd., Australia
Rainer Ruggaber	SAP, Germany
Omeir Shafiq	Digital Enterprise Research Institute (DERI), Austria
Carles Sierra	IIIA, Spain
Leon Sterling	Melbourne University, Australia
Hiroki Suguri	Comtec, Japan
Ingo Timm	Goethe-University Frankfurt/Main, Germany
Joerg Ziemann	IWi, Germany
Ingo Zinnikus	DFKI, Germany

Table of Contents

Security

Vertical Information Integration for Cross Enterprise Business Processes in the Energy Domain

Christoph Gerdes[1], Udo Bartlang[1], and Jörg P. Müller[2]

[1] Siemens AG, Corporate Technology, Information and Communications,
Munich, Germany
[2] Clausthal University of Technology, Germany

Abstract. The continuing growth and decentralization of power networks creates immense interoperability and integration challenges for ICT systems performing control and coordination tasks. On the one hand, large amounts of data coming from low-level field and automation systems need to be interpreted, aggregated, and made available to the business information systems to inform local decisions within power generation companies and operators; on the other hand, this *vertical integration* needs to be complemented by and connected to a *horizontal integration* capability which links the internal information and process models of different players in the market in (soft) real time, to inform and enable cross-enterprise coordination and optimization.

In this paper, we introduce an integration architecture that supports and combines vertical as well as horizontal integration, and methods to improve interoperability and increase automation of cross enterprise business processes in the energy domain. We support vertical integration by means of a novel decentral information aggregation and routing platform to manage large-scale data intensive systems. Horizontal integration is enabled by a peer-to-peer content (document) repository which is used to coordinate and integrate local processes in a cross-organizational fashion, thus allowing, e.g., reliable and timely provision of electricity outage reports and preparation of coordinated action plans. We evaluate important properties of these methods and report experimental results.

Keywords: Peer-to-Peer, vertical integration, content repository, business process management.

1 Introduction

Increasing demand for electrical energy has been leading to continuous extension of power grids world-wide. In Europe, national grids were joined to a synchronously operated AC grid. This union for the co-ordination of transmission of electricity (UCTE) provides electrical energy for more than 500 million consumers. This network enabled larger and more efficient power plants on the one hand and a maximum of reliability and availability on the other hand. Recent

K. Fischer et al. (Eds.): ATOP 2005 and ATOP 2008, LNBIP 25, pp. 1–28, 2009.

developments like de-central generation and de-regulation efforts, however, lead to rapid increase of load on electricity infrastructures. In consequence, large-scale blackouts like in August 2004 in the USA, on the Swiss-Italian border in 2003, and in the Weser-Ems area in Germany in 2006 endanger reliable electricity delivery. The latter left millions of households throughout Europe without electricity and resulted from lack of communication between transmission system operators (TSO). Initially a high voltage line was shut down over the Weser-Ems channel in Germany which caused a cascading effect — thereby overloading other lines until major parts of the European grid where separated. Efforts taken by individual TSOs to stabilize the network failed as they had no information on control actions taken by their colleagues in neighboring transmission areas yielding continuous aggravation until total disruption of service. In later analysis[1] the European commission emphasizes the importance to:

- Accelerate the adoption, in the context of a new Community mechanism and structure, of essential common binding network security standards;
- Enhance the coordination between transmission system operators to ensure an effective real-time operation of the European grid; efforts should be made to have a gradual evolution towards regional system operators; this should require effective unbundling as discussed in the Commission Strategic Energy Review;
- Improve investments in the European grid both to ensure its reliability and the construction of a truly competitive European market.

Already in 1999, the European transmission systems operators organization (ETSO) was founded to harmonize and develop the European electricity market. ETSO members include UCTE, the association of TSOs in Ireland (TSOI), the United Kingdom TSO association (UKTSOA), and the association of the nordic TSOs (NORDEL). ETSO takes care of cross TSO data exchange and standardization. ETSO also standardizes cross TSO processes like imbalance settlement, reserve resource planning, and outage transmission.

Illustrated by using the application scenario of electricity outage management as described by ETSO, the first contribution of this paper is a conceptual integration architecture for interoperability and automation of cross enterprise business processes in the energy domain. The architecture combines a *vertical* dimension, which supports the flow of information and coordination between low-level automation systems and enterprise systems, with a *horizontal* dimension, which links the internal information and process models of different players in the market, and enables cross-enterprise coordination.

The second, more technical contribution of the paper is that it illustrates two important functional building blocks to support successful integration:

- A decentrally organized information aggregation and routing platform to manage large-scale data intensive systems. Providing an interface of declarative querying and programmable data sources it abstracts from the underlying

---

[1] Cf. http://europa.eu/rapid/pressReleasesAction.do?reference=IP/07/110

physics; also, it can be extended to include assets unknown during design time as well add new functions for situation based analytics. Simulations show the performance of the indexing group which scales well to 100000 peers and beyond. From a business perspective, this approach can increase the efficiency of today's power networks as well as other industrial applications that rely on large, globally distributed networks with thousands of nodes.

- A peer-to-peer based content repository to substitute the centralized implementation of the ETSOVista platform's back-end system avoids a single point of failure in critical situations. From a technical point of view, the proposed system is able to benefit distributed collaboration in outage management processes by supporting a publish-subscribe mechanism to enable the rapid notification of critical events to interested parties. The evaluation shows that the system is robust against document losses and achieves good performance regarding document access. From a business point of view, the decentralized solution shows the potential to avoid vendor lock-in situations resulting from a proprietary market information aggregator.

A word on terminology: For our work, architectures and mechanisms for decentralized resource management, organization and coordination are at the heart of both multiagent systems and peer-to-peer computing. In this paper, we use the two terms often interchangeably. For a more detailed and more educated discussion of properties, commonalities, and differences between the two concepts, we refer to [1].

The paper is structured as follows: Section 2 provides the application background and describes the electricity outage scenario. In Section 3, the overall integration architecture is presented, followed by the definition of the technical building blocks: Information aggregation and routing (Section 4) and the distributed content repository (Section 5). Experimental results evaluating our approach are given in Section 6. The paper ends with a discussion of related work in Section 7 and a summary and outlook in Section 8.

2 Application Scenario

In this section, we present the application context of our work. We indicate the overall view of vertical and horizontal integration in distributed power networks. Subsequently, we describe a particular scenario to serve as a use case to illustrate our research: the distributed management of electricity outages.

2.1 Vertical and Horizontal Integration in Distributed Power Networks

Figure 1 illustrates the typical roles and relationships in a distributed power network. Generation companies (GenCos) operate power plants; they can be located at different levels of the physical energy network, ranging from supergrid (e.g., large coal power plants or nuclear plants) over high-voltage grid (e.g., industrial

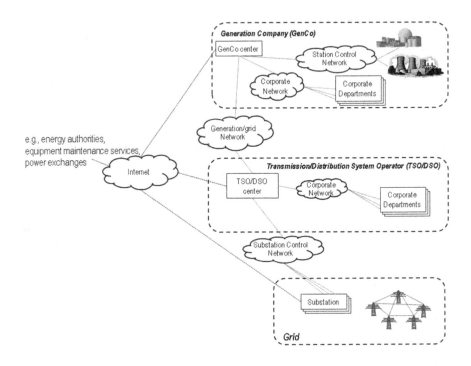

Fig. 1. Power Network Topology (inspired by [2])

powerplants) to medium- and low-voltage grids (wind or solar parks down to private solar installations).

The control center of a GenCo is responsible for coordinating two levels of activities, which in the sequel we shall call *vertical integration* and *horizontal integration*: firstly, using supervisory control and automation (SCADA) systems the GenCo operating center remotely controls the equipments located in the generation stations, with which it is normally connected via a dedicated plant control network to guarantee real-time control. These activities depend on field information and events coming from a multitude of sensors, devices, plants, and substations to be filtered, aggregated, and visualized. The process of gathering, aggregating, routing, and interpreting this information within an enterprise control system is called *vertical integration*.

Secondly, the information gathered using vertical integration is used as a basis for planning, enacting, monitoring, and coordinating both internal and cross-organizational business processes. Of particular focus for this paper are business processes involving cross-organizational interaction and coordination with the partners in the energy network, and, in particular the transmission system operators (TSOs), and the distribution system operators (DSOs). We call this type of activities *horizontal integration*. One example of this is the process of coordinating activities between a GenCo, TSOs, and DSOs in case of an outage. Vertical integration is used to determine type and extent of a local outage at the GenCo. In dealing with a local outage situation, the resulting information will inform decisions made in the business processes that guide coordination between the GenCo and its partners to prevent the effects of the local outage from spreading and causing malfunction in other parts of the network.

2.2   Use Case: Distributed Outage Management

In general, the propagation of an outage (document) involves the three principal actors. The first actor is a system operator (TSOs/DSOs) who has a complete overview of the tie line maintenance and operation and is in a position to provide a coherent picture of the situation at a given instance in time. The second actor is some market information aggregator, who may be a commercial entity that simply specializes in providing electricity market information and who makes the information available to the public. Such a provider may also make the information available to a selected distribution list as an additional service. Finally, the third actor is an information receiver or interested market participant who wishes to obtain such information.

The ETSOVista data platform is a service provided by ETSO aiming to facilitate access to information for all market participants and stake holders. Founded in 2006, it supports the publication of all information on current situation of the electricity market. A state of the art approach is to implement ETSOVista as a centralized web-based application with interfaces to aggregate and visualize respective data. For example, system operators can use ETSOVista's standardized interfaces to provide detailed information concerning their area of responsibility: in this context, a critical issue of availability is the knowledge of the outages.

In addition, ETSO has standardized an electronic document that system operators may use to transmit information about outages to an market information aggregator such as ETSOVista. An outage document is issued by a system operator and refers to information for generation over 100 MW network lines which have influence on the offered capacity. Outage events can be either planned, i.e., planned shutdown of an asset, or unplanned, i.e., the forced shutdown due to failure or other emergency situations. In the current release, the outage document is limited to outages of tie lines and network interconnections. Future extension to other outage object types is intended.

For example, the outage information publication process can be broken down to three sub-processes, namely (i) outage information creation, (ii) outage information modification, and (iii) outage information deletion:

- *Outage Information Creation:* whenever an outage situation occurs (either forced or planned) a system operator sends the information to the ETSO-Vista platform. The platform validates the conformity of the information received. If the information is incorrect the platform ignores the transmission and logs the incident. If the information is correct the platform shall enter it in its persistent data storage and shall publish it.
- *Outage information modification:* an outage situation may be modified to indicate its progress or to correct any data that is found to be invalid. Accordingly, the following possibilities exist:

- For an outage the following information may be revised: start date, start time, end date, end time, and affected interconnector.
- For an outage the following information may be added: start time, end date, end time, and affected interconnector.
- If an affected asset is incorrect or the planned maintenance is canceled prior to the start time, the outage in question has to be deleted and eventually new outage information has to be provided.

- *Outage information deletion:* a given outage may be deleted with an update that makes use of the *Delete* attribute. This has the effect of deleting the outage from the published list.

3   Overall Architecture

In this section, we show the overall view of the used ICT architecture. In addition, we indicate challenges to achieve vertical and horizontal integration, and consequently state our technical approach.

3.1   Overall View of the ICT Architecture

In this paper, we propose a decentralized architecture to support vertical and horizontal integration, as well as the coupling between vertical and horizontal activities. Figure 2 gives an exemplary view on the IT architecture of a distributed energy system including one ore multiple GenCos as well as TSO/DSOs. It also illustrates the two integration dimensions considered in this paper.

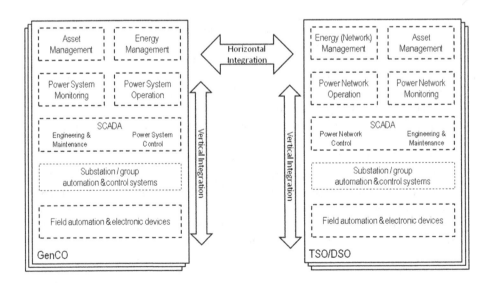

Fig. 2. ICT Architecture of a Distributed Energy System

The uppermost layer is the business systems layer including energy management, asset management as well as standard ERP systems. The ICT systems at this layer are instrumental in (internal and cross-enterprise) business process enactment; they need to be supported by appropriate business process models. They receive real-time decision-relevant information from the systems for power system/network monitoring and operation. These systems again rely on different types of supervisory control and data acquisition systems (SCADA), which collect and aggregate data from local field automation and control systems controlling individual power groups, subnetworks, or substations. At the bottom end of this information food-chain are numerous electronic devices and sensors producing large amounts of operation data.

Also note, that horizontal integration will take place in two interrelated ways: on the one hand, different types of business information systems supporting different business functions within a company (such as, e.g., asset management, energy management, and other ERP functions) need to be coordinated and integrated to optimize the overall performance of each individual company. On the other hand, horizontal integration entails the cross-enterprise coordination of business processes such as, e.g., dealing with an outage.

3.2 Challenges

Even considered in isolation, vertical integration raises a number of difficult challenges. Large amounts of data need to be handled, correlated and abstracted, routed upwards, interpreted and visualized to allow operators to obtain an up-to-date view of the status and performance of the plants/networks. The sources producing this data are largely distributed - due to the large data load, centralized processing is not feasible. Also, there are *interoperability barriers* at different levels. While there are a number of upcoming standards in the energy sector[2], there is still a certain heterogeneity of systems and interfaces, which makes the vertical information a challenging task. The same can be said for horizontal integration, where interoperability needs to be provided across business information systems and business process models of different companies, to enable timely and coordinated reaction to critical events.

In addition, due to changing regulations, market situations and technology innovations, the architecture displayed in Figure 2 needs to be open to change. For example, a regulatory change (e.g., new laws) may require modifications to be made to the internal or cross-enterprise business processes, which again may impact lower layers of the architecture. Also, new communication standards or middleware technologies may provide new, more efficient ways to realize the different layers of automation and control systems, which may affect the upper layers of the architecture. Ideally, our distributed energy system should be easily adapted to these changes at different levels.

---

[2] We refer, e.g., to the IEC 61850 standard series for communication of energy automation systems, where a common information model is being developed.

3.3   Technical Approach

To combine the requirements to deal with large amounts of data at different levels, to connect (locally autonomous) technical systems with business processes, and to provide internal and cross-enterprise interoperability and flexibility in the face of change, our overall research work combines a number of technology ingredients covering both design-time and run-time aspects:

- Design-time:

    - We provide a multiagent-based architecture to describe roles and capabilities of the parties in the distributed energy system, and to model (and subsequently enact) cross-enterprise coordination processes.
    - We use a model-driven system engineering approach (see, e.g., [3]) to enable the maintenance of process, service, and information models at different levels, and the top-down and bottom-up synchronization and adaptation between different layers based on model transformations.

- Run-time:

    - We support vertical integration by an information aggregation and routing approach based on a structured peer-to-peer framework (see, e.g., [4], [5]), enabling the decentralized management of ad-hoc queries as well as publish-subscribe style communication
    - We take a document-centric approach to horizontal integration by proposing a peer-to-peer content repository (see [6]) allowing different parties to publish, modify, version, and synchronize documents (e.g., outage reports), to subscribe and search for certain types of documents, and to route relevant documents to interested parties using content-based rules. This approach benefits both scalability and reliability, and ensures consistency of concurrent operations.

In this paper, we shall focus on the run-time aspects of our approach. In particular, in Section 4 we present a vertical integration approach based on a decentralized information aggregation and routing framework. In Section 5, we complement this approach by describing the architecture and methods of a peer-to-peer based distributed content repository to enable document-centric horizontal integration processes.

4   Information Aggregation and Routing

The state of the power grid is recorded by a large number of digital devices distributed over the entire supply territory. Sensing equipment includes intelligent electronic devices (IED), smart sensors and meters. In the context of vertical information integration, i.e., integration of field data with the business processes of the system operator, the digital devices act as data sources which provide data in a specified quantity and quality. In correlation with the kind of data source, the measured value its validity and the sampling interval, high volume measurement streams may occur. To make these streams usable in an operation context the raw data needs to be processed to information which is representative of the current network state. In traditional power grids, there exists a well defined power flow from few generators down to a large number of consumers. This allows operators to estimate the network state accurately without comprehensive measurements. In scenarios such as decentralized generation, power flows might reverse causing unforseen dynamics and failure situations which cannot be fully predicted by the system operator. Hence, in order to identify critical situations, timely collection and processing of high resolution data becomes mandatory. In this situation, in-network approaches are advisable as they limit the load on the communication infrastructure and yet yield a high quality of service (QoS) and fine granularity of measurements.

In this section, we introduce a data-centric perspective on multiple sensing equipment providing a unified access paradigm on distributed measurement data. Based on the standard query language (SQL), we developed a programming language to formally express an information interest and appropriate processing functions. Using declarative queries, measurement streams can be routed through the network, thereby being processed and aggregated at dynamically determined processing nodes. In the following, the integration architecture, query language and query execution subsystem are introduced. A set of examples show the capabilities of each component.

4.1   Vertical Integration Architecture

The foundation for information aggregation and routing is constituted by the query execution architecture. The architecture links all nodes of the network in an application layer overlay thereby providing a global address space for all assets in the network. The overlay manages the mapping from virtual peer addresses to physical hardware addresses thereby virtualizing network topologies and technology. The mapping supports both keywords as well as complex declarative queries. Keyword mappings are realized through a distributed hashtable (DHT) spanned over all network devices (Figure 3). In order to support complex queries, a subsection of the address space is dedicated to the so called index cloud. The cloud consists of dedicated index peers which manage device meta data and a query catalog. Additionally, data sources host a local query engine which is capable of processing and optimizing queries as described in Section 4.3. Power grid equipment has lifecycles of often up to 50 or more years hence yielding systems with a large variety of hardware with differing compute resources, communication standards and protocols.

Traditionally, all field data is transferred to a central service, however, with the limitations detailed in the above sections. The integration architecture introduced in this paper can achieve higher efficiency by pushing query engines into the network. This, however, must be either directly supported by the data sources other integration methods must be deployed. Our architecture supports three levels of integration: for data sources with sufficient compute resources,

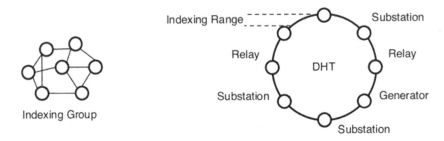

Fig. 3. Vertical Integration Architecture

the query engine can be directly hosted by the data source. Data sources which do not provide the required resources to support a query engine by themselves but have a device in their proximity are integrated by the neighboring query engine acting a as proxy reading individual measurements from the device, and processing them in the query context. Finally, data sources which do not support a common communication standard require an additional hardware component which acts as gateway to read, process, and forward data in the query context.

Device meta data provides information on device capabilities and attributes along with a device locator. Hence devices can be addressed based on its descriptions (e.g., "send a message to a device which can measure frequency"). The query catalog maintains all globally visible queries currently in execution. This information is used to optimize query execution and stream routing. Both concepts in combination enable locating information sources and routing their output to respective processing sinks (e.g., "send measurements from devices that can measure frequency to a device that can archive data"). To formally specify query and routing information, the following section introduces a query language especially designed for this purpose.

4.2   Query Language

The query language supports both snapshot queries (single result set) as well as queries initiating data streams. It allows us to apply filters on streams and to route streams to different nodes throughout the network. Despite known restrictions and flaws of SQL [7], we chose it due to the wide acceptance among developers and good integration with standard applications, such as JDBC. However, to meet the high performance requirements, query statements are compiled to an efficient encoding; as soon as they enter the network only this encoding is used. This improves execution performance and decreases network traffic. Given semantic equivalence, different query languages can be supported by adjusting the compiler. Representing the query, the compilation itself is a sequence of instructions, i.e., basic operations the query engine can perform to retrieve the query result. The query engine analyzes the instructions sequence and creates an execution plan as described in Section 4.3.

```
ALARMS@ -> SELECT * FROM MMXU WHERE Hz < 59.001
                WINDOW(now, forever, 1s)
                REPLICATION=3
                RESTRICT TO GenCo
                TRACEABILITY=ON
                RECEIVER(rcv_node)
```

Fig. 4. Example of how to retrieve and route information within the platform

Figure 4 provides an example query. It demonstrates an assignment specified through the right arrow, a standard *SELECT ... WHERE* clause and a
set of QoS constraints. In the example the result set is assigned to a variable
named *ALARMS*. Thereby the @ operator specifies where the variable is hosted.
ALARMS@ means the variable is globally visible and located in the indexing
cloud. *ALARMS@node1*, on the contrary would allocate a variable at node1. The
WINDOW operator specifies the activation interval of the data stream. The first
two parameters set start and end time while the third parameter specifies the
interval of execution, e.g., every 10 seconds. The window parameter implicity
controls response time and throughput and is one of the key QoS parameters.
In other words it advises the query engine to retrieve and deliver results sets
timely as specified. To achieve this goal the query engine coordinates all in the
query participating data sources and schedules their network and memory resource utilization. If this process of allocating resources fails, e.g., because of
resource shortage or other unavailability, the query will not be scheduled. The
REPLICATION parameter controls availability as it specifies the number of
copies the system keeps of the result set. A replication factor of 3, means that
the result set is replicated to three other nodes in the index cloud. Thereby each
replica inherits all other QoS parameters as specified in the query. *RESTRICT
TO* in one of the parameters to enforce security during query execution. In the
example *RESTRICT TO* restricts access to the result set and all intermediate
results which may be stored during query execution to the user or group identified by *GenCo*. Finally *TRACEABILITY* adds an additional attribute to the
result set containing information on all data sources that participated in the
query and each operation, i.e., individual execution plans, that were executed
in the process. This enables precise analysis and verifiability of the information
execution process. Finally the *RECEIVER* parameter specifies an receiver of
the result set. Thus it can be used to route a data stream to one or more receivers in the network. The parameter does not limit to a single receiver e.g.
*RECEIVER(SELECT * FROM NODES WHERE type='Archive')* would forward the stream to all nodes which are of type *'Archive'*.

Besides specification of queries the language supports imperative elements
and basic operators found in many other programming languages. Hence, the
language and its execution architecture make the network programmable enabling to define data processing filter functionality like the simple PID controller

in Program 1. Thus, instead of pulling high volume data streams to a single location, programs can be defined which process data in-network close to the data sources. Aggregated key indicators can then be calculated and sent to other nodes for further processing, stored in archives or visualized at control centers. This enables high performance applications such as high resolution monitoring of the network state. In [8] we introduced a special operator called MON_k which is capable of monitoring a large number of assets including detection of anomalies. Depending on the targeted accuracy and responsiveness of the detection, the MON_k operator causes intensive message exchange between involved assets. However, since communication is peer-to-peer and in-network, the operator scales well to a high number of network nodes.

```
FUNCTION PID(Pv, Sp)
  Kp -> 100
  Ki -> 0.9
  Kd -> 1000

  Error -> Sp - Pv
  @TotalError -> TotalError + Error

  Pgain -> Kp * Error
  Igain -> Ki * TotalError
  Dgain -> Kd * (Error - @Derror)
  @Derror -> Dgain

  return Pgain + Igain + Dgain
END
```

Program 1. Basic PID controller

4.3   Query Execution

The process of retrieving information specified through a complex query statement is non trivial in large-scale distributed systems. We apply a five step process for query execution starting with an analysis of the query statement, followed by locating respective data sources, building a distributed data structure which coordinates individual data sources to deliver the requested content, merging and filtering individual data items and finally generating a result set.

Once injected into the network, queries are compiled to binary form and loaded in a local query engine. An execution plan (e.g. Figure 5) is generated and scheduled for processing. The plan lists all actions necessary to deliver the requested result set. The plan depicted in Figure 5, for example, first checks locally if the query can be evaluated with local information alone. If so query execution is complete. Otherwise the query is optimized and rewritten for distributed execution. Query optimization is a complex procedure where the query is restructured to reflect the overlay topology, the specified QoS parameters as well as states of other concurrent queries scheduled in the same query engine. Afterwards a resolving action is triggered which determines which peer might provide the requested information and is able to allocate local resources to meet to constraints specified in the query. Subsequently, the query as a whole or in part is assigned to the peer accordingly. Intermediate results due to local computation or obtained through subquery assignment are stored in the local storage. The process continues until all requested information is contained in the local storage. During execution a number of events may cause query processing to fail. Without violating the QoS constrains the query engine tries to compensate failures by reissuing actions or assigning new subqueries an alternative sources. In case the maximum number of retries is reached, a timeout occurred, or the query is not computable, an exception is raised and the execution ends freeing all allocated resources.

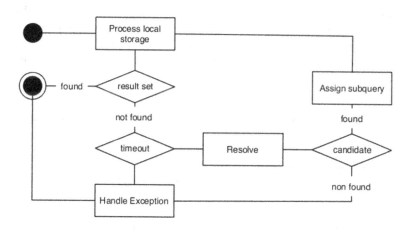

Fig. 5. Query execution plan

Deallocation is highly complex in cases of failures of complex queries with large numbers of peers involved since individual assets may be unreachable. To ensure appropriate deallocation of resources all variables in the query engines are temporary only. Variables reaching a defined age in a query engine's memory are automatically garbage collected. To persistently store results they must be forwarded to entities providing archiving functionality.

The vertical integration architecture provides a flexible high performance platform to manage large-scale data intensive systems. Based on peer-to-peer network virtualization and through providing an interface of declarative querying, it abstracts from the complexity of the heterogeneous and dynamic system. Since the platform is programable it can be extended to include assets unknown during design time and implement new functions to introduce new methods of analytics. Having unified access from high level IT systems down to individual automation equipment is the first key component to enable fully automated cross enterprise business processes. In the following sections a horizontal integration component is introduced which enables the flexible interlinking of individual business players.

5   Horizontal Integration Using a P2P-Based Content Repository

The ETSOVista transparency platform's main objective is to provide to the electricity market participants all the relevant, valued, and trusted information in a transparent way. That is, system operators shall use standardized electronic documents to transmit information about outages to the platform for diffusion to the market. As amongst the principle criteria of availability is the knowledge of the outages, we propose to substitute the centralized implementation of the platform's back-end system by a peer-to-peer based content repository [6] avoiding a single point of failure. In addition, the approach supports a publish-subscribe mechanism to enable the rapid notification of critical events to interested parties.

In the following, we present the overall architecture and exemplified methods of a peer-to-peer based, decentralized content repository to enable document-centric horizontal integration processes.

5.1   Modular Architecture of a P2P-Based Content Repository

The content repository enables the management of both structured and unstructured content: its repository model defines the meta model to identify and structure content data on a logical level—from a user's point of view; it supports to express functional operations on content data. The concrete implementation translates these operations into actual corresponding actions affecting its used (peer-to-peer) storage subsystems. The repository model adopts the *Content Repository API for Java* (JCR) [9], which is defined as open standard to improve application interoperability:

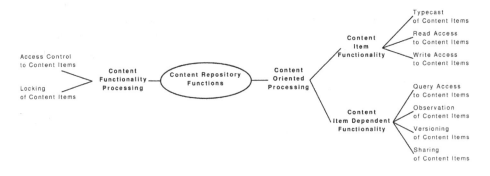

Fig. 6. Functional Components of the Content Repository

- The repository model offers a generic, hierarchical content data model and several levels of functionality for content services on a logical level: a repository consists of an unlimited set of named *workspaces*; each workspace establishes a single-rooted, virtually hierarchical, *n-ary* tree-based view of content *items*. E.g., a peer-to-peer workspace supports a decentralized document exchange.

- In addition to the basic repository model, a content repository is constituted by a set of essential functional building blocks, as illustrated in Figure 6.

- Documents may be accessed using either *direct* or *traversal* access. Each outage document can be uniquely identified to ease direct access. Consequently, it is independently addressable from its position within the workspace hierarchy. The traversal item access targets on walking through the content tree of a workspace, step by step, using (relative) paths. To support the verification of access rights, each document is allocated an unique identification of its sender and optionally (multiple) receiver identification(s) to restrict read access.

Figure 7 shows the modular content repository approach considering horizontal and vertical system decomposition [6]: on the one hand, the distribution degree of content repository functionality regarding the persistent storage support may vary—for example, the storage management for local or distributed workspaces. On the other hand, different modules, for instance, are responsible for different management tasks. Each of the architecture's layers is briefly introduced and discussed in the following:

The *content application layer* offers the *content repository* API. It hides sublayers to free users to deal with peculiarities of content storage.

The *content repository layer* represents the mapping of the logical repository model to corresponding system modules; at its core, it implements several registries and managers. For example, the *session* subsystem basically uses a *transient item state manager* to cope with a content item's transient state per session. The *workspace* subsystem uses several managers to deal with the repositories functional building blocks. It is responsible to create consistent items in persistent storage. For instance, a *query manager* is used to support query access to content items, a *version manager* is used to support versioning of content items, and an *observation manager* is used to support observations of content item changes. Such manager use the *persistent item state manager* to actually obtain read and write access to a workspace's content items—that is, to obtain an actual content item view of persisted data; it represents the connection between the workspace scope and the used persistent storage back-end subsystem; a persistent item state manager shall trigger the observation mechanism if interests in corresponding item changes exist—usually, reflected by some *access manager* of the *persistent storage layer*. This shall enable an observation manager to asynchronously subscribe for changes in a workspace. An *item access manager* uses a persistent item state manager to enforce its functions, that is, the support of access control for content items. Accordingly, the item persistent item state manager needs to obey such enforced restrictions.

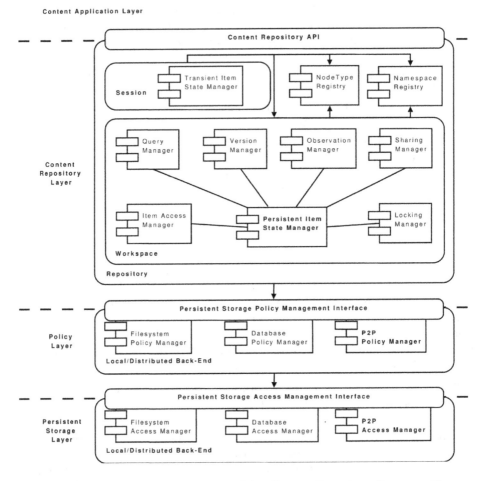

Fig. 7. Layered Architecture of the Modular Content Repository Decomposition

The *policy layer* administrates the scope of different storage policies that may be used by the content repository layer to actually access the persistent storage layer. Therefore, it uses *policy managers* matching corresponding *access managers* of the persistent storage layer. As illustration, the usage of a peer-to-peer policy manager enables the definition of potentially fine-granular policies at peer-to-peer data level—rather than on item level. Thus, each type of content or rather content instance may have its own policy; some examples of storage policies in peer-to-peer case may include the life of content, that is, if content shall be stored infinitely or temporarily.

The *persistent storage layer* defines the subsystem to deal with local or distributed persistent storage at data level. It is indirectly usable by the *persistent item state manager* of the *content repository layer* by exposing a generic *persistent storage access management interface*. Using this interface, several *access*

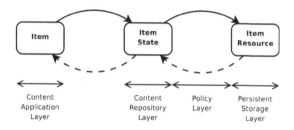

Fig. 8. Transformation Process of a Repository Item

managers for persistent storage may be used, for example, the *peer-to-peer access manager.* Such peer-to-peer access manager supports a mapping between a workspace view of content at item level and a raw data view at back-end storage level; thus, it is necessary to use some interpreter to recognize raw data as content items, that is, to retrieve item semantic from raw data resources.

Figure 8 illustrates the applied *naming concept* regarding the transformation process of a repository item (between logical and physical objects): (i) the *content application layer* actually deals with item *objects* existing in transient storage. (ii) The *content repository layer* has a more sophisticated view on items: the layer knows the internal state of an item as it is responsible to manage core repository functionality. However, at content repository level, an item and its represented content forms one logical unit. (iii) An item which shall be persisted needs to be transformed from its *item state* to a lower-level *item resource* object. Such a transformation process involves the *policy layer* to specify a policy for the corresponding *access manager* at *persistent storage level.* The *item resource* object resulting from this transformation shall reflect all necessary information to represent and reconstruct its item state. In addition, it contains policy information. An *item resource* deals with all the low-level details of actual data storage—which is transparent to the content repository layer.

As a result, the content repository system is able to support different content storage policies in a flexible way. For example, such policies may reflect how content may be actually persisted and accessed. It supports different granularity level hierarchies to be build by grouping aggregations of objects to represent larger objects (collections); regarding the granularity level, data objects may be restructured and build from atomic values on demand. Thus, content data must adhere to some global uniform semantics to deal with and ease content integration—specified by storage policies. For example, such concept facilitates the existence of multiple object copies but may hide their actual physical locations.

5.2   P2P-Based Methods for Persistent Storage Management

As most important feature, the peer-to-peer based content repository supports methods for *fault-tolerant* and *consistent* content management: as, once an outage document content is stored to the system, it shall not be lost. This raises

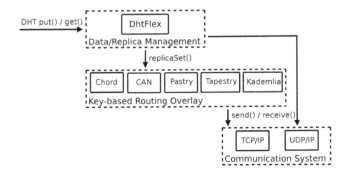

Fig. 9. Major Building Blocks of DhtFlex's System Environment

the challenge to coordinate concurrent activity in a dynamic peer-to-peer environment and to protect the consistency of created artifacts to keep content up-to-date across geographically distributed locations. For example, in case of the revision or addition of outage information, the same document identification is used and a new document version is created. This has the effect of canceling the previous transmission and replacing it with the new one.

The system uses *DhtFlex* [10], a distributed algorithm to enable flexible atomic data operations for replicated data at peer-to-peer persistent storage level—a method being trimmed for a highly concurrent and fluctuating environment. As illustrated in Figure 9 [10], DhtFlex is responsible for the complete data management, including replication handling.

The query model of DhtFlex supports simple DHT *put* and *get* operations for data items that are uniquely identifiable. In addition, techniques are used to extend a DHT in order to deal with the content management requirements. DhtFlex supports optimized operations for both immutable as well as mutable data resources and offers flexible consistency strategies. For example, once a certain version of an outage report is defined, it remains forever unchanged within the corresponding version chain.

Therefore, DhtFlex imposes an annotated data resource concept to typify replicated data. This allows the differentiation between mutable and immutable data items and thus an efficient processing for both data resource types. Especially for mutable data resources, DhtFlex provides strong consistency guarantees enabling atomic DHT *put* and *get* operations. Therefore, it exploits techniques of Leslie Lamport's famous *Paxos* algorithm [11] to coordinate the *recast* process of a data resource's replication group: DhtFlex serializes concurrent *put* and *get* requests over the *master* of a replication group in order to accelerate these operations; in addition, it is able to deal with master failures by automated handovers—ensuring consistency. DhtFlex allows system grows to large scales and updates to be made from anywhere in the system.

For example, the approach enables to implement a close-to-open model by retrieving the latest item resource via a *get* operation once the item should be locally opened and keep it as a cached copy by the *content repository layer* until access is closed. All succeeding requests to an item's potential child items can be satisfied using information from the cached copy. If the item should be modified, the locally cached copy is updated to reflect the changes; hence, *put* efforts and corresponding changes are locally buffered by a *session* before stored to the network in order to minimize local write latencies. Finally, once item access is closed, all cached changes are flushed to the peer-to-peer network and tried to be committed. This scheme works especially well when using versioning, as immutable item resources that store corresponding contents are never removed from the network; hence, links to certain versions of item resources could not be invalid as they cannot be removed from the system.

The support of *observations* at shallow operational scope relies on the usage of *special* observation resources. Using a subscribe-like feature [6], the basic eventing-notification mechanism can be implemented, which allows the triggering of a notification if a suited content resource for a certain path in the virtual tree of a workspace is stored. This is achieved by placing an observation resource as *subscription* at the corresponding peers, which perform matching tests reacting on the adding, removing, and modifying of affected item resources. The support of deep operational scope requires such observation resource to be attached to every item resource of the rooted subtree. As items are always added as the leaves of such tree, this method enables to pass and apply such deep observation pattern to the whole subtree.

Partitioning Strategy. DhtFlex employs a structured peer-to-peer overlay as *Chord* [4] for data resource placement: such overlay protocol can be used to determine the *root* of a resource, that is, the Chord peer which possesses the numerically closest matching identifier in comparison to the resource's identifier.

However, as a dynamic peer environment is assumed, network conditions can change over time. As a result, a resource's corresponding root may vary. Peers that enter or leave the network demand the used overlay protocol to adjust responsibilities for affected key ranges; for instance, gaps in the overlay resulting from crashed or temporarily unavailable peers need to be closed. As DhtFlex does support crash-recovery, as well as crash-stop failure models, it is able to exploit positive dynamics of a structured peer-to-peer overlay, where available peers may take over the key range of failed ones.

Replication Strategy. DhtFlex's partitioning strategy basically maps identifiers to values; thereby, a value may be an arbitrary object or item represented as data resource, which may be replicated and persistently stored. An object is retrieved by using the identifier under which it was published. DhtFlex uses replication in order to ensure high availability and durability of administrated data resources. Thereby, it supports a flexible degree of replication, that allows an adjustment per data resource type: if a peer leaves the system, for example, by crashing, its administrated data resources become unavailable. A replication mechanism increases data availability by storing data at several peers. But, in the face of concurrent modifications mutual consistency of replicated data resources may be violated, some replicas may not be up to date. The requirements of content repository functionality demands for DhtFlex to be able to get the current valid replica.

A replicated data item is independent of the peer on which it resides and may be regarded as virtual. This applied *virtualization* enables DhtFlex to employ structured overlay routing as partitioning strategy. Thereby, DhtFlex manages all replication functions; the overlay is accessed only to conduct necessary information to construct a *replication group*. A replication group configuration is a set of peers that are responsible to administrate a certain replicated data resource. The size of such set is defined by the resource's replication degree. A replication group of size n consists of one master and $n-1$ replicas.

Regarding the replication model, DhtFlex implements a *primary-copy* replication pattern [12] per replication group: a replication group's master is used to serialize and apply all updates to a mutable data object. In order to benefit the partitioning strategy, DhtFlex uses the unique identifier of a data resource to configure the corresponding root in the overlay as master. Accordingly, DhtFlex targets to fill the replication group set with the *available* $n-1$ peers succeeding a root in the overlay, the $n-1$ *root successors*. Hence, a replication group of size n shall contain those $n-1$ peers that are relevant to become a root for the key after network conditions change. Regarding fault-tolerance aspects, these $n-1$ peers are ideal candidates to place the replicas of a given data object.

The master of a replication group is responsible to ensure the replication factor for the data resources that fall within its key range. This means, in addition to their conservation in local storage, the master needs to replicate the resources to the remaining replicas. This implies, that changes on resources have to be propagated to all replicas in order to ensure consistency.

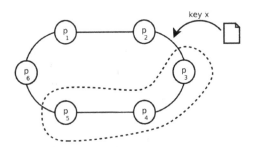

Fig. 10. Combination of Replication Strategy and Partitioning Strategy

The replication strategy in combination with the used partitioning strategy is exemplified in Figure 10. It shows a replication group consisting of one master peer p_3 and two additional replica peers: the master p_3 replicates the data object for identifier (*key*) x at peer p_4 and p_5. Hence, p_5 stores values that fall into the ranges $(p_2, p_3]$, $(p_3, p_4]$, $(p_4, p_5]$. As explained, the employed structured peer-to-peer overlay allows each peer to determine which peers should be contained in the replication group for a certain key.

6   Evaluation

The key contributions of this paper are (i) a vertical integration architecture coupling low-level field automation systems with business information systems using a decentralized routing and aggregation methods and a declarative query interface and (ii) a peer-to-peer content (document) repository which can be used to coordinate and integrate local processes in a cross-organizational fashion, allowing, e.g., reliable and timely provision of outage reports. The following paragraphs evaluate both contributions based on the application scenario in Section 2.

6.1   Aggregation and Routing

The declarative approach and utilization of peer-to-peer protocols introduces rather obvious benefits like scalability, resilience, resource virtualization and adaptiveness to the power network domain. With engineering and maintenance costs being major matters of expensive, self configuration and adaption to new devices and topologies yield immediate cost reduction for utilities. Efficient management of complex networks will become even more important in the near future. With the emergence of distributed generation retrieving detailed real time information on the current network state becomes more and more important as, for example, reversed power flows can circumvent protection systems and yield equipment failure. Among the challenges of retrieving a correct network state is the extraction of information from vast amounts of sensor data. The declarative approach proposed enables the calculation of key performance indicators in-network, and thus eliminates the need to transfer high volumes of data to a central point. The example Query 4 presented in Section 4.2 shows nicely how the complexity of the underlying network is hidden. Queries never use physical network addresses but virtual identifiers. Keywords get resolved and queries reevaluated periodically when messages are sent thus the platform adaptively reorganizes itself in the event of failure or the appearance of better suited nodes. Processing will still work even if small fractions of nodes are unavailable as is common in large networks.

Using a centralized meta data index is an efficient and entirely pragmatic approach but also a potential performance bottleneck. We ran extensive tests and simulations to optimize the meta data index performance. The testbed consisted of ten commodity PCs each equipped with relatively low end, Intel Pentium IV processors and 1GB of RAM. Since the project is in an early state of implementation, we are not interested in absolute peak transaction rates but rather how the system adapts to increased node numbers and update rates. As test data the configuration of up 100000 peers was loaded into the indexing group. Of each node 20 attributes where indexed. To simulate how the indexing group performs with increasing node numbers, we ran 10000 queries with numbers of peers ranging from 100 to 100000.

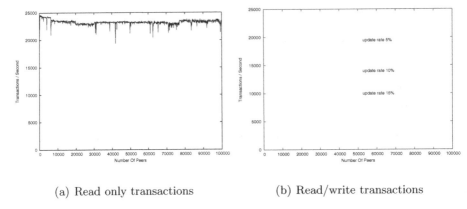

(a) Read only transactions   (b) Read/write transactions

Fig. 11. Queries are resolved through the query catalog of the centralized index. The catalog maps to nodes that are responsible for the data requested.

Figure 11a illustrates the results. Plotted are the transactions per second as measured directly on the indexing nodes, i.e., not including the time required for communication and compilation. The rate remains almost constant with a minimal decrease towards 100000 peers. As stated earlier, indexing nodes are optimized for read operations as we assume an update rate of below 1% in regular power networks. In consequence, Figure 11b shows the impact of high update rates on performance. While for low node numbers performance only deviates slightly from the read only case, transactions rates are down one third in the case of 100000 peers and an assumed 5% update rate and down to 19% for the 15% update rate case. However update rates of 5% or even 15% are not realistic as it would mean that a utility would lose or replace a large fraction of its network which in return would dramatically reduce read only transactions.

The average round trip time for a query was about 400ms in the case with 100000 peers. This includes parsing, compiling transferring, processing and receiving results. However, while it provides a rough idea on processing time, this figure has little value as it strongly depends on the network topology and may increase or decrease depending on the communication infrastructure used. Some power network applications are extremely time critical. A backup protection system as discussed in [13], [14], [15], and [16] requires full query execution and data delivery in about 200ms real time. In such cases, the node executing the protection logic would subscribe to necessary measurements in advance. Results would then be delivered to a local cache from which they can be taken for state assessment. In the context of the application scenario of Section 2, these performance measures are sufficient.

In order to achieve a highly efficient outage report process, network failures must be detected automatically. The programmability of the vertical architecture reflects this aspect as new filters and detection algorithms can be implemented on demand. Since these programs run in-network, their analysis can be based on high detail measurement data enabling early detection of complex failure patterns.

6.2   P2P-Based Content Repository

The evaluation of the peer-to-peer based content repository highlights two important properties considering the decentralized management of different versions of outage documents: (i) the availability of a certain document version. (ii) The latency to retrieve a certain version.

For example, the DhtFlex approach ensures reliability of different data resource versions using replication as redundancy scheme: a certain number of identical copies are stored at different peers. As a data resource's replication factor ρ influences its availability, the value of ρ should be set appropriately depending on the demanded degree of availability. As in worst case, DhtFlex only requires a single copy of the ρ replicated (immutable) data resources to be available to progress successfully, the probability P_{fail}—the failure of a data resource's whole replication group—is given by the following equation (we assume that peers fail independently and that all peers have an identical (average) availability α_{peer}):

$$P_{fail} = P(all\ \rho\ replica\ peers\ fail) = P(one\ replica\ peer\ fails)^{\rho} = (1 - \alpha_{peer})^{\rho} \tag{1}$$

A resource's replication factor ρ can be adjusted depending on the desired availability aim, as stated by the following formula: $\rho = \frac{log(P_{fail})}{log(1-\alpha_{peer})}$. Figure 12(a) depicts the probability P_{fail} to actually lose an immutable data resource—depending on different values for α_{peer} and ρ: one observation is that comparatively small values for the size of a replication group suffice to reduce the probability loosing a certain data resource significantly.

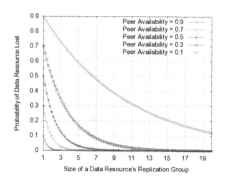
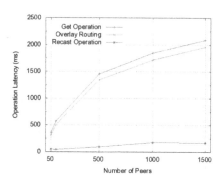

(a) Worst Case Probability a Document Version is Lost

(b) Latency of DhtFlex for Immutable Data Resources using Iterative Overlay Routing

Fig. 12. Evaluation of Availability and Performance Properties

The evaluation of performance properties to retrieve a certain outage document version uses an experimental setup integrating a *King* data set [17]. This approach enables to gain estimations of DhtFlex's communication costs based on real measurement data of thousands of Internet hosts. Figure 12(b) indicates the latency of DhtFlex for operations on *immutable* data resources, for example, outage document versions. All shown latencies represent the average value of ten measurements per operation; each data resource is allocated to a replication group of six (different) peers. The results show that a *get* operation is strongly affected by the costs to perform peer-to-peer overlay routing, which increase with the number of peers—the operation itself introduces, however, rather constant overhead. As the *recast* operation does not require overlay routing, its latency is comparatively small. In addition, outage document versions may be arbitrarily cached at client-site to avoid overlay lookup latencies and thus to reduce the latency of *get* operations—this is an important remark as these are supposed as the most requested kind of operation for such resources.

As a result, the peer-to-peer based content repository is able to ensure high availability of outage documents and to achieve good performance properties regarding their data access. This may benefit the adoption of the decentralized solution in comparison to the state of the art system (see Section 2.2).

7   Related Work

In the context of wide area sensor network Aberer et al. [18] published research that provides similar concepts to the approach taken in Section 4. Our architecture, however, was heavily influenced by applicability in current industrial systems. Our sensor model is determined by IEC 61850 which supports an integrative approach with current automation equipment. Compiling queries and programs to binary form allows us to run query engines on low cost embedded devices as well as desktop PCs.

A good overview of distributed databases is given in [19]. [20] provides an overview of current research topics on data stream management. In [21], D. Kucuket et al. introduce a streaming database solution to monitor power quality. Mariposa [22] introduces an architecture for wide area distributed databases in perspective of traditional distributed data management systems (DBMS). The approach includes a micro economic paradigm used for query and storage optimization. AURORA [23], STREAM [24], Cougar [25] and others discuss general query processing in sensor networks. AURORA allows users to create queries in a graphical representation. STREAM and Cougar extend the SQL with temporal semantics but do not provide the extensions of a programming language.

A considerable body of research is available on peer-to-peer systems, including DHTs [4], [26], and gossip based algorithms [27]. In contrast to peer-to-peer systems deployed in the Internet, in industrial systems, we find a more comfortable environment in some respect: we can expect lower churn rates and less problems with network address translation. However, we must adapt algorithms originally designed for media distribution in the Internet to the resource-constrained environment of industrial systems. Hence, issues such as determinism and real-time capabilities must be addressed. In previous work [5] [28] [8] we showed already the potential of peer-to-peer algorithms in industrial domains beyond content distribution.

Peer-to-peer systems generally lack capabilities to support content repositories. In addition, most of these systems use a rather monolithic approach and usually do not target consistency of concurrent operations. Moreover, the systems commonly do not offer some degree of flexibility regarding certain properties, as different availability demands. In order to delimit our approach of a peer-to-peer content repository, we subsequently present selected related work. It is worth mentioning that to our knowledge, our work is the first peer-to-peer implementation available, which addresses the powerful features of JSR-170.

For instance, the Cooperative File System (CFS) [29] provides a peer-to-peer infrastructure for wide-area storage and focuses on guarantees for efficiency, robustness, load balancing, and scalability. CFS offers a simple file-system interface, which interprets constituent blocks that may be stored at different peers as files. On bottom, CFS is based on a Chord DHT routing scheme for the lookup support of data blocks. CFS basically offers a read-only system from a user's point of view where consistency is hardly a problem. In contrast to our approach, only a single user, that is, the publisher, is able to modify its own data. However, CFS does not support a publish-subscribe mechanism nor our multi-level naming concept.

OceanStore [30] is designed as an Internet-scale, persistent peer-to-peer data store for incremental scalability, secure sharing, and long-term durability. Data objects are identified by global unique IDs and persisted in an underlying DHT. For an efficient storage, OceanStore splits up data objects into blocks. Multiple users are supported to work on the same data objects, respecting concurrent modifications. There exists also the possibility to equip data files with ACLs. Unlike our work, there are no private storage sections available, nor exists the possibility to store sensitive data locally publishing only metadata, but allowing a transparent retrieval. In addition, no advanced features like observations or type concepts are offered and imposed.

OGSA-DAI [31] is a middleware that enables heterogeneous data resources, e.g., underlying relational or XML databases, to be queried, updated, transformed, compressed, and delivered via web services within a Grid environment. Regarding security, OGSA-DAI establishes a role-based model to grant data access permissions, mapping credentials to corresponding underlying database roles. In contrast to our work, OGSA-DAI targets on concepts of a more generic middleware layer, especially integrating client–server solutions. For the horizontal integration, however, we focus on peer-to-peer techniques with the aim of eliminating central entities in the network. None the less, our repository solution may be integrated to OGSA-DAI as data storage.

8   Conclusion and Outlook

In this paper we introduced an integration architecture and methods to improve interoperability and increase automation of cross enterprise business processes.

While the focus of this paper is on the energy domain, we believe that the results are not restricted to this area of application. The vertical integration approach illustrated in this paper constitutes a high performance platform to manage large scale data intensive systems. Providing an interface of declarative querying and programmable data sources it abstracts from the underlying physics and can be extended to include assets unknown during design time as well add new functions for situation based analytics. Simulations show the performance of the indexing group which scales well to 100000 peers and beyond. Everything considered, the architecture increases the efficiency of today's power networks as well as other industrial applications that rely on large, globally distributed networks with thousands of nodes. Considering horizontal integration, the approach of using a peer-to-peer based content repository to substitute the centralized implementation of the ETSOVista platform's back-end system avoids a single point of failure in critical situations. From a technical point of view, the proposed system is able to benefit distributed collaboration in outage management processes by supporting a publish-subscribe mechanism to enable the rapid notification of critical events to interested parties. The evaluation shows that the system is robust against document losses and achieves good performance regarding document access. From a business point of view, the decentralized solution shows the potential to avoid vendor lock-in situations resulting from a proprietary market information aggregator.

What we have not yet considered in this paper is support of modeling and enacting the cross-enterprise business processes which will be required to operate on top of the document repository. In the future, we shall investigate the suitability of previous work on model-driven design and enactment of cross-organizational business processes (see, e.g., [3],[32], [33]). Also, there has been considerable research in agent-supported market mechanisms for efficient resource allocation[3], which can be employed on top of our run-time infrastructure. A further area of future of work will be to support interoperability and automation of outage report publishing at the system operator's side. This would eliminate the need to manually commit a report to the market information aggregator. At the side of an interested market participant, future work may turn towards the development of techniques to establish a business logic to automatically react to (critical) outage events.

References

1. Fischer, K., Müller, J.P., Stäber, F., Friese, T.: Using peer-to-peer protocols to enable implicit communication in a BDI agent architecture. In: Bordini, R.H., Dastani, M., Dix, J., Fallah, A.E. (eds.) PROMAS 2006. LNCS (LNAI), vol. 4411, pp. 15–37. Springer, Heidelberg (2007)
2. CRUTIAL: Analysis of new control applications. Deliverable D2, Critical Utility Infrastructural Resilience, EU Project IST-FP6-STREP-027513 (2006)

---

[3] Just one example out of many is the work on agent-based auction done at EPRI, see http://www.agentbuilder.com/Documentation/EPRI/index.html

3. Roser, S., Bauer, B., Müller, J.P.: Model- and architecture-driven development in the context of cross-enterprise business process engineering. In: SCC 2006: Proceedings of the IEEE International Conference on Services Computing, Washington, DC, USA, pp. 119–126. IEEE Computer Society, Los Alamitos (2006)
4. Stoica, I., Morris, R., Karger, D., Kaashoek, M.F., Balakrishnan, H.: Chord: A scalable peer-to-peer lookup service for internet applications. In: SIGCOMM 2001: Proceedings of the 2001 conference on Applications, technologies, architectures, and protocols for computer communications, pp. 149–160. ACM, New York (2001)
5. Stäber, F., Gerdes, C., Müller, J.P.: A peer-to-peer-based service infrastructure for distributed power generation. In: Proc. of 17th IFAC World Congress, Seoul, Korea, Intl.l Federation of Automatic Control (2008)
6. Bartlang, U., Stäber, F., Müller, J.P.: Introducing a JSR-170 standard-compliant peer-to-peer content repository to support business collaboration. In: Cunnigham, P., Cunnigham, M. (eds.) Proceedings of eChallenges e-2007 Conference. Information and Communication Technologies and the Knowledge Economy, vol. 4, pp. 814–821. IOS Press, Amsterdam (2007)
7. Date, C.J.: A critique of the SQL database language. SIGMOD Rec. 14, 8–54 (1984)
8. Gerdes, C., Müller, J.P.: Data centric peer-to-peer communication in power networks. In: Proceedings of the First Workshop on Global Sensor Networks (GSN 2009) at KIVS 2009, Kassel, Germany (2009) (forthcoming)
9. Day Management AG.: Content Repository API for Java^{TM} technology specification, Java Specification Request 170, version 1.0 (2005)
10. Bartlang, U., Müller, J.P.: Dhtflex: A flexible approach to enable efficient atomic data management tailored for structured peer-to-peer overlays. In: Mellouk, A., Bi, J., Ortiz, G., Chiu, D.K.W., Popescu, M. (eds.) Proc. Third International Conference on Internet and Web Applications and Services, vol. 3, pp. 377–384. IEEE Computer Society Press, Los Alamitos (2008)
11. Lamport, L.: The part-time parliament. ACM Trans. Comput. Syst. 16, 133–169 (1998)
12. Gray, J., Helland, P., O'Neil, P., Shasha, D.: The dangers of replication and a solution. In: SIGMOD 1996: Proceedings of the 1996 ACM SIGMOD international conference on Management of data, pp. 173–182. ACM, New York (1996)
13. Wang, X.R., Hopkinson, K.M., Thorp, J.S., Giovanini, R., Coury, K.B.D.: Developing an agent-based backup protection system for transmission networks. In: Power Systems and Communication Systems Infrastructures for the Future (2002)
14. Stedall, B., Moore, P., Johns, A., Goody, J., Burt, M.: An investigation into the use of adaptive setting techniques for improved distance back-up protection. IEEE Transactions on Power Delivery 11, 757–762 (1996)
15. Kezunovic, M.: Intelligent systems in protection engineering. In: Proc. of International Conference on Power System Technology, vol. 2, pp. 801–806 (2000)
16. Kim, M., Damborg, M., Huang, J., Venkata, S.: Wide-area protection using distributed control and high speed communications. In: 14th Power Systems Computation Conference (2002)
17. Gummadi, K.P., Saroiu, S., Gribble, S.D.: King: estimating latency between arbitrary internet end hosts. In: IMW 2002: Proceedings of the 2nd ACM SIGCOMM Workshop on Internet measurment, pp. 5–18. ACM, New York (2002)
18. Aberer, K., Hauswirth, M., Salehi, A.: Infrastructure for data processing in large-scale interconnected sensor networks. In: International Conference on Mobile Data Management, 2007, pp. 198–205 (2007)
19. Oezsu, M.T., Valduriez, P.: Principles of Distributed Database Systems. Prentice-Hall, Englewood Cliffs (1999)

20. Golab, L., Oezsu, M.T.: Issues in data stream management. SIGMOD Rec. 32, 5–14 (2003)
21. Kucuk, D., Boyrazoglu, B., Buhan, S.: Pqstream: A data stream architecture for electrical power quality. In: International Workshop on Knowledge Discovery from Ubiquitous Data Streams (2007)
22. Stonebraker, M., Aoki, P.M., Litwin, W., Pfeffer, A., Sah, A., Sidell, J., Staelin, C., Yu, A.: Mariposa: A wide-area distributed database system. VLDB Journal: Very Large Data Bases 5, 48–63 (1996)
23. Cherniack, M., Balakrishnan, H., Balazinska, M., Carney, D., Cetintemel, U., Xing, Y., Zdonik, S.: Scalable Distributed Stream Processing. In: CIDR 2003 - First Biennial Conference on Innovative Data Systems Research, Asilomar, CA (2003)
24. Garofalakis, M., Gehrke, J., Rastogi, R.: Data Stream Management: Processing High-Speed Data Streams (Data-Centric Systems and Applications). Springer, New York (2007)
25. Gehrke, J., Madden, S.: Query processing in sensor networks. IEEE Pervasive Computing 3, 46–55 (2004)
26. Rowstron, A., Druschel, P.: Pastry: Scalable, decentralized object location, and routing for large-scale peer-to-peer systems. In: Guerraoui, R. (ed.) Middleware 2001. LNCS, vol. 2218, pp. 329–350. Springer, Heidelberg (2001)
27. Boyd, S., Ghosh, A., Prabhakar, B., Shah, D.: Gossip algorithms: design, analysis and applications. In: Proceedings IEEE INFOCOM 2005. 24th Annual Joint Conference of the IEEE Computer and Communications Societies, March 13-17, 2005, vol. 3, pp. 1653–1664 (2005)
28. Friese, T., Müller, J.P., Smith, M., Freisleben, B.: A robust business resource management framework based on a peer-to-peer infrastructure. In: Proc. 7th International IEEE Conference on E-Commerce Technology, pp. 215–222 (2005)
29. Dabek, F., Kaashoek, M.F., Karger, D., Morris, R., Stoica, I.: Wide-area cooperative storage with CFS. In: SOSP 2001: Proceedings of the eighteenth ACM symposium on Operating systems principles, pp. 202–215. ACM Press, New York (2001)
30. Kubiatowicz, J., Bindel, D., Chen, Y., Czerwinski, S., Eaton, P., Geels, D., Gummadi, R., Rhea, S., Weatherspoon, H., Wells, C., Zhao, B.: OceanStore: an architecture for global-scale persistent storage. In: ASPLOS-IX: Proceedings of the ninth international conference on Architectural support for programming languages and operating systems, pp. 190–201. ACM, New York (2000)
31. Karasavvas, K., Antonioletti, M., Atkinson, M., Hong, N.C., Sugden, T., Hume, A., Jackson, M., Krause, A., Palansuriya, C.: Introduction to OGSA-DAI services. In: Herrero, P., Pérez, M.S., Robles, V. (eds.) SAG 2004. LNCS, vol. 3458, pp. 1–12. Springer, Heidelberg (2005)
32. Kahl, T., Zinnikus, I., Roser, S., Hahn, C., Ziemann, J., Müller, J.P., Fischer, K.: Architecture for the design and agent-based implementation of cross-enterprise business processes. In: Gonçalves, R., et al. (eds.) Enterprise Interoperability II: In Proceedings of the 3rd International Conference on Interoperability of Enterprise Software and Applications (I-ESA 2007), pp. 207–218. Springer, Heidelberg (2007)
33. Stiefel, P., Müller, J.P., Bessling, S., Hausknecht, C., Dokters, T.: Realizing dynamic product collaboration processes in a model-driven framework: Case study and lessons learnt. In: Proceedings of the 14th International Conference of Concurrent Engineering, Lisbon, Portugal, pp. 983–990 (2008)

Agents for Cross-Organisational Business Interoperability

Iain Duncan Stalker[1] and Nikolay Mehandjiev[2]

[1] School of Science and Technology, University of Teesside,
Middlesbrough TS1 3BA, UK
i.stalker@tees.ac.uk
[2] Manchester Business School, The University of Manchester,
Manchester M15 6PB, UK

Abstract. Increasing complexity of products and services together with shrinking lead times means that demands are often best satisfied through dynamic networks of collaborating enterprises. Businesses seek agile partnerships where companies focus on core business activities and partners provide complementary expertise. Successful collaboration demands a tight yet flexible integration of business processes. In this paper we focus on issues of process interoperability and the use of agents to support *cross-organisational process interoperability*. We maintain that an informed decision on the place of agents within this context demands a systematic approach: such an approach forms the core contribution of this paper. We apply a modified version of the *function-behaviour-structure* (FBS) framework of Gero as an organising schema to develop a clarifying structure; and to help determine the role of software agents. In particular, we use the formal elements of the FBS framework to identify those areas where agents may be applied. We highlight the need to combine this with appropriate mechanisms to promote *semantic interoperability*.

Keywords: Process interoperability, agents, system design, semantic interoperability.

1 Introduction

Increasing complexity of products and services together with shrinking lead times means that demands are often best satisfied through dynamic networks of collaborating enterprises. Businesses seek agile partnerships. Effective cross-organisational collaboration enables a company to focus on its core business within a dynamic network of partners which provide complementary expertise. This allows companies of all sizes to pursue immediate opportunities in a chosen market through participation in virtual enterprises (VEs) and dynamic supply chains. Moreover, the trend towards eBusiness places substantial demands on software infrastructures to ensure robust intersystem communication, meaningful information exchange and successful coordination of processes and activities. Interoperability at all levels is paramount and significant advances in enabling

K. Fischer et al. (Eds.): ATOP 2005 and ATOP 2008, LNBIP 25, pp. 29–46, 2009.

software technologies are needed to support this. Compatibility of business processes and activities must be realised through *process interoperability*. As the information processing infrastructures of the participants are typically linked, a frictionless information exchange requires *interoperability at the systems level*. Activities arise within the context of compatible legal and organisational structures predicating *interoperability at the business level*. Moreover, any successful collaboration is informed and underpinned by a shared understanding and this reveals a fundamental need for *semantic interoperability*.

The nature of a collaborative business network is such that a seamless coordination of processes through cross-organisational workflows is fundamental to its effective operation and the fulfilment of the purpose for which it formed. This provides the focus for interoperability issues. We see interoperability as a systemic property of the set of collaborating entities, which emerges as a consequence of their interaction, rather than as an individual property of system components. Consider the following definition of the IEEE of interoperability as the "... *ability of two or more systems or components to exchange information and to use the information that has been exchanged*" (IEEE, 1990). This has the following consequences for the mechanisms which underpin our approach to interoperability:

Process interoperability is currently supported only in a limited manner by state-of-the-art approaches. Consider, the process interoperability support offered by current Workflow Management System (WfMS), is predicated upon standard cross-organisational reference processes which are separate from the internal workflow processes of individual organisations. The two are linked through (implementations of) *ad hoc* interfaces of individual suppliers: this creates inflexible and proprietary solutions. Instead, we make use of collaborating software agents to achieve a goal-driven dynamic formation of both the team and the workflow coordinating team activities. Intelligent agent technology can provide the capabilities for deliberative reasoning; dynamic goal-oriented behaviour; and explicit declaration of interaction intent and structure. Agents are therefore used to represent collaborating business entities, providing natural representations in software for business autonomy, information hiding, self-interested behaviour and coalition formation. Agents are also a natural choice to support an ontology-based approach to semantic interoperability: they employ sophisticated communication mechanisms, based on explicit declaration of intent and ontological commitment; and provide the negotiation and reasoning capabilities necessary to maintain a devolved ontology model (cf. Section 4).

Semantic interoperability is based on the use of ontologies; and negotiation mechanisms to find common ground and identify shared ontological commitments among interacting group members. This leads to a core ontology common to all group members and a number of peripheral ontologies, each of which extends this core and is specific to a sub-group or individual organisation. Novel negotiation protocols, informed by the theory of utility and supported by rigorous ontology mappings, enable the evolution of the core and the peripheral ontologies:

for example, to incorporate new capabilities and services within the task group. Automatic reasoning within this context is underpinned by the use of Formal Concept Analysis [4] and Lattice Theory [3]. The resultant model, e.g. [2], which we call Devolved Ontology, integrates centralised and distributed approaches to ontology engineering.

In this paper we focus primarily on issues of process interoperability and the use of agents to support *cross-organisational process interoperability.*/ Our approach to semantic interoperability is discussed elsewhere, see for example [2], though we do touch upon this in Section 4. The approach reported here differs from other efforts, for example, [11,21,14], in the use of a formal model of the cognitive aspects of our domain constructed *a priori.* This allows us to determine the place of agents in a systematic fashion rather than developing *ad hoc* solutions.

We treat workflow configuration as a design problem. Design problems are typically under-defined, that is, the information needed to properly define a particular design problem is not available from the problem statement [22,23]. Some form of preliminary exploration is needed to clarify the structure of the problem (cf. decision or design) space and a significant part of any design effort is devoted to this learning. An *a priori* structuring of the cross-organisational aspects is an invaluable aid to preliminary exploration in business process coordination and workflow configuration. Moreover, an informed decision on the place of agents in decentralised workflow management systems demands a systematic approach and this, again, motivates some *a priori* structuring.

We suggest the *function-behaviour-structure* (FBS) framework [1] as an organising schema to conceptualise design of workflow structures and to help determine the role of software agents. FBS has been applied in a number of engineering domains such as civil engineering, process engineering and even software engineering, but not yet to constructing workflow software. We emphasise that here we are using FBS as an informing framework rather than proposing it as an alternative to existing approaches to the development of agent-based systems and management of cross-organisational workflows. In particular, we use its formal elements to develop a systematic approach to identify areas where agents may be applied, highlighting potential contributions, to the design and construction of decentralised workflows.

This paper is an elaboration of earlier work [5] and is structured as follows. In Section 2 we present the function-behaviour-structure framework of Gero [1]: we use a slightly modified version of this to develop a framework for cross-organisational team and workflow formations, clarifying the interactions between these. In Section 3 we use the framework to identify potential areas for the application of agents. In Section 4 we briefly discuss semantic interoperability as a necessary complement to process interoperability through agents, before reflecting on our contribution, discussing some issues we feel it appropriate to clarify and cosidering how the approach may be evaluated in Section 5. We close with some concluding remarks in Section 6.

2   FBS

The function-behaviour-structure (FBS) framework [1] underlies a knowledge-based approach to conceptual design and is motivated by the following presupposition:

> ... the metagoal of design is to transform function F ... into a design description D in such a way that the [design] artefact being described is capable of producing these functions. [1]

The design description documents the structure of the (*design*) *artefact* which is the intended product of a conceptual design effort. In our case, the artefact is a process: a global workflow linking participants in a VE. As there is generally no function in structure nor structure in function, the transformation from function to description proceeds in stages; and the FBS framework, illustrated in Fig. 1, was devised to elaborate these.

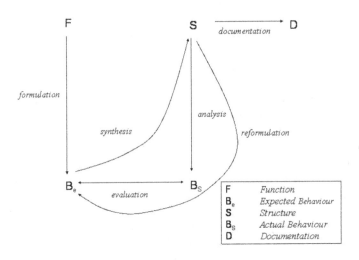

Fig. 1. The Function-Behaviour-Structure (FBS) Framework of [1]

The FBS framework identifies a number of categories of (domain) knowledge and separates this from the computational processes (transformations) which operate (act) upon it. With an identified function (or set of functions), F, we associate a number of expected behaviours, B_e, through which to realise this (*formulation*). We identify (a partial order of) components which exhibit these behaviours and assemble these into an appropriate structure, S (*synthesis*). We use appropriate techniques to predict the behaviours, B_S, of the resulting structure (*analysis*) and compare these with those expected (*evaluation*). If the two sets of behaviours match, then we formalise the design (*documentation*); otherwise, we return to and possibly revise the set of expected behaviours and synthesise a new structure (*reformulation*): strictly speaking, reformulation is the full loop from S to S through B_S and B_e, which takes into account the information obtained through analysis and evaluation.

2.1 Modes of Reasoning and Enlarged FBS

The notions of *function, behaviour* and *structure* identify categories of knowledge which are useful in the design process without being prescriptive. In applying the FBS framework to team and workflow formation, we find it useful to insert an additional category, *capability*, between function and behaviour[1]. We consider formulation as associating function with capability and we use the term specification to denote the association of capability with behaviour. By decomposing function into subfunctions and mapping these onto necessary capabilities, we provide a first step in identifying potential team members, by matching desired capabilities with those possessed by a given resource. This will become clearer in the following discussion of applying the FBS to team and workflow formation. For ease of exposition, we consider a (cross-organisational or individual) (business) process to be formalised as a workflow.

2.2 Applying FBS to Team and Workflow Formation

We apply the FBS framework once we have established the desired outcome of the global workflow. The design of a workflow is intimately related to the formation of a core team of partners who will work together on a project, such as car assembly. However, this is not necessarily straightforward. We distinguish two modes of interaction between the team formation and workflow design: team formation precedes the workflow design; and team formation is interwoven with the workflow design. We could consider a third possibility: a core team assembles prior to workflow design, but is enlarged during workflow design as additional long term requirements are identified; this is a combination of the two previous modes.

Team formation precedes workflow formation. We view this as an independent, preliminary application of the FBS framework. Here, the design artefact denotes the team to be assembled and the function is the capacity to realise, i.e. the ability to perform or produce, the global business process for which the team is assembled. This capacity translates into a set of capabilities (cf. formulation), such as car engine assembly, or parts manufacture such as the production of a car body. A potential participant in a VE is a *resource* possessing certain capabilities expected of a particular *resource class* (cf. [6]). Thus, subsets of the capabilities needed to realise the global business process can be used to identify relevant resource classes and thus potential team members. Since in team formation we do not need to go to the level of behaviours, we think of capability as abstract behaviour and do not distinguish between formulation and specification. Thus, we identify capability with behaviour here and use it to synthesise a team structure.

---

[1] Rather than revising Fig. 1 to reflect this insertion, we refer the reader to the central column of Fig. 3 to see where this is located.

We examine the interdependencies of (the capabilities of) these resources and use the information to help to establish a team structure: for example, if one resource coordinates input from a number of resources, then this might suggest assigning management responsibilities to it, e.g. a partner responsible for assembling a car might manage those partners which supply the necessary components; this corresponds to synthesis, cf. Fig. 1. We analyse the team structure and the capabilities of the members to ensure that all phases and aspects of team interaction are supported by the core competencies (cf. actual behaviours in Fig. 1) of the team (cf. analysis in Fig. 1). We compare the competencies with the identified capabilities (cf. evaluation in Fig. 1). At this stage we might recognise that while the competencies subsume the necessary capabilities, our team lacks necessary competence to support an important aspect of the team interactions which was overlooked during the initial formulation: for example, by focusing on the physical artefact in car assembly, we may have neglected to ensure that our team has the necessary competence to support interorganisational accounting. Thus, we revise our initial set of capabilities to accommodate this and recycle through the FBS (cf. reformulation in Fig. 1).

Having established a core team of partners, we can apply the FBS to the different phases of the team operation to design appropriate workflow structures to support these. Where appropriate this would include the formation of a subteam, or task force, to address a particular phase: this is interwoven with the workflow design as suggested below, with the members chosen from our core team. For example, in the case of car assembly, we would cycle through the FBS to coordinate the supporting processes of parts manufacture and timely delivery to support a consistent throughput at the assembly location; in a wider sense we can use the distinctions of the FBS to design workflows to support the global business process, including bidding for contracts, or accounting and financial processes.

The application of FBS to team formation reveals an immediate potential for integration of model-driven approaches with agent-based approaches: an agent representing a partner within a given VE offers one or more services; potentially, these services can be described using fragments of languages which already exist in the domain of workflow management, for example, in the XML-based *eXchangeable Routing Language* (XRL) [7].

Team formation is interwoven with the workflow design. In this case, we use the formation of a team within the FBS framework. Here, the design artefact is a global workflow and the function is the realisation of global business process. With the function we associate a number of capabilities. When team formation is interwoven with the workflow design, we distinguish formulation and specification. We identify the capabilities needed as in the case when team formation precedes workflow formation, using team structure to inform the workflow structure.

Each capability is realised by a particular resource through a set of behaviours, or tasks, which we associate with it. The explicit statement of these expected behaviours denotes specification. We examine the interdependencies of the resulting behaviours: for example, some behaviours, or tasks, must follow or require information from others, others are independent, some may be alternatives and still others need to be carried out a number of times to achieve the desired end. These interdependencies can be classified as *sequential, parallel, selective* and *iterative* [6]. For example, in the car assembly, the manufacture of an axle must precede its attachment to the chassis (sequential); whereas, the manufacture of a dashboard is independent of manufacturer a disc brake (parallel). Identifying the interdependencies of tasks and behaviours allows us to partially order them into a global structure: this is referred to as *routing* [6]. This forms part of synthesis of Fig. 1. We examine the global workflow, using suitable tools and techniques, to confirm that it achieves the desired top level goal, by comparing this analysis with our formulated expected behaviours (cf. analysis and evaluation in Fig. 1).

Again, the application of FBS reveals a potential for integration of model-driven approaches with agent-based approaches: the analysis of the workflows can be undertaken using specialised Petri Nets, referred to as *workflow nets* in [6]. Ideally, the predicted behaviours should be a safe superset of the expected behaviours: that is, there should be no undesirable additional behaviours deriving from the proposed workflow structure, for example, *deadlocks,* where a process reaches an impasse, or *livelocks,* where a process falls into an infinite loop [6]. If the analysis and evaluation reveal inadequacies in our proposed workflow structure, we use this information to revise our set of expected behaviours (cf. reformulation of Fig. 1).

We can interpret the global workflow structure developed as a syntactic structure which has as its semantics the realisation of the global business process (cf. [1]). This reveals another potential integration of agent based approaches and model-driven approaches: not only can the description of services offered by particular agents, or resources, be supported through the use of XRL [7], so can the sharing of any semantic information (electronically) by agents during this stage.

2.3   Product-Process-Team

In many domains knowledge about the final product to be realised through the cross-organisational collaboration provides information which is invaluable when it comes to identifying the dependencies of the activities of the partnership members and these in turn influence the structure of the team. For example, the structure of a car and in particular its composition from identifiable components imposes a sequence on the tasks in the assembly process. Also, each component must have been manufactured, quality tested and delivered prior to assembly. Moreover, the need for a given component or the need for a given skill in the assembly process identifies necessary expertise which must be embodied by some partner(s) in the network producing the car. Formally, the semantics of the product informs the semantics of the process and the semantics of the process informs the semantics of the team. As an analogy we can think of a client-server relationship existing between the product and process; and also between the process and team. We reflect this client-server relationship by a directional arrow in (the UML diagram of) Fig 2.

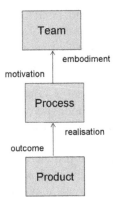

Fig. 2. Product-Process-Team Dependencies

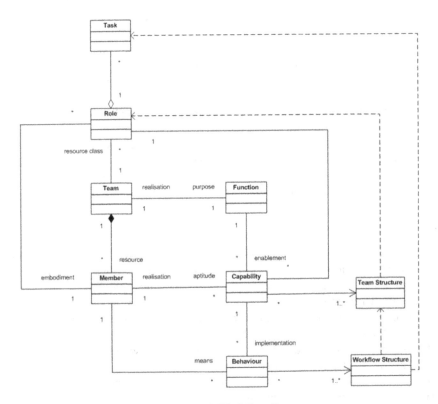

Fig. 3. Team and Workflow Structures

Using this observation to inform the application of the FBS framework (discussed above) allows us to develop a model which clarifies the structures of teams and workflows and there interrelations. We illustrate this model in (the UML diagram of) Fig. 3.

3   Application of Agents

Using the model of the strategic level developed in the preceding section, we now examine (some of) the transformations among the categories distinguished above to identify potential opportunities for the application of agents. We are guided by the widely accepted definition of a (software) agent as a computer system capable of flexible, autonomous action which subsists within some environment. The capabilities of such a system were distilled into three expectations by Wooldridge and Jennings [8], namely:

- *Proactiveness* - an agent acts in a goal directed manner under its own initiative;
- *Reactivity* - an agent perceives its environment and responds appropriately, in a timely manner to changes to this; and
- *Social ability* - an agent communicates, as necessary, with other agents (including human agents) to achieve its goals.

In each case we consider the application type and the suitability of agents. We note that Wooldridge [9] presents the domain of workflow and business process management as a notable application of multiagent technology (p. 245), including ADEPT [11,10]. Of particular interest is the broad classification of applied agents into two groups by Wooldridge [9]:

- *Distributed systems* where agents become processing nodes in a network; and
- *Personal software assistants* where agents act as proactive, intelligent assistants to facilitate user tasks.

Representing each participant in a VE as an agent, or indeed, as a team of agents, corresponds to the notion of a distributed system above. In the each of the applications discussed below, we include a *coordinator*. This is a personal software assistant to facilitate the designer of the workflow.

3.1   Formulation and Specification

Formulation and specification are prime candidates for the introduction of personal software assistants, in particular, *a goal decomposition agent* to help the human designer. The goal decomposition agent may use one or more knowledge sources: for example, the appropriate agent has access to two knowledge sources, one of which associates (sets of) function(s) and (sets of) capabilities, for example standard decompositions of global service(s) into component services, and one which associates capabilities with (sets of) behaviour(s), for example component services as a set of behaviours. Alternatively, it may be appropriate to consider more than one agent, each agent equipped with knowledge required to refine one level of abstraction, along the continuum from function to capability to behaviour, to a less abstract level, reflecting a recursive application of formulation. This decision depends on the application requirements and cannot be made in the general case.

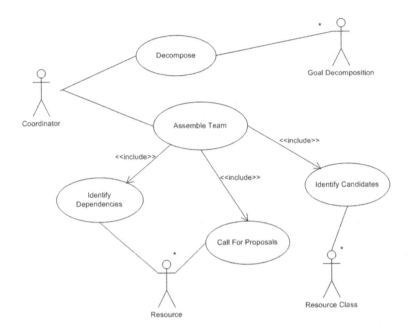

Fig. 4. Formulation in Workflow Design and Team Formation

In either case, a (possible) functional view of agents in formulation is illustrated in the use case diagram of Fig. 4.

The coordinator obtains from a (team of) goal decomposition agent(s) a set of services (capabilities) and tasks (behaviours) which are needed to fulfil the given top-level goal. If team structure is not predefined, then the coordinator can use the decomposition to assemble an appropriate team. This will involve making a call for proposals to relevant resources, identifying dependencies of tasks and resources and entering into negotiations. Depending upon the number of potential candidates, the coordinator might make use of one or more resource class agents to identify candidate team members before calling for proposals. A *resource class agent* would essentially wrap a library of resources, identifying a number of resource classes, agents belonging to these and the appropriate addresses, for example, in the form of Universal Resource Locators.

In Table 1 we consider the three characteristics identified in the introductory remarks at the beginning of this section, cf. [8] for each actor in use case diagram of Fig 4. In particular, a tick in a cell indicates that the given characteristic (column) is definitely demonstrated by the appropriate actor (row); a cross indicates that the given characteristic is not shown; and where the cell is left blank, we are noncommittal. For example, for the goal decomposition agent, we are noncommittal about whether it requires reactivity or social ability to fulfil its given function. There might be a team of goal decomposition agents which work together and in such a case, reactivity and social ability are certainly exhibited. We consider the positive presence of at least one of these characteristics,

Table 1. Actors in Formulation in Workflow Design and Team Formation

Actor	Use Case	Proactivity	Reactivity	Social Ability
Coordinator	Decompose Assemble team	✓	✓	✓
Goal Decomposition	Decompose	✓		
Resource	Identify Dependencies, Call for proposals			✓
Resource Class	Identify Candidates		✗	

as shown through a tick, to be sufficient motivation to explore the possibility of agents for the given function fulfilled by the actor. In the use cases presented, the resource class agent is an interesting actor. We have anticipated in the name that it will be an agent, but since in a general sense none of the characteristics is exhibited and we can clearly infer that no reactivity is needed, it is fair to propose that this agent be replaced by some other device, for example a look up table. In such a case, the device could be wrapped using by agent to endow it with communication abilities and knowledge of what service it provides; and thus allow it to participate in the agent based system, rather than functioning as an isolated set of methods.

3.2   Synthesis

Synthesis is also an area where we could consider personal software assistants. For example, in constructing the global workflow, we might make use of a *routing agent*. The routing agent contributes by determining a partial ordering of the appropriate tasks, according to the dependencies established as a consequence of consultation and negotiation between resources and the coordinator; thus, removing the need for this to be done manually. Technically, synthesis involves identifying structural elements which exhibit one or more of the desired behaviours; discovering the dependencies among these; composing these structural elements into a global structure which ideally retains the necessary behaviours. Naturally, determining the dependencies among structural elements is a non-trivial, knowledge-based task and we should note that these dependencies are not merely temporal. Synthesis can be informed by existing work, for example, process views [12] admit of safe abstractions of local workflows, removing detail irrelevant to the global perspective where synthesis occurs; again providing for integration of model-based and agent-based approaches. A (possible) functional view of synthesis is illustrated in Fig. 5. The use case *Establish Dependencies* parallels the use case *Identify Dependencies* of Fig. 4 However, the focus in the former is at the task level with a view to determining sequence, parallelisation, selection and iteration of these tasks, whereas in the latter, the focus is on which tasks and process requires inputs and interactions with other with a view to establishing a team structure.

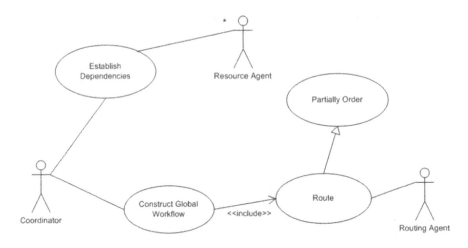

Fig. 5. Synthesis of Global Workflows

Table 2. Actors in Synthesis of Global Workflows

Actor	Use Case	Proactivity	Reactivity	Social Ability
Coordinator	Establish Dependencies, Construct Global Workflow	✓	✓	✓
Resource Agent	Establish Dependencies	✓		✓
Routing Agent	Route	✓	✗	✗

As before, in Table 2 we consider the three characteristics—proactiveness, reactivity and social ability—for each actor. Of particular interest here is the *routing agent*. Strictly speaking, to fulfil its function it does not require reactivity nor social ability, since we assume that the routing is undertaken once the dependencies among the resources are know. Thus, there is a case for having a "non-agent" to fulfill the routing function, for example, an appropriate automated tool from model-based approach to workflow construction. Again, the device could be wrapped using by agent to endow it with communication abilities and knowledge of what service it provides. Moreover, here the wrapping would provide a systematic way in which to integrate model-based tool into an agent-based system.

3.3   Analysis and Evaluation

There exist a number of tools for analysing workflows, e.g. [7]. An agent which is able to interpret the results of the analyses and use these in evaluation of

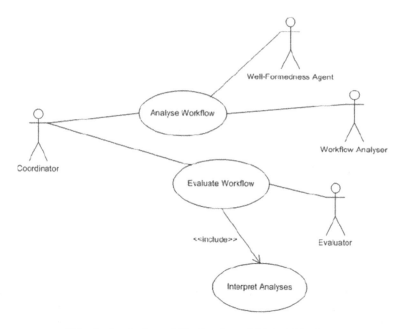

Fig. 6. Analysis and Evaluation of Global Workflows

workflows is a potential application for a personal software assistant, with a capacity to compare of the predicted behaviours with the expected behaviours. Where the comparison indicates inadequacies in the global workflow, the evaluator can communicate this information to those agents which participate in reformulation.

It might be convenient to have such a *workflow analyser* work in conjunction with a *well-formedness agent* which can ensure the validity of formal representations, such as XRL, which are used to represent the workflow. We illustrate such a scenario in the use cases of Fig. 6. Evaluation is often used to select among candidate proposals from project partners: the best chosen based upon the information obtained from analysis and comparison with appropriate ranking criteria.

Again, in Table 3 we consider proactiveness, for each actor in use case diagram of Fig. 6. As for the routing agent of the previous subsection, there is a case for having a non-agent to fulfill the analysis and evaluation functions; for example, appropriate automated tools from model-based approaches. These could be wrapped using by agents provide communication abilities and knowledge of what services provided, as a way in which to systematically integrate model-based techniques into an agent based system.

3.4 Reformulation

We treat reformulation as a revision of the formulation and synthesis stages, taking account of the additional information obtained through analysis and

Table 3. Actors in Analysis and Evaluation Global Workflows

Actor	Use Case	Proactivity	Reactivity	Social Ability
Coordinator	Analyse Workflow, Evaluate Workflow	✓	✓	✓
Well-formedness Agent	Analyse Workflow	✓		✓
Workflow Analyser	Analyse Workflow		✗	✗
Evaluator	Evaluate Workflow		✗	✗

evaluation. For example, preferring a particular workflow from a number of alternatives based upon analysis and evaluation might lead to a reallocation of services or a re-ordering of tasks. The agents responsible for formulation and synthesis assume responsibility for reformulations.

4   Semantic Interoperability Through Devolved Ontology

While multiagent systems offer much to foster the open nature of agile partnerships, for example, *ad hoc* interaction with new arrivals is supported through agent communication languages and standardised exchanges of messages for common conversation patterns (*interaction protocols*), there are limitations. To communicate effectively our agents must use a common vocabulary and agree on the semantics of the terms in it. Typically, communication in multiagent systems presupposes a common ontology[2] which is fixed in both content and semantics. Yet, the very nature of agile partnerships suggests neither a fixed ontology nor a unique semantics is appropriate. A fixed ontology precludes the enrichment of the partnership with a new range of services: the necessary concepts to describe this are typically not contained in the ontology. Such enrichments often arise within the partnership, when an existing partner introduces a new service; and are concomitant with the arrival of a new partner. The diversity of backgrounds means that partners often interpret the same term differently. Formally, each maintains a different view of the same concept and these may be inconsistent or even contradictory. As such the semantics of a given term is fluid within a partnership. More interestingly, a partner can learn the view of another, entertaining simultaneously a number of views of a single concept and choosing the most appropriate according to context.

---

[2] An *ontology* is a formal (partial) account of a domain of interest: this can be used to realise a controlled vocabulary to support communication.

We have devised a model of an evolvable, devolved ontology to promote *ad hoc* semantic interoperability in open environments and agile partnerships. We have developed a formal framework for devolved ontologies and use this to address novel concepts arising within an agile partnership. Technical details of this are not presented here; see, for example [2]. This is based on the use Formal Concept Analysis [4], lattice theory [3] and aspects of *Partially Shared Views* (PSV) [13].

Informally, a devolved ontology comprises of a core ontology and a number of peripheral ontologies. The core ontology provides a common ground for understanding among partners and is central to the partnership. The concepts included within this are agreed through negotiation of all partners. As such, the responsibility for the evolution and maintenance of the core is shared by the partners. Each peripheral ontology represents an extension of the core ontology into an application domain. The responsibility for the evolution and maintenance of each peripheral ontology *devolves* upon the appropriate partner or partners. This includes the responsibility for extending the core into the particular context and ensuring that the peripheral ontology remains consistent with the core. Moreover, we recognise the existence of interapplication domains or ontologies. For example, two partners may share a number of concepts which are not part of the core. The responsibility for the initial extension of the core into the interapplication ontology devolves upon two agents jointly; the responsibility for the further extension devolving onto the appropriate single agent. Thus, a devolved ontology exhibits a recursive structure. Agents entering into an (independent) agreement prior to the formation of the partnership should strictly be treated as a federation. For the purposes of the negotiation of the partnership core the federation is essentially a single agent.

Since the participants in agile partnerships are fundamentally self-interested, we supplement our framework with appropriate mechanisms to capture this. We make use of the theory of utility to develop negotiation protocols [2].

5   Discussion

Beginning with the FBS framework of Gero [1], we have developed a model to clarify the strategic aspects of team and workflow formation in agile partnerships. Our aim here was to present a framework which can be used systematically to identify potential opportunities for the application of agent technology to foster cross-organisational (business or production) process interoperability.

We have shown how we can use this framework systematically to identify where agents might be applied. In particular, we have clarified the decision space for cross-organisational process design and coordination, using FBS to distinguish a number of categories of knowledge and the transformations between these categories. Elements of this framework were used in CrossWork project [19] to inform the decision of where to apply agents in a set of concrete usage scenarios: for example, agents were used in team formation, see [20]. The approach also partly-informed software architectural design decisions in the ongoing European Project SUDDEN (www.sudden.org.uk).

We reiterate that here we are using FBS as an informing framework rather than proposing it as an alternative to existing approaches to the development of agent-based systems. We feel it important to clarify this as there exist a number of well-constructed approaches which we use with our framework; in particular, *Aalaadin* [16] and *Gaia* [17]. Moreover, we are fully aware that work in this area continues, for example, recent developments include the model-based methodology of Jarraya and Guessoum [15]. Additionally, we are not proposing the approach as a way in which to manage, especially at an operational level, cross-organisational workflows. Again, we have used the framework with existing approaches; for example, in CrossWork we appealled to the three-tier model developed in the CrossFlow Project [24].

We emphasise that the core contribution of the work expounded here is a systematic way in which to inform the decision of where and whether to use agents in coordinating decentralised, cross-organisational (business) processes. We have proposed elements of a generic framework which could be specialised to a particular application according to end-user requirements. Indeed, applying the proposed elements to as many concrete usage scenarios as possible, offers a means, perhaps, the only means of evaluating our work. It is a systematic approach to inform decisions on the use of agents and as such must be evaluated on its utility in comparison with the typically *ad hoc* approaches that we have observed. Such an effort forms a key part of our ongoing work.

6   Conclusion

Approaches to business processes and the intimately related workflow systems have been traditionally based on two alternative approaches: model-driven, e.g. [6], in which a predefined (workflow) model, guides the execution of a global business process; and agent-based (e.g. [10]), in which a workflow emerges from the interaction of agents associated with different participants in the global business process. Each alternative has particular strengths and weaknesses; and while there have been (early) attempts to obtain the "best of both worlds" by combining the two, cf. [14], which typically, have followed *ad hoc* conceptualisations of the process of workflow design and management. An informed use of agents in cross-organisational (business) processes demands a more systematic approach. We propose function-behaviour-structure [1] as an organising schema to structure the process of workflow design and construction, which then helps us to identify the roles of software agents in the workflow design process. The FBS is particularly appealing as an organising schema because:

- *It is noncommittal about the expression of the categories of knowledge.* For example, in the case where the design artefact is actually a system, our initial function set might be expressed as a set of top-level use cases which we progressively refine; alternatively, our function might be a set of data flow diagrams. Behaviours could be expressed through state diagrams or activity diagrams, etc. In the case of workflows, our structure might simply be a Petri net.

- *It provides a starting point for identifying and classifying relevant domain knowledge, a useful prelude to developing an ontology for the domain(s) of interest.* For example, using an object-oriented approach, we identify categories of objects some of which are simply items which will be manipulated, rather than having any responsibilities, and typically, these can be associated with concepts of our domain of interest.
- *It does not prescribe the form of the operations on or transformations between the categories of knowledge.* This allows for the inclusion within it appropriate models of these transformations. For example, we might map from function to behaviours through a goal to task decomposition; or, if appropriate, we may appeal to a data-centric approach such as Jackson Structured Design; or, of course, agent based approaches.

The use of agents to support cross-organisational process interoperability reduces the burden on the designer, for example, by (partially) automating negotiation between and coordination of the participants in an agile partnership. However, an agent-based approach, like any automated approach, not only removes the onus from the user, it also removes a certain amount of control. Thus, we need to ensure that we promote an interactivity at each stage. For example, we could use the coordinator to feed back some of the design choices for confirmation by the designer and allowing the him to supervise the system, thus returning control without the burden.

References

1. Gero, J.S.: Design prototypes: A knowledge representation schema for design. AI Magazine, 26–36 (Winter 1990)
2. Stalker, I.D., Mehandiev, N.D.: A Devolved Ontology Model for the Pragmatic Web. In: Schoop, M., de Moor, A., Dietz, J. (eds.) Proceedings of the First International Pragmatic Web Conference (PragWeb 2006). Lecture Notes in Informatics, vol. 89 (2006)
3. Birkhoff, G.: Lattice Theory, 3rd edn. AMS Colloquium Publ., Providence (1967)
4. Ganter, B., Wille, R.: Formal Concept Analysis. Mathematical Foundations. Springer, Heidelberg (1999)
5. Stalker, I.D., Mehandjiev, N.D.: 'Agents for Cross-Organisational Business Interoperability'. In: Proceedings of ATOP 2005, Workshop of AAMAS 2005 (July 2005)
6. van der Aalst, W., van Hee, K.: Workflow Management: Models, Methods, and Systems, Cooperative Information Systems. The MIT Press, Cambridge (2002)
7. van der Aalst, W.M.P., Verbeek, H.M.W., Kumar, A.: XRL/Woflan: Verification of an XML/Petri-net based language for inter-organizational workflows. In: Altinkemer, K., Chari, K. (eds.) Proceedings of the 6th Informs Conference on Information Systems and Technology (CIST 2001), Informs, Linthicum, MD, pp. 30–45 (2001)
8. Wooldridge, M., Jennings, N.R.: Intelligent agents: theory and practice. The Knowledge Engineering Review 10(2), 115–152 (1995)
9. Wooldridge, M.: An Introduction to Multiagent Systems. Wiley & Sons Ltd., Chichester (2002)

10. Jennings, N.R., Faratin, P., Norman, T.J., O'Brien, P., Wiegand, M.E., Voudouris, C., Alty, J.L., Miah, T., Mamdani, E.H.: ADEPT: Managing Business Processes using Intelligent Agents. In: Proceedings of BCS Expert Systems 96 Conference (Intelligent Systems Integration Programme Track), Cambridge, UK, pp. 5–23 (1996)

11. Jennings, N.R., Faratin, P., Norman, T.J., O'Brien, P., Odgers, B., Alty, J.L.: Implementing a Business Process Management System using ADEPT: A Real-World Case Study. Int. Journal of Applied Artificial Intelligence 14(5), 421–465 (2000)

12. Liu, D.-R., Shen, M.: Workflow modeling for virtual processes: an order-preserving process-view approach. Information Systems 28(1) (2003)

13. Lee, J., Malone, T.W.: Partially shared views: A scheme for communicating among groups that use different type hierarchies. ACM Transactions on Information Systems 8(1) (1990)

14. Myers, K.L., Berry, P.M.: Workflow Management Systems: An AI Perspective. Technical Report, Artificial Intelligence Center, SRI International, 333 Ravenswood Ave, Menlo Park, CA 94025 (January 1999)

15. Jarraya, T., Guessoum, Z.: Towards a Model Driven Process for Multi-Agent System. In: Burkhard, H.-D., Lindemann, G., Verbrugge, R., Varga, L.Z. (eds.) CEEMAS 2007. LNCS, vol. 4696, pp. 256–265. Springer, Heidelberg (2007)

16. Ferber, J., Gutknecht, O.: Aalaadin: a meta-model for the analysis and design of organizations in multi-agent systems. In: Proceedings of International Conference on Multi-Agent Systems (ICMAS 1998) (July 1998)

17. Zambonelli, F., Jennings, N.R., Wooldridge, M.: Developing Multiagent Systems: The Gaia Methodology. ACM Transactions on Software Engineering Methodology 12(3), 317–370 (2003)

18. Kollingbaum, M.J., Norman, T.J.: 'NoA - A Normative Agent Architecture'. In: Proceedings of IJCAI 2003, pp. 1465–1466 (2003)

19. Grefen, P., Eshuis, R., Mehandjiev, N., Kouvas, G., Weichhart, G.: CrossWork: Internet-Based Support for Process-Oriented Instant Virtual Enterprises. In: IEEE Internet Computing (2009) (to appear)

20. Stalker, I.D., Carpenter, M., Mehandjiev, N.D.: Establishing Agile Partnerships in Open Environments: Extended Abstract. In: Meersman, R., Tari, Z., Herrero, P. (eds.) OTM 2006 Workshops. LNCS, vol. 4277, pp. 15–16. Springer, Heidelberg (2006)

21. Huhns, M.N., Singh, M.P.: Managing Heterogeneous Transaction Workflows with Co-operating Agents. In: Jennings, N., Wooldridge, M. (eds.) Agent Technology: Foundations, Applications and Markets. Springer, Heidelberg (1998)

22. Navinchandra, D.: Exploration and Innovation in Design: Towards a Computational Model. Springer, Heidelberg (1991)

23. Simon, H.A.: The structure of ill-structured problems. Artificial Intelligence 4, 181–201 (1973)

24. Grefen, P., Aberer, K., Hoffner, Y., Ludwig, H.: CrossFlow: Cross-Organizational Workflow Management in Dynamic Virtual Enterprises. Computer Systems Science & Engineering 15(5), 277–290 (2000)

Enhancing Interoperability: Ontology-Mapping in an Electronic Institution

Henrique Lopes Cardoso, Daniel Dinis Teixeira, and Eugénio Oliveira

LIACC, DEI / Faculdade de Engenharia, Universidade do Porto
R. Dr. Roberto Frias, 4200-465 Porto, Portugal
hlc@fe.up.pt, daniel.teixeira@fe.up.pt, eco@fe.up.pt

Abstract. The automation of B2B processes requires a high level of interoperability between potentially disparate systems. We model such systems using software agents (representing enterprises), which interact using specific protocols. When considering open environments, interoperability problems are even more challenging. Addressing business automation as a task that intends to align businesses through a tight integration of processes may not be desirable, because business relationships may be temporary and dynamic. Furthermore, openness implies heterogeneity of technologies, processes, and even domain ontologies. After discussing these issues, this paper presents, in the context of an Electronic Institution, an ontology-mapping service that enables the automation of negotiation protocols when agents may use different ontologies to represent their domain knowledge. The ontology-mapping service employs two approaches used for lexical and semantic similarity, namely *N-Grams* and *WordNet*, and poses few requirements on the ontologiès' representation format. Examples are provided that illustrate the integration of ontology-mapping with automated negotiation.

Keywords: Automated negotiation, Open environment, Heterogeneity problem, Ontology-mapping.

1 Introduction

Technological support to the creation of B2B relationships is arising in many forms. The most ambitious ones intend to automate (part of) the process of creation and execution of contracts, mainly through multi-agent system (MAS) approaches.

The agent technology roadmap [1] identifies as key problem areas the development of infrastructures for open agent communities, as well as the need for trust and reputation mechanisms. Electronic institutions, together with ontologies and related services, address the needed infrastructures. Norms, electronic contracts and their enforcement are pointed out as means to achieve trust in open environments.

A keyword in these recommendations is *open*. In open environments interoperability problems are exacerbated, posing further challenges on the efforts to solve them. In fact, addressing an open environment implies that one intends to accommodate a wider range of agent architectures, technologies, or representation formalisms. Appropriate tools are needed in order to assist interoperation among such disparate systems.

K. Fischer et al. (Eds.): ATOP 2005 and ATOP 2008, LNBIP 25, pp. 47–62, 2009.

We will start by briefly discussing the implication of openness in business automation approaches using MAS, according to our view. We will then concentrate on the issue of ontologies in open environments, giving a motivation for the ontology-mapping approach that we describe throughout the rest of the paper.

1.1 Open Agent Communities for Business Scenarios

Today's business environments are characterized by a high degree of specialization and frequent market changes. The *Virtual Enterprise* (VE) concept is, as a consequence, a major trend in enterprise interoperability. A VE has been defined as "a temporary consortium of autonomous, diverse and possibly geographically dispersed organizations that pool their resources to meet short-term objectives and exploit fast-changing market trends" [2]. In outsourcing or supply chain configurations, a tight integration of partners using information technology approaches (focused on managing inter-organizational workflows with, e.g., Web-services, SoA, and service composition with BPEL) provides a fine-grained engagement between parties that leads to middle- or long-term relationships. However, flexible and dynamic relationships are the trend in a very competitive market. Because of this, we address interoperability in open business scenarios at a legal/contractual level [3]. Contracts formalize partners' commitments in a way that allows for their monitoring and enforcement.

In "breeding environments" [4] potential partners are already acquaintances and typically have previous common business experiences. This facilitates the construction of business agreements, as parties can rely on relational contracts [5], which specify continuous relationships that are naturally self-enforceable. However, in open environments potential partners may not be acquaintances, meaning that a business engagement may comprise entities that have never worked together in the past. In this more open setting formal contracts and their enforcement are a means to ensure trust.

Looking from a MAS perspective, while agent theory describes agents as autonomous self-interested entities, preferably interacting in open environments, an important issue arises when attempting to apply agents in real world scenarios: how to ensure cooperative outcomes in scenarios populated with self-interested agents? A possible answer to this problem is to regulate the environment, providing incentives for cooperative behavior through normative constraints [6].

Taking the aforementioned roadmap [1] into account, we have been developing an Electronic Institution (EI) platform motivated by the need to develop services that assist the coordination efforts of agents which, representing different real-world entities, interact with the aim of establishing business relationships. We therefore aim at agent-based B2B contracting, focusing on process automation. Some of the services we developed are depicted in Figure 1. The negotiation and establishment of electronic contracts are important in business interactions among companies that rely on running their businesses electronically.

The establishment of contractual agreements is supported with negotiation mediation, based on appropriate negotiation protocols and contract templates, defined using an institutional ontology. The validation and registration of contracts allows for their

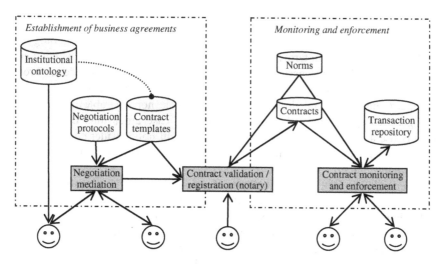

Fig. 1. Some services in an Electronic Institution

"legal" existence. Contracts are created as a result of a successful negotiation. However, we do not assume that agents will always have their negotiations mediated within the EI. As such, agents may opt to use institutional services for compliance checking only. An enforceable normative environment is established by rendering a contract monitoring and enforcement service, which registers transactions and verifies norm applicability, as well as the fulfillment of signed contracts.

Although aiming to address open environments, we do have a set of assumptions regarding agents' interoperability. First of all, agents must be able to 'speak' a common language (ACL in the agents' world [7]). We also assume that there is a common understanding on domain-independent business vocabulary, concerning terms such as 'proposal', 'price', 'delivery' or 'payment'.

We have also assumed in the past that agents have common domain ontologies, an issue that we have later addressed by adding ontology-based services to our infrastructure. This paper describes how such services have been integrated with the contract negotiation phase. Before we describe our approach, in the next subsection we will identify this problem more clearly.

1.2 Ontologies in Open Environments

An intrinsic problem that must be dealt with when approaching open systems is that each of a set of heterogeneous entities may potentially use a different domain ontology. There may be syntactic or semantic discrepancies in these ontologies: the same information may be stored in different representation formats, diverse terminologies for the same concepts may exist, or even the same terminology may be used for distinct concepts. This heterogeneity is a critical impediment to efficient business information exchange and to the automation of B2B processes.

The most simplistic way of solving this problem (often called the *interoperability* or *heterogeneity problem* [8, 9]) would be to define either a common ontology (used by all) or a shared one (in terms of which everyone can communicate) which could be understood by all agents participating in business interactions (inside a "breeding environment" [4] common domain ontologies might prevail). However, open environments (where a central design is neither possible nor desirable) populated with heterogeneous agents make the common ontology case unfeasible. Each agent will typically use a different ontology, and enterprises will not consider converting all the content of their ontologies if the target ontology is less expressive or not considered as a *de facto* standard.

The Foundation for Physical Intelligent Agents (FIPA) [10] has analyzed the interoperability problem in heterogeneous Multi-Agent Systems (MAS) and has proposed an Ontology Agent (OA) for MAS platforms [11]. Among other responsibilities, the OA may provide the translation service of expressions between different ontologies or different content languages by itself, possibly as a wrapper to an ontology server. In this paper we present an implementation of such a service, embedded in an Electronic Institution. The ontology-mapping service is aligned with a negotiation mediation service, allowing negotiation to take place between entities using different domain ontologies.

The rest of the paper is structured as follows. Section 2 contextualizes the usage of an ontology-mapping service in agent-based automated contracting. Section 3 details the service itself. In Section 4 examples that exploit the service are provided. Section 5 concludes.

2 Interoperability in Agent-Based Automated Contracting

There is a strong research effort towards the automation of B2B contracting processes. In particular, multi-agent systems technology is being used to establish business contracts by automatically negotiating agreements.

An Electronic Institution (EI) is a software platform that aims at (i) supporting agent interaction as a coordination framework, making the establishment of business agreements more efficient; and at (ii) providing a level of trust by offering an enforceable normative environment [12]. The ontology service described in this paper is essential to serve the first of these aims. Particularly when addressing an open environment, where a central design is not possible, agents representing different enterprises (henceforth *enterprise agents*) may use different domain ontologies, which have to be matched in order to make the (automated) establishment of agreements possible.

The EI will offer a set of services related to contract establishment and execution. A major service concerns negotiation mediation, through which an enterprise agent may automatically find and negotiate with potential partners. Negotiation is typically based on appropriate negotiation protocols and contract templates. The beginning of the negotiation mediation process is where ontology services come into play.

In open environments, different domain-dependent vocabulary may be used by different business entities. Ontology services are important to allow for negotiation to take place. Figure 2 illustrates these concepts.

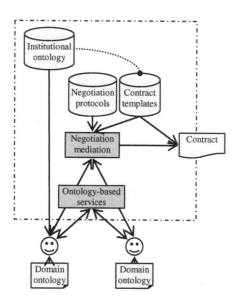

Fig. 2. The interplay between negotiation mediation and ontology services

The negotiation mediation service acts as a mediator between an enterprise agent and a set of potential partners (other enterprise agents). Each of these has a set of competences based on certain classes of components that it is able to supply. When asked for, each enterprise agent can negotiate the supply of a component of a certain class, if that class is in his competence list. Figure 3 illustrates the start of the negotiation process when there is no ontology service for solving the heterogeneity problem: enterprise agents on the right side may be prevented from participating in the negotiation because of an ontology mismatch.

The ontology-mapping service can be used when some enterprise agent does not understand the content of a CFP message (i.e. the component class under negotiation). The agent may recur to the service in order to find out if he supplies components of a class matching the one asked for. Figure 4 illustrates this process. In this case an enterprise agent on the right hand side is able to participate in the negotiation thanks to the ontology-mapping service, which gave him a mapping between the asked component class and one described in his ontology. In order to reduce the potentially large space of mapping attempts that the ontology-mapping service has to do, some heuristics may be used to preselect only those classes that have a potential to successfully map with the target class.

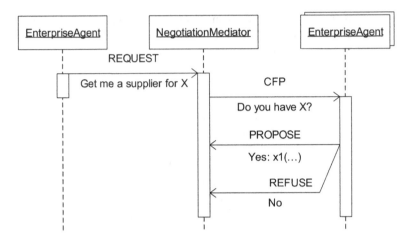

Fig. 3. Negotiation-mediation without an ontology-mapping service

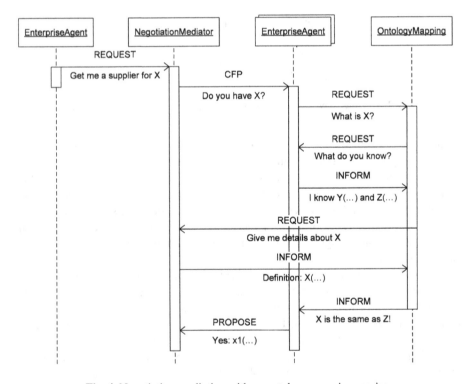

Fig. 4. Negotiation-mediation with an ontology-mapping service

This kind of service is mostly important if we consider that the negotiation process is to be automated through the use of enterprise (software) agents. In the next section we detail the workings of the ontology-mapping service.

3 Ontology-Mapping Service

Our background scenario is based on a set of enterprise agents requesting or supplying certain classes of components, for which they use a negotiation mediation service. Despite their potential interest in the same components, it is not guaranteed that they use the same names to define them. Suppose that a customer wants an 'alarm' and a supplier has exactly the component that this customer is looking for; however, in the supplier's ontology the component is known as a 'siren'. An automated negotiation process will fail if this ontology mismatch is not dealt with. Our approach is based on a service whose aim is to make a mapping between concepts defined in two different ontologies.

This section describes how the mapping process takes place. This process is based on the principle that if two different ontologies represent the same domain, then there is a high probability that the described concepts have a similar syntax and share similar attributes [8]. We will start by describing the minimum set of assumptions that enable the usage of the ontology-mapping service.

3.1 Assumptions on Ontology Representation

Even in open environments, a minimum set of conventions is needed to enable the interaction between heterogeneous agents, be it an ACL, negotiation protocols, and so on. In the B2B domain, it is generally assumed that parties have a common understanding on domain-independent business vocabulary. Concepts like proposal, deal or price must be part of a common base ontology. If we want enterprise agents to automatically negotiate contracts, they should also have a common understanding of what a delivery or a payment means.

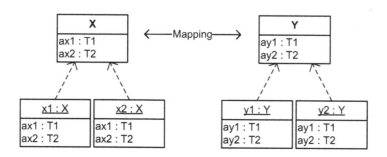

Fig. 5. Classes, attributes and components

In order to render an ontology-mapping service, a minimum set of requirements is also needed regarding the representation of components in different ontologies. Each ontology must be describable in terms of classes and attributes (see Figure 5). Each component is an instance of a class that defines its type. Each class has a name and a set of typed attributes. The mapping-service will be based on matching class names and class attributes.

Since we set the foundations of our approach on lexical and semantic similarity tools (in this case using *WordNet* – an English-based tool), an additional assumption that we make regarding the to-be-matched ontologies is that they are based on the English language.

The following subsection describes how the mapping process takes place.

3.2 Ontology-Mapping

Ontology mapping is the process of finding correspondences between the concepts of two ontologies. If two concepts correspond, then they mean the same thing or closely related things. The mapping process is based on two approaches. The first approach is *N-grams* [13]: an algorithm that takes as input two strings and computes the number of common sub-strings between them. The other approach consists of using *WordNet* [14], which is a free lexical database containing semantic and lexical relations between words. Succinctly, the *N-Grams* algorithm computes a lexical similarity between two words, while *WordNet* computes a semantic one. These two approaches are applied to the names of the classes and also to their attributes, obtaining an overall mapping score between two classes, as explained below.

N-Grams. The *N-Grams* [13] algorithm takes as input two strings and computes the number of common *n-grams* between them. An *n-gram* is a sequence of *n* characters; for each string, the algorithm computes the set of all possible *n-grams* that are in each string. A pre-processing step consists of normalizing both strings: all non-alphanumeric characters are replaced with '_'. The second step is to get the *n-grams* from each string (sub-strings of length *n*). Finally, the algorithm counts the number of *n-grams* of the first string that match an *n-gram* of the second string. The number of matches is used to calculate the outcome of the algorithm – a value of similarity is obtained from the formula:

$$Value = \frac{number\ of\ matches}{number\ of\ n\text{-}grams\ in\ first\ string}$$

The value obtained is within the range [0.0; 1.0]. The algorithm is parameterized with the value of *n* (the size of each *n-gram*). In our approach we chose a value of *n=3* to produce *3-grams*.

The *N-Grams* similarity approach has been used as an alternative to word-based systems. It has the merit of being robust in misspelling cases, which can be expected to occur in a scenario with multiple ontologies for the same domain.

WordNet. *WordNet* [14] is a lexical database designed for automatic processing that provides an effective combination of traditional lexicographic information and modern computing. *WordNet* contains thousands of words, including nouns, verbs adjectives and adverbs. These words are grouped into sets of cognitive synonyms (*synsets*), each expressing a distinct concept.

Other comparable systems exist [15], but with essentially different purposes, e.g. *CYC* (a general knowledge base and commonsense reasoning engine) or *EDR* (a dictionary with a bilingual English-Japanese emphasis). Comparing to *WordNet*, *CYC* is a more general-purpose system, while *EDR* has a different scope. *WordNet* fits our purposes for being an essentially linguistic knowledge base for English.

Furthermore, we make use of *WordNet::Similarity* [16], a *WordNet*-based Perl module [17] that calculates the similarity or relatedness between a pair of concepts, according to several different measures, such as Resnik, Jiang-Conrath, Leacock-Chodorow, Hirst-St.Onge, Wu-Palmer, among other. Measures of similarity quantify how much two concepts are similar, based on information contained in a hierarchical model. For instance, an 'automobile' can be considered more like a 'boat' than a 'tree', if 'automobile' and 'boat' share 'vehicle' as a common ancestor. Measures of relatedness compare concepts using relations like "has part", "is made of" or "is an attribute" instead of a hierarchical model. For instance a 'wheel' would give a good relatedness with a 'car', since a 'wheel' is an attribute of a 'car' [16].

In previous work [8] we concluded that the most appropriate measure for our scenario is Leacock-Chodorow (LCH), a similarity measure based on path lengths between concepts. LCH finds the shortest path between two concepts and scales that value by the maximum path length in which they occur. We then normalize that value to obtain a result within the range [0.0; 1.0].

In our domain, class and attribute names are not necessarily words appearing in *WordNet*. When names are made from word compositions, it may be the case that they are not part of *WordNet*'s database (e.g. while "photographic equipment" can be found, "vision angle" cannot). In such cases, a pre-processing step dividing the names into words is needed in order to try to find individual word mappings (e.g. the words "vision" and "angle" may be found in *WordNet*), which are then averaged if a mapping is found for them.

Mapping Process. Since we do not know at the beginning if two words have a lexical or semantic similarity, the ideal would be to apply both measures for each pair of words. However, this may not be feasible for performance reasons, because *WordNet::Similarity* [17] has a client/server architecture with socket communications, which introduces a large latency. For this reason, we firstly apply *N-Grams* and only if the result is not satisfactory we make use of *WordNet::Similarity*.

Ontology mapping starts with a list of component classes that can be matched with the requested (i.e. target) component class. Each class in the list will be tested. We choose the best matching class provided that it has a satisfactory value. The following algorithm implements this overall mapping process:

```
1. Let bc be the best matching class and bs its matching score
2. For each class c in the list
      a. Compute c's matching score with target class
      b. Update bc and bs
3. If bs is satisfactory then return bc, otherwise return null
```

The matching score (2.a above) between a class and the target class is the average of two values: the similarity score of their names and their attributes. The attribute matching process is done only for attributes of the same type, and is successful only if there is a mapping for every attribute of the target class. The following algorithm shows how the matching score between two classes is calculated:

```
1.  Compute the class name similarity score ns
2.  Compute the attribute list similarity score as
        a. Let as be the attribute list similarity score
        b. For each attribute at in the target class attribute list
                i. Find the "unmatched" class attribute a with best
                   similarity score
               ii. Update as
              iii. Mark a as "matched"
3.  Return the average of ns and as
```

Similarity is calculated by first applying *N-Grams* and eventually using *Word-Net::Similarity*, as described in the following algorithm:

```
1.  Compute the N-Grams similarity score ngs
2.  If ngs is satisfactory then return ngs
3.  Compute the WordNet::Similarity similarity score wns
4.  Return max of ngs and wns
```

As explained above, both ngs and wns are within the range [0.0; 1.0].

One might think that this approach is rather vulnerable to homonym-like pairs of strings: although syntactically very similar, they could mean entirely different things, and *N-Grams* will give them a high similarity score. While this is the case, it is unlikely that in such a situation the concepts described will have similar attributes, and thus this problem is somewhat contained. In other words, since a matching process involves calculating $1+n$ similarity scores (where n is the number of attributes), the homonym problem is unlikely to hinder our approach.

The following section describes an example that shows a scenario with suppliers and customers having different ontologies and where this mapping process is applied.

4 Example

In order to exemplify the usage of the ontology-mapping service and the mapping of several classes, a scenario is described in the following subsections. The scenario includes suppliers and customers interested in components from the domotics domain. It was tested in our Electronic Institution platform developed with the JADE framework [18].

Ontologies were created using the Protégé ontology editor [19] and saved in OWL files. This format allows defining classes of components in an object oriented model, where sub-classes inherit attributes from super-classes. Each enterprise agent instantiates components in an OWL file extended from the ontology definition.

4.1 Scenario

The scenario contains six agents (see Figure 6). Five of them are suppliers (Supply1 to Supply5) and one is a customer (Request1). The customer uses the same ontology (B) as Supply1, Suply2 and Supply3. On the other hand, Supply4 and Supply5 have defined their components based on a different ontology (A). The arrows in Figure 6 show which classes of components are supplied by each of the suppliers. The customer Request1 is interested in composing a package with four different components: a 'Command', a 'Switch', an 'Alarm' and a 'Camera'. In ontology A these kinds of components are known, respectively, as 'Control', 'Cutout', 'Siren' and 'Photographic_Equipment'.

Suppliers Supply4 and Supply5 need to use the ontology-mapping service if they are to enter the negotiation for each of the requested components. Supply4 is the only agent who has a 'Camera' ('Photographic_Equipment' in his ontology); therefore, it is absolutely necessary that the mapping is correctly done; otherwise, Request1 will not be able to negotiate this component, which will prevent him from composing the intended package.

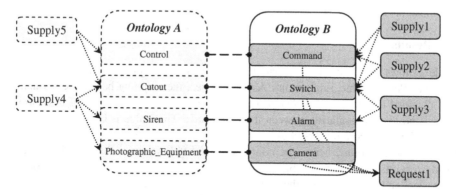

Fig. 6. Scenario: agents, ontologies and classes of components

In addition to the class names, the ontologies also differ in the attribute names for each class. Table 1 summarizes the attribute names for both ontologies. We can notice that the attribute named 'price' is the only one which is actually the same in both ontologies. For all other attribute names, some are lexically similar, while others have only a semantic resemblance. For instance, 'has_wireless' in ontology B is lexically similar to 'wireless' in ontology A. On the other hand, the attribute 'sight_grade' in ontology A has no lexical similarity with the attribute 'vision_angle' in ontology B, and yet they mean the same thing. Hence it is easy to anticipate that the mapping of the attributes 'wireless' and 'has_wireless' will be solved by using *N-Grams*, while *WordNet::Similarity* will help on solving the pairing of attributes 'sight_grade' and 'vision_angle'.

Table 1. Class attributes for ontologies A and B

Ontology A		*Ontology B*	
Attribute	*Class*	*Attribute*	*Class*
Price	*all*	price	*all*
Range	Control	reach	Command
Cipher	Control	code	Command
num_button	Cutout	number_button	Switch
Decibel	Siren	db	Alarm
Wireless	Photographic_Equipment	has_wireless	Camera
sight_grade	Photographic_Equipment	vision_angle	Camera
lens_dimension	Photographic_Equipment	lens_size	Camera

According to this scenario, we expect that the ontology-mapping service is able to map classes from ontology A with classes from ontology B. For instance, when Supply4 receives a CFP from the negotiation mediator (see Figure 4) asking for a 'Camera', he looks at his ontology and does not find that class. Consequently, he will ask the ontology-mapping service, which will give him the respective mapping, telling him that 'Camera' represents a concept similar to 'Photographic_Equipment'. Additionally, the service will also give him a mapping between the attributes of 'Camera' and those of 'Photographic_Equipment'.

4.2 Results

Table 2 shows the values obtained with the mapping process applied to the classes 'Camera' and 'Photographic_Equipment'. As we can see, the mapping between class names was obtained using *WordNet::Similarity* [17], after a foreseeable failure of *N-Grams* – there is no lexical similarity between the two words. This value is 0.81 and represents 50% of the final score for this class[1]. Attribute 'price' has a perfectly matching attribute according to *N-Grams*, hence the confidence of 1.00. Attribute 'has_wireless' had a satisfactory matching with attribute 'wireless' using *N-Grams* (0.64). As for attributes 'lens_size' and 'vision_angle', they both did not get a satisfactory result using *N-Grams*. A better result was obtained using *WordNet::Similarity*: 'lens_size' matched 'lens_dimension' with 0.85; 'vision_angle' matched 'sight_grade' with 0.73. These results were obtained by averaging the mappings of two pairs of words composing the attribute names. The global score for attribute matching is the average of each individual attribute matching score: (1.00 + 0.64 + 0.85 + 0.73) / 4 = 0.81. The final score is then the average of both (class and attributes) scores: (0.81 + 0.81) / 2 = 0.81.

Table 2. Mapping results for classes 'Photographic_Equipment' and 'Camera'

Ontology A	*Ontology B*	*Confidence*		
Photographic_Equipment	Camera	0.81 (*WN::Sim*).	0.81	
price	price	1.00 (*N-Grams*)		
wireless	has_wireless	0.64 (*N-Grams*)	0.81	0.81
lens_dimension	lens_size	0.85 (*WN::Sim*)		
sight_grade	vision_angle	0.73 (*WN::Sim*)		

The ontology-mapping service gave results of high confidence for all the classes considered. Results are summarized in Table 3.

The user interface at Figure 7 shows, for Supply4 (who had components belonging to classes 'Cutout', 'Siren' and 'Photographic_Equipment'), that all these classes were correctly mapped by the ontology-mapping service. Supply5 also had a list of mapped classes for 'Control' and 'Cutout'.

---

[1] The actual score obtained by *WordNet::Similarity* for mapping the class names 'Camera' and 'Photographic_Equipment' is 2.99, which was then normalized to the range [0.0; 1.0].

Table 3. Confidence values for each class mapping

Ontology A	*Ontology B*	*Confidence*
Control	Command	0.97
Cutout	Switch	0.82
Siren	Alarm	0.90
Photographic_Equipment	Camera	0.81

Figure 8 shows information regarding the negotiation of the four components that were part of the package intended by Request1. In the second column we can see the number of agents who negotiated those components. Looking again at Figure 6, we can conclude, that all agents who had a component to supply were involved in the negotiation, regardless of the ontology they had adopted. Three agents negotiated the 'Command' component: Supply1, Supply2 and Supply5. All agents negotiated the 'Switch' component. Two agents negotiated the 'Alarm' component: Supply3 and Supply4. Finally, the only supplier who had a 'Camera' – Supply4 (a 'Photographic_Equipment' in his ontology) – was the only one who entered the negotiation of that component.

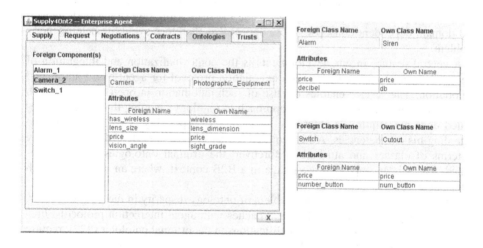

Fig. 7. Mapped classes for Supply4

Component	Agents Negotiating	Current Winner	Round	Utility
Command_2	3	Supply1 Ont1	10/10 --> OVER	29.999998
Camera_2	1	Supply4 Ont2	10/10 --> OVER	2.8922763
Alarm_1	2	Supply3 Ont1	10/10 --> OVER	1.4962795
Switch_1	5	Supply5 Ont2	10/10 --> OVER	8.935559

Negotiation: 1200190958843

Fig. 8. Negotiations

The use of the ontology-mapping service made it possible for agent Request1 to successfully negotiate all the components of the package it intended to assemble.

5 Conclusions

The heterogeneity problem in ontology specification is a strong impediment to the development of interoperable automated tools. In our case, we address this interoperability issue from a multi-agent system perspective: agents need to solve their ontological differences in order to be able to automatically negotiate on behalf of their owners. Although ontology schema mapping is, in general, not likely to be fully automated, we have implemented an approach with such an aspiration in mind. However, as noted in [20], some schema semantics is often not explicit and thus cannot be automatically processed, and therefore matching tools should be used to determine match candidates, to be confirmed by the user. Also, the user should be empowered to manually specify matches that the system was not able to find, and therefore appropriate user interfaces should be developed with this concern.

The research literature devoted to Electronic Institutions does not emphasize the importance of having ontology mapping services. In this respect, our approach is original, as far as we know. Some authors [21] point out the need for having a common ontology available for all parties inside the institution, describing both general and domain-dependent concepts. These approaches therefore avoid the heterogeneity problem.

A central feature in our developments is the contextualization and integration of the ontology-mapping service with a negotiation protocol for agent-based automated negotiation. The service enables the use of such automation in open settings, which would otherwise be unfeasible. The approach to ontology mapping that we have integrated does not require an enterprise agent to reveal possibly sensitive information regarding his competencies. All is required is that he is able to describe his ontology in terms of classes and attributes. Moreover, the original ontologies can be maintained, which is an important advantage in a B2B context, where an ontology switch can be an expensive task.

Other authors have tackled the problem of ontology disparity in the past. However, most of them do not integrate their approaches with agent interaction protocols. Furthermore, some approaches force modifications in the original ontologies [22], require the inspection of instances described in those ontologies [23], impose the creation and usage of a new merged ontology [24], or assume more requirements on the original ontologies' representations [25]. An approach to ontology alignment in MAS communication is presented in [26]; in this case, an upper ontology describing general concepts that are the same across all domains is assumed to exist.

We are aware that our experiments are based on simplified artificial scenarios. In fact, most experiments reported in the literature so far, are toy problems. Real experiments with ontology mapping and integration are missing, probably caused by the lack of available real-world ontologies on the Web. The basic principle that we rely on – the fact that two different ontologies representing the same domain will describe concepts with (probably) a similar syntax and share similar attributes – leads us to believe that our approach is sensible. However, as pointed out above, this process is far from being a solution to enable automatic negotiation when using real-world ontology schemas. More likely, an improved version of this ontology-mapping tool could be used as an assistant to find potential matches.

Acknowledgments. The authors would like to thank Andreia Malucelli for her PhD work on the ontology-mapping service. The first author is supported by FCT (Fundação para a Ciência e a Tecnologia) under grant SFRH/BD/29773/2006.

References

1. Luck, M., et al.: Agent Technology: Computing as Interaction (A Roadmap for Agent Based Computing). In: AgentLink (2005)
2. Davulcu, H., et al.: Modeling and Analysis of Interactions in Virtual Enterprises. In: Ninth International Workshop on Research Issues on Data Engineering: Information Technology for Virtual Enterprises. IEEE Computer Society, Los Alamitos (1999)
3. Lopes Cardoso, H., Oliveira, E.: Electronic Institutions for B2B: Dynamic Normative Environments. Artificial Intelligence and Law 16(1), 107–128 (2008)
4. Camarinha-Matos, L.M., Afsarmanesh, H.: Elements of a base VE infrastructure. Journal of Computers in Industry 51(2), 139–163 (2003)
5. Hviid, M.: Long-Term Contracts and Relational Contracts. In: Bouckaert, B., Geest, G.D. (eds.) Encyclopedia of Law and Economics, Volume III: The Regulation of Contracts, pp. 46–72. Edward Elgar, Cheltenham (2000)
6. Castelfranchi, C.: Engineering Social Order. In: Omicini, A., Tolksdorf, R., Zambonelli, F. (eds.) ESAW 2000. LNCS, vol. 1972, pp. 1–18. Springer, Heidelberg (2000)
7. FIPA-ACL. Message Structure Specification, http://www.fipa.org/specs/fipa00061
8. Malucelli, A.: Ontology-based Services for Agents Interoperability. Faculdade de Engenharia, Universidade do Porto, Porto (2006)
9. Willmott, S., Constantinescu, I., Calisti, M.: Multilingual Agents: Ontologies, Languages and Abstractions. In: Workshop on Ontologies in Agent Systems, 5th International Conference on Autonomous Agents, Montreal, Canada (2001)
10. FIPA. Foundation for Intelligent Physical Agents, http://www.fipa.org
11. FIPA-OSS. Ontology Service Specification, http://www.fipa.org/specs/fipa00086
12. Lopes Cardoso, H., et al.: Institutional Services for Dynamic Virtual Organizations. In: Camarinha-Matos, L.M., Afsarmanesh, H., Ortiz, A. (eds.) Collaborative Networks and Their Breeding Environments – 6th IFIP Working Conference on Virtual Enterprises (PRO-VE 2005), Valencia, Spain, pp. 521–528 (2005)
13. Damashek, M.: Gauging Similarity via N-Grams: Language-independent Sorting, Categorization, and Retrieval of Text. Science 267, 843–848 (1995)
14. Princeton University. WordNet: a lexical database for the English language, http://wordnet.princeton.edu
15. Lenat, D., Miller, G., Yokoi, T.: CYC, WordNet, and EDR: Critiques and Responses. Communications of the ACM 38(11), 45–48 (1995)
16. Pedersen, T., Patwardhan, S., Michelizzi, J.: WordNet:Similarity - Measuring the Relatedness of Concepts. In: Nineteenth National Conference on Artificial Intelligence (AAAI 2004), San Jose, CA (2004)
17. Pedersen, T.: WordNet:Similarity, http://wn-similarity.sourceforge.net/

18. JADE. Java Agent DEvelopment Framework, `http://jade.tilab.com`
19. Stanford Center for Biomedical Informatics Research. The Protégé Ontology Editor and Knowledge Acquisition System, `http://protege.stanford.edu`
20. Rahm, E., Bernstein, P.A.: A survey of approaches to automatic schema matching. The International Journal on Very Large Data Bases 10(4), 334–350 (2001)
21. Dignum, F.: Agents, markets, institutions and protocols. In: Sierra, C., Dignum, F.P.M. (eds.) AgentLink 2000. LNCS, vol. 1991, pp. 98–114. Springer, Heidelberg (2001)
22. Bailin, S.C., Truszkowski, W.: Ontology Negotiation between Scientific Archives. In: Thirteenth International Conference on Scientific Statistical Database Management. IEEE Computer Society Press, Fairfax (2001)
23. Wiesman, F., Roos, N.: Domain independent learning of ontology mappings. In: Third International Joint Conference on Autonomous Agents & Multi Agent Systems. ACM Press, New York (2004)
24. Pinto, H.S., Gómez-Pérez, A., Martins, J.P.: Some Issues on Ontology Integration. In: Workshop on Ontology and Problem-Solving Methods: Lessons Learned and Future Trends. CEUR Publications, Stockholm (1999)
25. van Eijk, R.M., et al.: On Dynamically Generated Ontology Translators in Agent Communication. International Journal of Intelligent Systems 16, 587–607 (2001)
26. Mascardi, V., Rosso, P., Cordì, V.: Enhancing Communication inside Multi-Agent Systems - An Approach based on Alignment via Upper Ontologies. In: Baldoni, M., Baroglio, C., Mascardi, V. (eds.) Int. Workshop on Agent, Web Services, and Ontologies Integrated Methodologies (MALLOW-AWESOME 2007), Durham, pp. 92–107 (2007)

Emergent Process Interoperability within Virtual Organisations

Martin Carpenter, Nikolay Mehandjiev, and Iain Duncan Stalker

School of Informatics, University of Manchester, P.O. Box 88, Manchester, M60 1QD, UK
m.carpenter@manchester.ac.uk

Abstract. The current speed of market change means that business opportunities today are increasingly short-lived. To successfully pursue these opportunities, enterprises increasingly establish virtual organisations, drawing upon established networks of partners having complementary skills and expertise. The formation of a virtual organisation traditionally derives from a top-down decomposition of a business goal into a set of activities, followed by a recruitment of members to implement these activities. As this essentially presupposes a closed-world context, it does not foster innovative solutions and will fail if a decomposition cannot be found or the recruited members cannot work with each other. The approach proposed here aims to address these challenges through innovative use of agent technology, allowing process interoperability to emerge as a result of shared interests and complementary expertise of individual agents. Members of the virtual organisation are drawn from a comparatively stable yet open business ecosystem or virtual breeding environment [1] in response to a business opportunity which is "pinned" to a notice board as soon as it appears. We show how this approach can complement top-down decomposition, using a simple case study and a prototype. The prototype is implemented in JADE.

1 Introduction

The dynamic and opportunistic nature of many contemporary markets, together with current trends towards shrinking lead times and volatile demand, mean that business opportunities are increasingly short-lived. To flourish in such an environment and make the most of business opportunities, enterprises face a growing need to share information and to collaborate with others throughout the value chain. This fosters focus on core competencies within a network of complementary expertise and resources. Such collaborations are often result in a *Virtual Organisation (VO)* [2]. Our working definition of a VO is "an aggregation of autonomous and independent organisations connected through a network and brought together in response to a customer need" [3]. This underlines its transient and goal-centred nature.

The speed with which a VO and its business process can be configured is often of a crucial importance in capitalising on a particular business opportunity. Thus, automated software support for VO formation would be a significant advance for business interoperability and process management.

A VO requires recruitment of appropriate members and the creation of a global cross-organisational business process to coordinate the complementary skills of

K. Fischer et al. (Eds.): ATOP 2005 and ATOP 2008, LNBIP 25, pp. 63–79, 2009.

members. Conventional approaches to VO formation (cf. Section 2) typically favour a top-down decomposition of the business goal into process activities, followed by a stage of matching organisations to these. Agent technology is often utilised in both stages providing: deliberative goal-driven reasoning over domain knowledge to automate goal decomposition and process refinement; and interaction protocols to structure and manage recruitment.

In this paper we focus on contexts where VOs form within a network of potential partner companies having recurrent dealings with each other, as exemplified by the Upper Austrian Cluster of Automotive Excellence [4]. We appeal to the concept of a *virtual breeding environment*, henceforth VBE, - [1] as a suitable theoretical model for such stable yet open business ecosystems. We examine conventional approaches to virtual organisation formation within a VBE and note several difficulties, most notably an (over-) dependence on a centralised top-down decomposition, see Section 2. The results of this examination motivate our proposing a novel approach, in which members of a congregation form a VO where the global cross-organisational business process *emerges* as a natural corollary (see Section 3); a top-level goal decomposition arises as an adjunct to the natural interactions of the participants.

The aim of the current paper is to expound the underlying principles of the approach. As such, the technical details are kept to a minimum and the examples made deliberately simple. Throughout the paper we indicate potential problems we observe in existing approaches and use these to motivate our proposal. Nevertheless, we would emphasise that we see our approach as complementary to existing approaches and conclude that in many cases, the ideal would be a hybrid, as we discuss in Section 5. The proposed ideas are illustrated using a simple case study (see Section 4): implemented as a multi-agent system built using JADE (jade.tilab.com); ontologies are used to (formally) describe the problem, constraints and dependencies.

2   Preliminaries

In this section we introduce the notion of a virtual breeding environment and examine the constraints on virtual organisation formation within the specific classes of VBE addressed by the work presented. We use these to prepare the ground for our approach (see Section 3).

2.1   Application Domain

Within the current paper we are interested in contexts where VOs form within a network of potential partner companies having recurrent dealings with each other, as exemplified by the Upper Austrian Cluster of Automotive Excellence [4]. While such contexts are encountered in VO literature, see for example, [3], they are usually treated as incidental to the process of virtual organisation formation. One exception to this is the idea of a virtual organisation breeding environment. This idea was originally introduced by Hamideh Afsarmanesh and Luis M. Camarinha-Matos in [1] and later developed into the core application context behind the Ecolead European project.

A concise definition of a VBE was given by the same authors in a later paper,[5] as:

A VBE is an association of organisations and their related supporting institutions, adhering to a base long term cooperation agreement, and adoption of
common operating principles and infrastructures, with the main goal of increasing both their chances and preparedness towards collaboration in potential
virtual organisations

A fuller development of this idea with numerous real world examples can be found
in [6].

Since this idea describes an automotive cluster quite well we have adopted VBEs
as the basic theoretical grounding for the work reported within this paper. The concept
however has a very general scope and we modify it.

In particular we do not require the member companies to share a base long term cooperation agreement or common operating principles. Instead we rely on the fact that
the companies within the VBE joined it in order to constructively participate in VO formation. As argued by Sen within [7] the social control exhibited as a result of repeated
interactions within a stable group often suffices to ensure cooperative behaviour without
the use of explicit, formal penalties.

In addition we highlight two important features:

1. *The set of processes available for composition is not fixed.* The VBEs studied within
   this work are open systems with new members joining and existing members leaving during the lifespan. Moreover, new processes can be made available as these are
   developed by existing members. Perhaps, the most significant reason derives from
   the self-interested nature of the participants: the set of processes offered by each is
   typically in proportion to the perceived return on investment (of effort) of a given
   opportunity. For instance, a large order might motivate a participant to buy in new
   machinery; a less appealing proposition is likely to be met with disinterest.
2. *The success of a VO depends upon shared interests of its participants.* Certain companies within the VBE might prefer not to work together. This brings to the fore
   the need to co-optimise the membership of a VO with the global business process
   under construction.

2.2 VO Formation Within VBEs

In this section we consider the opportunities and challenges attaching to the formation
of a VO within a VBE. We identify two phases in the establishment of a VO:

1. *Team formation*, where the members of the VO are chosen from potential candidates.
2. *Detailed process configuration*, where those members (selected) determine how to
   work together.

These phases are potentially distinct, however, as a VO assembles for a specific purpose,
it is important to consider the services offered by each team member during team formation. Notwithstanding, seeking to merge the two phases by combining all processes

of a potential team, raises two major difficulties: VBE members might be reluctant to reveal processes in detail to a (central) planning mechanism, compromising any guarantee of a workable solution; and the space of possibilities quickly becomes intractable. An alternative is to treat the first phase as fully separate from the second. This can lead to the formation of a team where the detailed processes (of the members) do not fit together well. This typically requires a revision of the team or the acceptance of less than optimal solution. We believe that a hybrid solution should yield best results: team formation is guided by partial feedback on how well the processes of potential team members combine and integrate.

We briefly examine some conventional approaches for VO formation, and then explore in detail the top-down techniques to service composition using there. In particular, we consider the applicability of these, noting shortcomings and potential problems. We conclude this section with an examination of an alternative approach.

Conventional Approaches to VO Formation. VOs are transient structures assembled to achieve a particular goal or fulfil a given function. Automated approaches to the creation of such goal-driven assemblies typically pursue a (centralised) top-down (functional) decomposition, as exemplified by the software support found within the Service-Oriented Architectures and Web Service communities. Here the aim is to create a composite service to respond to a service request [8]. A service request is received by a central agent which decomposes the request into subtasks. Each of these is matched to a service provider advertising services sufficient to meet the needs of the given subtask. The matching of task requirements to service descriptions (*matchmaking*) is analogous to consulting a *Yellow Pages*. An alternative is to issue a *call for proposal(s) (cfp)*, for example using the *Iterated Contract Net Protocol* (see www.fipa.org): we refer to this as the *Contract-Net Approach (CNA)*. Again an agent decomposes a given request into subtasks. The agent then decides to out-source a number of these and in each case makes a cfp, describing the nature of the subtask and soliciting proposals to address this. An agent interested in responding to a cfp submits a proposal, i.e. bids, to supply a necessary service. The (initial) agent chooses from these offers (or rejects these and reissues the cfp, perhaps slightly revised). This is often supplemented by the use of *Library Agents* as a mechanism to manage complexity: the initial agent sends a cfp to the Library Agents, each of which issues a cfp to an appropriate subset of the agents which have registered with it.

Top-Down Techniques for Service Composition. Both CNA and the Web Service model distinguish two distinct phases: decomposition and matchmaking. The first of these entail decomposing the original request into a set of sub requests, the second locating appropriate providers for them. Such approaches often consider the interactions among the service providers only once these have been (independently) matched to given subtasks. However, if the selected providers have processes which do not integrate, then revision of the choices is required. Similar difficulties arise if one company is reluctant to work with another, perhaps owing a lack of trust or a previous (bad) experience. Furthermore, certain subgroups of companies may have established close relationships, through previous partnerships and thus, have a good coordination of their actions. Decomposing an initial problem into a set of subproblems presupposes a hierarchy of tasks, or other such semantics, to guide this decomposition. Moreover, an prerequisite to success is that there exist good matches of abstract tasks obtained through such a decomposition to concrete processes available. Hierarchies to support such matches have been developed and studied in the context of (hierarchical) planning [9,10]. The utility of these is strongly dependent upon the properties of:

- *Ordered Monotonicity* which requires [9] *"For all abstract plans, all refinements of those plans leave the literals established at the abstract level unchanged."*
- *Downwards Refinement* [10] which guarantees that an abstract plan can be refined into a plan at the next level of abstraction down.

Even when these hold, hierarchies constrain the set of solutions considered [9], which restricts creative solutions. To counter these difficulties, methods for automatically generating efficient hierarchies have been proposed [9]. These techniques require the specification of a set of available operators for a given domain. However within the context of our research a complete or comprehensive set of available processes is difficult to obtain, as discussed above in Subsection 2.1. This makes (convincing) top-down decomposition challenging, if not impossible: consider, incomplete information regarding available processes within a given domain not only hinders matchmaking, it also frustrates the manual creation of appropriate (task) hierarchies.

An interesting development, presented in [11], is to have an agent which *intelligently* coordinates a response to an identified customer need. These agents, however, are used in a conventional top-down fashion: they procure solutions using an auction analogous to a CNA; and the subtask allocation is derived from the top-level goal in a traditional manner. While this an iterative approach and can address multiple criteria, in our opinion, it sacrifices many of the benefits afforded by peer-to-peer negotiation: to which we appeal to in our approach.

A Bottom-Up Approach. Our approach, expounded in Section 3, is inspired by the notion of a *Blackboard System (BBS)* [12,13]. A BBS formalises the metaphor of a group of experts working on a problem and communicating ideas using a blackboard. The blackboard becomes a repository of information which is globally accessible and records the problem specific information available from each expert. The flow of information between the blackboard and each expert is bidirectional: an expert both contributes and extracts information. Ideally, the contributions are revised, extended and restructured to yield a solution to the problem. Traditional implementations make use of a single, central blackboard and a scheduler, the *focus mechanism* or *blackboard control*, which manipulates the flow of data and the order in which the experts are consulted. Multi-agent systems (MAS), however, allow this to be extended [14]. In particular, each expert can have greater autonomy and communicate with others directly in addition to using the blackboard (control) as an intermediary.

3   A Notice Board Approach to Virtual Organisations

We propose a novel agent-based approach which uses notice boards and peer-to-peer negotiation to address the formation of a VO and the coordination of a cross-organisational business process within congregations. Each notice board serves as both a repository of information and as a communication channel. Combined with appropriate negotiation protocols, this promotes an *emergence* of solutions in which the VO and its process are co-designed in a dynamic and automated manner. We see this as a complementary approach to conventional top-down decomposition.

3.1   Problem Set Up and Consequences

Typically the problem of supporting the formation of virtual enterprises has been considered to be broadly equivalent to that of constructing a composite web service, namely constructing the single best team to solve a specific problem. Within a VBE, such as the Austrian automotive cluster, VO formation typically occurs within the following context:

1. A large company external to the VBE decides to seek an external supplier for a specific part or service and makes an open offer for bids. In the case of the automotive domain this corresponds to an OEM seeking a supplier for a given module.
2. The existence of this opportunity is made visible to members of the VBE and this motivates the formation of one or more potential VOs.
3. The potential VOs plan in sufficient detail to allow them to tender for the proposed contract and proceed to do so.
4. The original external company chooses their preferred VO for the contact.
5. The chosen VO then makes truly detailed plans and moves into actual production. In the case of the automotive domain this step involves several stages of prototype design and typically takes several months before full scale production can commence.

A system aiming to support virtual organisation formation within this context should not try to support the production of a single, 'best' team but rather to support the general formation of virtual organisations. Indeed it is arguable if the concept of the 'best' VO has any meaning during the VO formation phase: the final evaluation criteria are not known and so any evaluation criteria must arise within the VBE.

As there is no entity within the VBE with the authority to impose an evaluation scheme, any evaluation scheme must arise through the combined judgement of the companies within the VBE. The natural self interest of these companies makes it likely that they will differ in their judgement of the worth of particular teams, with a particular preference for teams of which they are a member. A proposal that a supplier should be allowed to join an existing, partially formed, team can consequently only be fairly evaluated by the existing members of that team. Thus a system to support VO formation within a VBE should support the formation of multiple teams while allowing the existing members of a partially formed VO to evaluate any potential further contributions to that VO. The approach proposed within this paper offers support for both of these features.

The context above also affects the nature of the output of any system supporting VO formation. In contrast to many related systems, and especially to those composing web services, there is a considerable period of time between the system identifying a potential VO and that VO moving into production. A set of companies produced as the output of such a system is thus not required to have a detailed, immediately executable plan to meet the business opportunity as a VO,[1] but rather to believe that they will be able to produce such a plan. Delaying the commitment of companies to specific processes as long as possible allows the process of VO formation to retain maximal flexibility and is thus desirable.

The system proposed within this paper allows companies to propose contributions using a formalism which focuses purely on their intended effects, rather than the process used to achieve those effects. This allows for a full exploration of the space of potential virtual organisations. In consequence the system cannot provide an absolute guarantee that a complete solution produced can later be developed into a virtual organisation. In the current context this corresponds to a team entering negotiations to prepare a bid and failing to agree on what bid to propose. While this is undesirable in principle there are no major costs associated with this in this context. Additionally the complexity of the bid preparation process means that no system could ensure that its complete solution could always be completed. Finally the system contains several features which mitigate the chances of this occurring.

In summary the system the principal goal of the system proposed within this paper is to facilitate the overall formation of virtual organisations within a virtual breeding environment. It achieve this goal by producing sets of companies who are likely to be able to combine to meet the goals of the business opportunity.

3.2 Notice Boards and Partial Solutions

To structure our exposition, it is convenient to distinguish three stages in the establishment of a VO within a congregation: a request is made visible to the agents within the congregation; a team (or set of teams) to fulfil a given request *emerges* as agents volunteer contributions and agree to provide (sub)services; and a solution *emerges* from the (final) coordination of actions among team members. We examine each of these in more detail. We first clarify the notions of partial and complete solutions; and formally define a notice board.

Definition 1. (Partial Solution). *Suppose we have a consistent set of goals. A* partial solution *is any set of tasks (or activities) which satisfies a subset of our set of goals. This is in contrast with a* complete solution *which is a set of tasks (or activities) which satisfies all of our goals.*

Remark 1. A global goal can be represented as a conjunction of one or more subgoals. This applies independently of how such a set of subgoals is achieved: whether through a top-down decomposition or as an adjunct to a bottom-up approach. Accordingly, we overload the term partial solution to apply more informally to any set of activities arising in the pursuit of complete solution to an identified global goal: here the subgoals are left implicit.

Remark 2. A complete solution is necessarily a partial solution. However, a complete solution is (typically) not a unique combination of partial solutions.

---

[1] As would be required in for instance web service composition.

Definition 2 (Notice Board). *A* notice board *is a communication device which contains the following information:*

1. *A precise statement of the top-level goal or service for which the VO is to be assembled and for which a global process is sought. The notice board goal identifies which request the notice board represents.*
2. *Utility information defining the worth of the request. The utility information for the request includes the information required for each agent to decide on the perceived worth of the request. This might include the company issuing the request and the number of items requested.*
3. *A set of partial solutions (cf. Definition 1).*

For convenience, we denote the above categories of information $\mathcal{G}, \mathcal{U}$ and $\mathcal{S}$, respectively; and we denote the corresponding notice board $\mathbb{NB} = \langle \mathcal{G}, \mathcal{U}, \mathcal{S} \rangle$.

In addition to recording the evolution of a set of partial solutions (ideally into a complete solution), a notice board serves in the coordination of information exchange during team formation.

Making a Request Visible. Requests are made visible to agents within the congregation through a system of notice boards. A notice board is created for every request which comes into the system.

Team Formation. A teams develops incrementally: initially it can offer only a partial solution (to a request); the team grows as additional members join and contribute towards a complete solution. This is driven by the agents' monitoring notice boards within the system, looking for promising partial solutions to extend and proposing extensions where appropriate [2]. A proposed extension triggers negotiation among the existing team members and the proposing agent (*candidate*): this concerns the admissibility of the candidate as judged by the existing team members; a simple model might involve a blacklist reflecting the preferences of the existing members, where if the candidate is not on this, then he is admissible; more sophisticated models would also consider how well processes integrate. To facilitate team formation a notice board includes information on the partially formed team as part of a partial solution. Thus, the noticeboard also enables the team extension negotiations. At this stage each partial solution is owned by a group of companies who are provisionally happy to work together and have each promised to provide a process to the team. The details of the processes promised are left purposefully vague to maintain the maximum possible flexibility. A possible partial solution representation technique is presented in in Subsection 3.4.

Final Coordination. This final stage is triggered once a partial solution on a notice board has been extended into a complete solution. In this case we have a team of agents

---

[2] We do not discuss the technical details of creation of notice boards, nor how an agent is made aware of notice boards in the system. One possibility is that once a agent receives a service request, it arranges for a notice board to be created. This notice board is wrapped by an agent, which registers with the *Directory Facilitator* and makes a broadcast message to notify agents of its creation.

who expect to solve the problem. Nevertheless, the actual details of how the team will work and interact are yet to be made precise. As our aim in the present paper is to present a mechanism for emergent process interoperability arising from VO formation in congregations, we consider this stage out of scope of the present discussion.

Nevertheless, we note that this stage presents significant challenges and is likely to require much human input. *Inter alia* the following issues will need to considered:

1. A precise product specification. This will include details of raw materials, component interfaces, tolerances, etc. In some cases this will include explorations to arrive at a detailed configuration of part of the final product, which can only be considered once substantial detail is available; and may involve further negotiation [15].
2. A detailed statement of each agent process (cf. local workflow) to a level sufficient to support the composition of a global process (cf. global workflow).
3. The actual global workflow for the combined process.
4. Contractual matters including the division of proceeds; timelines; change request management; recourse upon contractual breaches; etc.
5. If the team is assembled to respond to an invitation to tender, then a price needs to be agreed.

Potentially, these stages are interdependent. Consider, a company might be willing to modify its processes to fit better with the processes within the team only if it is given a greater share of the revenue. Moreover, contractual details and price agreement will generally require human intervention. As such, a full automation of this stage seems unlikely in all but very simple cases. A more realisable objective would be to reduce the onus on the (human) user, by automating the more routine tasks involved.

3.3   Summary

The following set of pictures offers a useful summary guide to the overall operation of the bottom up team formation system. The first depicts a newly created noticeboard, and later pictures depict the stages of solution development. For clarity only the creation of one, simple, complete solution is shown. In the general case multiple solutions of differing forms would be explored.

As an aid when considering these pictures consider the opportunity to require the production of a water tank. Agent A is then a large company which can produce the water tank if someone can supply them with a specifically configured reservoir - this is represented by the resource in the intermediate state. Agent B can supply such a reservoir, and so offers to do so. This triggers negotiations between the two companies which conclude successfully, and the extension request is granted. This then produces a complete solution. The companies within this solution are then notified and move onto a more detailed discussions of how they wish to work together.

3.4   Technical Details

We present and discuss some of the more technical aspects of our proposal.

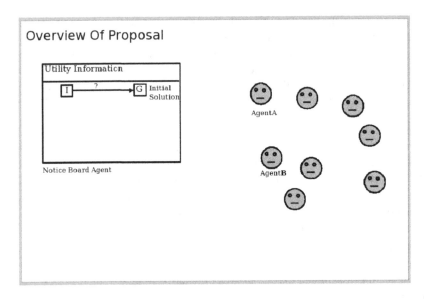

Fig. 1. The opportunity is noticed and a noticeboard is created

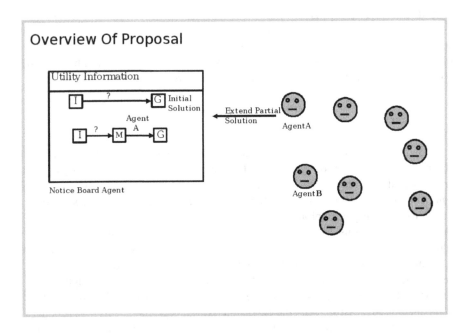

Fig. 2. Agent A extends the initial solution

Representation. The representation of partial solutions is facilitated through creation of an ontology to realise a vocabulary to describe the objects and states (of interest) which exist within the application domain, together with a constraint language. A partial

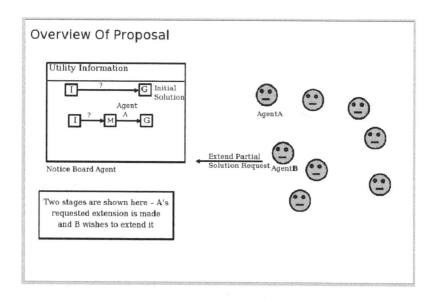

Fig. 3. Agent B wishes to further extend the extended solution

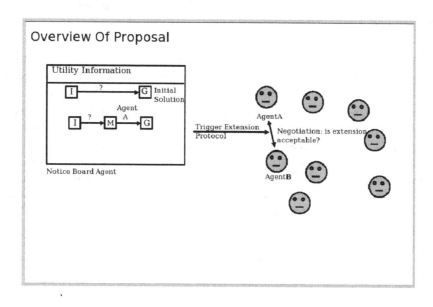

Fig. 4. The proposed extension is verified

solution is represented as a set of states connected by transitions. Each transition is labelled with either the name of the agent which has promised to supply it or a question mark ("?") to indicate that it is indeterminate. We refer the latter case as an *unlabelled*

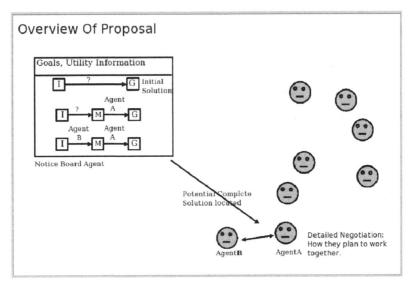

Fig. 5. A complete solution has been located

transition. Each state is represented by a set of objects from the domain ontology together with constraints on their attributes.

Extending Partial Solutions. To extend a partial solution new states are added and connected to existing states using appropriate transitions. There are two basic ways in which to extend an existing partial solution: a *right extension* (cf. forward chaining), where a given state S is transformed into a state S' by a transition T, $S \xrightarrow{T} S'$; and a *left extension* (cf. backward chaining), where a given state S is derived from a state S' by a transition T, $S' \xrightarrow{T} S$; naturally, there is the possibility of an extension achieving both of these simultaneously. We illustrate these, without loss of generality, from a goal process: the goal process of the notice board is represented by a pair of states, the start and the goal state distinguished for the case-in-hand, connected by an unlabelled transition. For instance the following goal process (partial solution) indicates that the goal is to repaint a green ball red. [3]

$$(ball(colour == green)) \xrightarrow{?} (ball(colour == red))$$

Suppose an agent is prepared to strip the paint from that ball as a potential intermediate step, then this is a right extension.

$$(ball(colour == green)) \xrightarrow{PaintStripperAgent} (ball(colour == blank))$$
$$\xrightarrow{?} (ball(colour == red))$$

---

[3] The system described in the later case study uses a more complex, non linear state representation. A simpler one is used below for clarity of exposition.

Alternatively, suppose an agent can paint a blank ball red as a potential intermediate step, then this is a left extension.

$$(ball(colour == green)) \xrightarrow{\quad ? \quad} \begin{array}{l} (ball(colour == blank)) \\ \xrightarrow{PainterAgent} (ball(colour == red)) \end{array}$$

Naturally, if an agent can provide both of these, we have a (simultaneous) left and right extension, which in this case yields a complete solution

$$(ball(colour == green)) \begin{array}{l} \xrightarrow{Paint\&StripAgent} (ball(colour == blank)) \\ \xrightarrow{Paint\&StripAgent} (ball(colour == red)) \end{array}$$

The idea of using such a resource language to describe a distributed planning problem is taken from [16] where a similar system is used to merge plans in an efficient manner.

Learning Opportunities. In the basic system above the notice board serves only to coordinate the communications within the system. Uplifting a noticeboard to an agent status offers an opportunity to extend its role. For example, one possibility would be to enable the reuse of previous partial solutions in a manner analogous to case based planning, see e.g. [17]. The notice board agent could persist beyond the life of the project and respond to related future requests. Alternatively, the information could be used to inform the appropriate ontological structures and problem-solving mechanisms; or passed onto an agent responsible for maintaining, indexing and answering queries concerning previous partial solutions. Such reuse is useful both for speeding the generation of new virtual organisations and for the speedy location of substitute organisations if a problem occurs with one of the partners after the team has formed.

Requirements on Agents. The system outlined above devolves significant responsibility upon the process agents and thus demands of them several types of reasoning. The primary requirement on an agent is that it contribute processes to the partially formed virtual organisations. This splits into two parts, namely:

1. Identifying when it wants to contribute a process. This motivates the inclusion of utility information, i.e., data which can be used to inform an agent's preferences. This is peculiar to a given domain.
2. Recognising when it can make a useful contribution. An agent must be cognisant of its own capabilities and be able to query a notice board to determine states which can form (part of) an input to an owned process. Thus, an agent concentrates on expressing *what* it can do, such as paint stripping (a declarative statement) rather specifying *how* it achieves its activities (a procedural or operational statement).

Finally were the process provider agents to contribute one of their processes whenever it was possible for them do so there would be a real risk of an undesirable quantity of partial solutions being produced. Thus the process provider agents should possess some measure of the degree of "usefulness" of its processes to a given partial solution. Within the current context of automotive manufacturing such knowledge is naturally present - a company will know the sorts of product in which their processes are typically used.

4   Case Study

To explore the technical feasibility of the notice board system, a testbed was created using JADE (jade.tilab.com). This test bed implemented a technically complete version of the noticeboard system and has been run on many small case studies.

Concepts and Problem-Solving Methods (PSMs). The chosen case study within this paper was inspired by one encountered within the Crosswork European research project. The basic concept within the case study is the creation of a virtual organisation to produce a watertank.

Overall there are five agents within study, including:

1. A watertank constructor agent who can construct the type of watertank required if provided with certain components. (a Grommet, a reservoir, a lid and a pump)
2. A set of agents who each provide one of these required components

4.1   TestBed

The case study demonstrates one of the simple ways in which noticeboard virtual organisation can operate. In this case the scenario flow is:

1. A virtual organisation must be found to produce a watertank
2. A corresponding noticeboard is created
3. The watertank constructor notices that it can construct this kind of watertank and adds an appropriate partial solution to the noticeboard
4. Companies who can provide the individual components notice this and offer to do so, thus eventually forming a complete solution

The initial solution within this case study is simply : $[\phi] \xrightarrow{?} [Watertank]$.

The partial solution generated once the watertank constructor agent has extended this initial solution can be seen in diagram 6. Finally the complete solution can be seen in diagram 7.

This scenario demonstrates how backwards chaining works within a noticeboard system - essentially companies within the system recognise that they could make some form of product if they were supplied with certain other products.

This differs from traditional top down approaches since the knowledge used to decompose the watertank into a set of subcomponents here comes purely from the watertank constructor agent it self.

Indeed the set of components that it needs only includes those components for which it needs an external contractor. A different watertank assembly company, or the same company producing a different form of watertank, might need to be supplied with a very different set of subcomponents.

The noticeboard system also supports forwards chaining - in this case an agent recognises that a process they can provide is likely to be useful for the type of product being

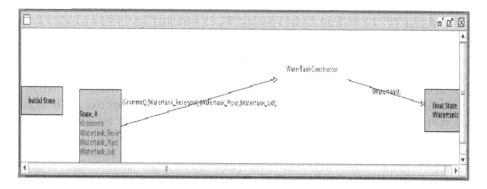

Fig. 6. The initial partial solution

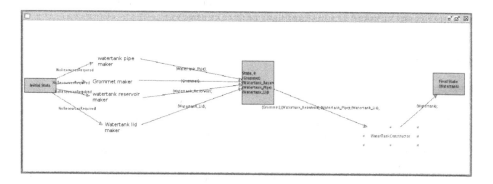

Fig. 7. The final solution

produced and offers it. For example here the producer of watertank reservoirs might notice a solution involving the production of watertanks and offer to supply relevant forms of reservoir.

4.2 Implementation and Results

The system was implemented using a (single generic type of) process agent. This agent queries a notice board agent for partial solutions to extend. Since the focus was on core technical feasibility a single notice board agent was created and the tests stopped once a single complete solution had been generated. In addition the process provider agents used contained simplified reasoning - each was responsible for one specific process and were totally cooperative. Thus, while all of the required negotiation stages actually took place, they were always successful. None the less the tests provided a good measure of the technical progress of the implementation of the system. Indeed these tests emphasised the importance of controlling the numbers of partial solutions generated within the system.

5   Conclusion

Congregations [18] capture the stable yet open business ecosystems in which VOs often form to capitalise upon business opportunities arising in dynamic and complex markets. Conventional approaches to formation of VOs in such congregations typically yield suboptimal solutions. We have proposed a novel notice board based approach to workflow composition which we believe offers a powerful, complementary approach. Through this VO processes and VO structure are co-optimised. The power of our approach derives from a focus on peer-to-peer negotiation. This encourages process interoperability to *emerge* as a result of shared interests of agents (cf. entities, institutions) within a network of complementary expertise. In particular, we have indicated how this circumvents a number of problems which derive from conventional approaches to VO formation, especially within congregations. The simple case study fosters confidence in the core ideas of the approach and highlights areas of further work. Additionally, we plan to investigate situations where this approach works in tandem with conventional top-down decompositions, allowing more flexible search solutions.

References

1. Camarinha-Matos, L.M., Afsarmanesh, H.: Elements of a base ve infrastructure. Computers in Industry 51, 139–163 (2003)
2. Mowshowitz, A.: Virtual organization. Commun. ACM 40(9), 30–37 (1997)
3. Faisst, W.: Information technology as an enabler of virtual enterprises: A life -cycle-oriented description. In: Proceedings of the European Conference on Virtual Enterprises and Networked Solutions (1997)
4. Consortium: Intra- and inter-organisational business models. Public Deliverable to work package 1 Crosswork European research project (2004)
5. Afsarmanesh, H., Camarinha-Matos, L.: A framework for management of virtual organization breeding environments. In: CamarinhaMatos, L., Afsarmanesh, H., Ortiz, A. (eds.) Collaborative Networks and Their Breeding Environments. International Federation for Information Processing, vol. 186, pp. 35–48. Springer, Heidelberg (2005)
6. Consortium, E.: D22.1 key components, features and operating principles of the virtual organisation breeding environment (2005)
7. Sen, S.: Believing others: Pros and cons. Artificial Intelligence 142(2), 179–203 (2002)
8. McIlraith, S., Son, T., Zeng, H.: Semantic web services. IEEE Intelligent Systems and their applications 16(2), 46–53 (2001)
9. Knoblock, C.A.: Automatically generating abstractions for planning. Artificial Intelligence 68(2), 243–302 (1994)
10. Bacchus, F., Yang, Q.: The expected value of hierarichical problem solving. In: National Conference on Artifical Intelligence (AAAI 1992), pp. 364–374 (1992)
11. Oliveria, E.: Agents' advanced features for negotiation and coordination. In: Mutli-agents systems and applications, pp. 173–186 (2001)
12. Carver, N., Lesser, V.: Evolution of blackboard control architectures. Expert systems with applications 7(1), 1–30 (1994)
13. Hayes-Roth, B.: A blackboard architecture for control. Artif. Intell. 26(3), 251–321 (1985)
14. Craig, I.: Blackboard Systems. Ablex, Norwood (1995)

15. Lander, S.: Distributed search and conflict management among heterogeneous reusable agents. Ph.D. thesis, University of Massachusetts, Amherst (May 1994)
16. de Weerdt, M., Bos, A., Tonino, H., Witteveen, C.: A resource logic for multi-agent plan merging. Annals of Mathematics and Artificial Intelligence 37(1-2), 93–130 (2003)
17. Spalzzi, L.: A survey on case-based planning. Artif. Intell. Rev. 16(1), 3–36 (2001)
18. Brooks, C.H., Durfee, E.H.: Congregation formation in multiagent systems. Autonomous Agents and Multi-Agent Systems 7(1-2), 145–170 (2003)

Analysis and Support of Organizational Performance Based on a Labeled Graph Approach[*]

Mark Hoogendoorn[1], Jan Treur[1], and Pınar Yolum[2]

[1] Vrije Universiteit Amsterdam, Department of Artificial Intelligence
De Boelelaan 1081a, 1081 HV Amsterdam, The Netherlands
{mhoogen,treur}@cs.vu.nl
[2] Bogazici University, Department of Computer Engineering,
TR-34342 Bebek, Istanbul, Turkey
pinar.yolum@boun.edu.tr

Abstract. Organizational performance analysis enables organizations to un-
cover unexpected properties of organizations and allow them to reconsider their
internal workings and provide support for this. To perform such an analysis and
obtain appropriate support, in this paper organizations are modeled as labeled
graphs that capture the interactions of the entities and the characteristics of
those interactions, such as their content and frequency, through labels in the
graph. Algebraic representations and manipulations of the labels enable analysis
of a given organization. Hence, well-known phenomena, such as overloading of
participants or asymmetric distribution of workload among participants can easily be detected and supported. A case study performed within the domain of incident management is described to illustrate the approach.

1 Introduction

Performance of multi-agent organizations is based on agents that serve as a kind of
engines and that interact to carry out their tasks. Usually models of multi-agent organizations represent organizations by roles that agents adopt. Structure and behavior of the
organization are specified in terms of the relations between the roles, and the agents
should (ideally) comply to these definitions that are imposed upon them. Analysis of
such an organization model may check if the model satisfies desired properties such as
the possibility of completing a desired task given that all agents comply with the requirements of the organization. However, such an analysis is not sufficient to analyze
an executing organization. The main reason is that many design-time choices become

---

[*] This paper is an extended version of Hoogendoorn, M., Treur, J., and Yolum, P., A Labeled
Graph Approach to Analyze Organizational Performance. In: Nishida, T. (ed.), *Proceedings
of the 2006 IEEE/WIC/ACM International Conference on Intelligent Agent Technology (IAT
2006)*, IEEE Computer Society Press, 2006, pp. 482-489. and Hoogendoorn, M., Treur, J.,
and Yolum, P., A Labelled Graph Approach to Support Analysis of Organizational Performance. In: Fischer, K., Berre, A., Elms, K., and Muller, J.P. (eds.), *Proceedings of the Workshop on Agent-based Technologies and applications for enterprise interOPerability, ATOP'05*,
pp. 49-60

K. Fischer et al. (Eds.): ATOP 2005 and ATOP 2008, LNBIP 25, pp. 80–97, 2009.
© Springer-Verlag Berlin Heidelberg 2009

specific during execution. Agents choose who they want to interact with as well as how often they want to do so during run-time. For example, among two agents that enact a merchant role, one might be preferred over the other because the agent has better capabilities, more work capacity. Such interactions of agents at run-time can give rise to situations that can only be detected during execution. For example, one merchant agent will be more loaded than the second merchant due to one of such local decisions. Moreover, the agents participating in an organization may be designed and developed by independent parties, which requires them to interoperate and execute intelligently at run-time. In other words, such facts about the workings of a multi-agent organization cannot be discovered from a static representation of an organization during design time, but can only be analyzed during the execution time.

Whereas there is a vast literature in design of multi-agent organizations, there is little work on the analysis of executing multi-agent systems [13, 14]. This paper provides a complementary treatment of multi-agent organizations, where in addition to existing design time dynamics of the organizations, a graph representation is used to analyze executing organizations. Executing multi-agent organizations are analyzed by logging the performance of the organization in traces. Graph representations are useful for analyzing organizations; for example for understanding the structure of an organization through theoretical concepts.

This paper in the first place presents a formal specification language based on a graph representation. The relationships between participants in the organization are represented by a directed graph and labels in this graph are used to give semantics to the relationships. Once the labeled graphs are constructed, they can be used to analyze the functioning of the organization at runtime, i.e. analyze traces of the execution of the multi-agent system. Organization designers or analyzers can study the graph to understand the shortcomings of the organizations and to restructure the organization as they see fit; such interventions can be incorporated in software agents supporting the roles in an organization. This paper further shows that rules related to the organizations can be developed and automatically checked against the labeled graphs. As a concrete example, detection of overloaded agents is used.

The rest of this paper is organized as follows. Section 2 gives a representation of organizations as labeled graphs. Sections 3 discusses the usage of the graph for external analysis. Section 4 presents a case-study and Section 5 introduces a support agent for roles in the organization. In Section 6 related work is discussed, and finally, Section 7 concludes the paper and presents future work.

2 Organizations as Labeled Graphs

A directed graph $G = (V, E)$ constitutes the basis of the description of an organization in this paper. V denotes the set of nodes, which represent agents that enact a role. Note that for the sake of simplicity it is assumed that one agent can play only one role at a time. E denotes the edges in the graph, which represent the interactions between agents. Graph-based representations are typically used to model processes in areas such as (distributed) workflow management, business process design, organization modeling and organizational performance measurement. Usually the graphs have no labels or simple labels; such as a number that denotes the strength of a link. However, in real organizations edges denote different types of relationships with different properties. To represent such relationships, this paper provides a more complex structure of the labels and formalizes the structure with an algebra.

The example organizations considered here contain agents that fulfill tasks, assign subtasks to other agents, and thus run a business together. There are two primitive concepts we consider: workloads and capacities. An edge e connecting u and v means in this particular application that u requires some work to be done by v; i.e., edge e denotes a request for *workload*. As in real life, u could request different tasks to be performed by v. A label on an edge specifies the task type and the strength of the task (i.e., how intensive the work is). The label also includes a list consisting of tasks the current task at hand originates from.

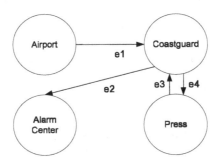

Fig. 1. An example organization graph

Example 1. Consider the organization in Figure 1. The figure gives a simplified representation of the disaster prevention organization in case of a plane crash in the Netherlands in the form of a labeled graph. Four agents enact the roles as shown in Figure 1: First of all, the airport role is present. This role takes care of the communication with airplanes and is the one that receives the mayday calls. After it has received a mayday call from a plane above the sea, it will contact the coastguard immediately to start a rescue task. The call causes the coastguard a lot of work, as they are in charge of the entire fleet of rescue ships. For possible precautions or backup from the land, the coastguard can contact the alarm center role which will arrange this type of help. The press is also represented as a role as they often request information regarding the number of casualties, information about the cause of the crash, and so on. The coastguard is responsible for fulfilling this task, which is called Inform.

Each agent in the organization has a certain capacity for each of the tasks that it can perform. Hence, the nodes of the graph are also labeled to denote the capacities of agents. First, a description of a formal language for the labels is given. Next, the capacities of the nodes will be discussed. Finally, the workload is defined.

2.1 Formal Specification Language

The formal language presented in this section is based on many-sorted algebra. The sorts of the label specification language are shown and explained in Table 1. Based on these sorts, functions are defined to combine these sorts into labels. Statements of this

Table 1. Sorts used in the label algebra

Sort	Description
Value	Sort for real values.
Timepoint	Sort for moments.
TimeInterval	Sort for names of intervals that contain two time-points of sort Timepoint.
Node	Sort to identify a node.
Edge	Sort to identify an edge.
Task	Sort to identify tasks.
Load	Sort to identify loads.
LoadValue	Sort for a Load Value pair.
LoadValueList	Sort for a list of LoadValue pairs.
Label	Sort to identify a label.
LabeledLoad	Sort for a pair containing a LoadValueList and a Label.
TaskSubtaskList	Sort for a list of tasks with a subtask relationship between them.
TaskList	Sort for a list of tasks.
Capacity	Sort to identify a capacity.
CapacityValue	Sort for a pair containing the Capacity and a Value.
OverallCapacity	Sort to identify the overall capacity.
OverallCapacity Value	Sort for a pair containing the OverallCapacity and a Value.
EdgeActivation	Sort for specifying the Value of the amount of activations of an Edge during a certain TimeInterval

language are equations as the examples accompanying the function definitions show. Throughout the text, when sorts and functions of the algebra are meant, they are denoted in Courier font.

First of all, a function is defined to construct a list containing pairs of subtasks. In general, the relation between tasks could be more general than the subtask relationship; for example, by incorporating information on the alternative tasks as well. However, the focus here is on dividing a task into smaller pieces that will be performed by agents, hence, only concentrating on the subtask relationship.

```
taskSubtaskPair: Task x TaskSubtaskList → TaskSubtaskList
```

Considering Example 1 one could express that the Rescue task has as a subtask LandOp which includes the operations that take place on land. Formally this can be expressed as follows:

```
tS=taskSubtaskPair(Rescue,
      taskSubtaskPair(LandOp, null))
```

Besides that, another function is specified which expresses a regular list of tasks without the subtask relationship between them.

```
taskList: Task x TaskList → TaskList
```

For example, a list containing the tasks that can be performed by the coastguard:
```
tL = taskList(Rescue, taskList(Inform, null))
```

For expressing the load three sorts are used: (i) the list which specifies the task from which this task originates, (ii) the node that carries the load, and (iii) the time interval for which this all holds. Intuitively, a load captures the intensity of the task a node has to do in a given time interval.

```
loadFor: TaskSubtaskList x Node x TimeInterval → Load
```

In the running example, the load for the coastguard can be expressed for TimeInterval I (for example 8 hours) and the Rescue task:

```
L = loadFor(tS, Coastguard, I)
```

A load is accompanied by a value expressing the amount of work caused by the load.

```
loadValuePair: Load x Value → LoadValue
```

For the Load defined above the value is set to 5:

```
LV = loadValuePair(L, 5)
```

Constructing a list from these LoadValue pairs can be done by means of a function. A communication from a role to another role can cause different kinds of load, therefore there is a need to express more than one load for each edge.

```
loadValuePairList: LoadValue x LoadValueList → LoadValueList
```

In the case of the example, only one LoadValue is present:
```
LVL = loadValuePairList(LV, null)
```

Now that the load caused by a connection in a graph can be fully specified it is combined with a label identifier.

```
loadLabel: LoadValueList x Label → LabeledLoad
```

The label specified above is now called L1:

```
LL = loadLabel(LVL, L1)
```

Now a label identifier is associated with an edge.

```
labeledEdge: Edge x Label → LabeledEdge
```

Example:

```
LE = labeledEdge(e1, L1)
```

Finally, at runtime an edge will be activated a certain number of times over a certain period, which can also be expressed in the algebra:

```
edgeActivation: Edge x TimeInterval  x Value → EdgeActivation
```

For example, the edge E1 was activated 2 times during TimeInterval I:
```
EA = edgeActivation(e1, I, 2)
```

Capacities can also be expressed by means of the functions. Capacities belong to nodes, as they are the ones that need to carry the load. The next Section will go into more detail on expressing the capacities. The capacity of a node is the amount of task it can do in a certain time period. The amount of task is denoted by a `TaskList` and the time period is denoted by a `TimeInterval`.

`capacityOf: TaskList x Node x TimeInterval → Capacity`

A value can be added to the capacity, for example, during the time-interval for which the capacity is specified, one man-hour is available for rescuing.

`capacityValue: Capacity x Value → CapacityValue`

Besides a capacity for specific tasks, a node also has an overall capacity. This overall capacity exists independent of types of tasks it can do.

`overallCapacity: Node x TimeInterval → OverallCapacity`

A value can again be added to this kind of capacity. It can for example say that during the time-interval of a day a maximum of 8 man-hours are available for a specific node.

`overallCapacityValue: OverallCapacity x Value → OverallCapacityValue`

Using the basic ontology of this algebra, its relations can be expressed, and logical relationships can be defined: The primitive terms used in the label algebra are defined by a many-sorted signature. The signature takes into account symbols for sorts, constants, functions and relations, including the equality relation. Among the relations, the equality relation has a special position: the identities (equations) between algebraic term expressions. Further relations can be defined by a relation symbol instantiated with term expressions. Logical relationships involve conditional statements involving relations, both the equality relation and other relations. For simplicity these logical relationships are assumed to be in a clausal format. Examples of constants are names of values, examples of function symbols are +, x, etc. examples of relation symbols are = and <. An examples of such a logical relationship is

if t1 < t2 then f(t1) < f(t2)

If no other relations than the equality relation occur, the algebra is called functional.

2.2 Capacities

The capacity of a node should be represented flexibly so that realistic situations can be modeled. The following scenarios are seen frequently. For these scenarios, it is assumed that the unit of capacity is man-hours. The maximum man-hours available is fixed: in this case to eight man-hours.

1. **Fixed Capacities:** An agent has a fixed number of hours it can spend on each task as dictated by its role. The sum of these hours should not be more than the maximum amount available.

2. **Constant Task-Specific Capacities:** This time an agent is told how many hours it can spend on each individual task. For example, if the role enacted by this agent has two tasks, coordinating the rescue operations and informing the press, then a possible restriction could state that the agent playing the role can spend at most 5 hours on the rescue operations and 5 hours on informing the press. Of course, working on the rescue operations task for 5 hours still leaves 3 hours for the informing the press task. That is, the maximum number of hours is still constant.
3. **Group-Restricted Capacities:** This time the restriction is not on individual tasks but on sets of tasks. For example, a role can spend a maximum 5 hours on the rescue operations and informing the press and maximum of 4 hours on writing reports. The choice of distributing the 5 hours between the rescue operations task and the informing the press task is up to the agent that plays the role. However, the time spent on the rescue operations and informing the press together cannot exceed 5 hours.
4. **Flexible Capacities:** An agent can decide to work any number of hours on any of its tasks, as long as a certain maximum is not exceeded during the time-interval for which this capacity holds.

It is actually easy to see that both Scenarios 1 and 4 can be modeled in terms of Scenario 2. To model the first scenario, the only thing that needs to be ensured is that the total of the fixed capacities adds up to the maximum. This already defines the scenario in terms of constant task-specific capacities. For the fourth scenario, the individual restriction for each individual work has to be set to the maximum 8 hours. Additionally, Scenario 2 can be modeled a special case of Scenario 3 where each set consists of one task. Hence, accommodating Scenario 3 enables accommodating the remaining scenarios. For the sake of simplicity, disjoint sets of tasks are assumed for a specification of the capacity.

Example 2. To give an example, consider the node `Coastguard`, having capacity for tasks `Rescue` and `Inform`. The capacity of the `Coastguard` concerning the `Rescue` task in the `TimeInterval I` is 8. For the `Inform` task this maximum is set to 2. Combined however, the overall capacity is set to 8, meaning that for the `Inform` and `Rescue` tasks together the time spent can not exceed 8. According to the formal notation as introduced in Section 2.1, the example can be formalized as shown below.

```
c1 = capacityOf(taskList(rescue, null), Coastguard, I)
cval1 = capacityValue(c1, 8)
c2 = capacityOf(taskList(inform, null), Coastguard, I)
cval2 = capacityValue(c2, 2)
co = overallCapacity(Coastguard, I)
coval = overallCapacityValue(cO, 8)
```

2.3 Workloads

A workload of a node is the amount of work it is required to do. Much work has been done to define the concept of workload more precisely, however there is still little consensus on a single definition. In [8] the 'human workload' is described as follows: "The intrinsic difficulty of the activities that an operator must perform establishes the target or nominal level of workload. The difficulty of a particular task may be influenced by any one or several of the following factors: (1) the goals and performance criteria set for a particular task; (2) the structure of the task; (3) the quality, format, and modality in which information is presented; (4) the cognitive processing required; (5) the characteristics of the response devices."

In operations management [12] research has been performed to define the time required to do a job in order to generate a unit of output, which is called work measurement. The initiator of this type of measurement was F.W. Taylor with his scientific management approach. It has however fallen into disfavor because it focuses on routine, repetitive tasks, but recently the labor-intensive service companies have resulted in a new popularity (e.g. hospitals that measure times spent by care takers).

The workload of an agent in this paper is determined based on the tasks assigned to it now, how often these assignments take place, and how much of these tasks are delegated to other agents. In general, the agent would perform a percentage of the tasks on its own and assign the remaining tasks to other agents; i.e., create workloads for others. In principle, the newly created workload should be less than that of the initial workload of the agent. The workload of an agent is only determined during execution. Hence, it is not possible to know the workloads exactly during design time and distribute work accordingly.

3   Specification for Labels With Respect to Loads

As has been mentioned before, labeled organization graphs can be used to analyze an organization. It can first be used to model the capacities and the workloads, and thereafter can be applied to analyze a trace representing the state of affairs within a multi-agent system during a certain period.

3.1   Calculations for Values of Loads

The workload of a node v during an interval I for a task t can be calculated in the following way: Let *workload(e,t)* be the workload for task t caused upon one activation of edge e. This number can be derived from the labeled algebra. First, look up the `task-SubtaskList` associated with this `Task t: taskSubtaskList(t, TSL)`. Thereafter get the label for edge e: `labeledEdge(e,L1)`. Now, look up the identifier of the `LoadValueList` via the `Label: loadLabel(LVL, L1)` and scan all entries of the `LoadValueList` for a `Load` in which the `TaskSubtaskList` starts with an element in `TSL` or starts with `t`, and holds for `TimeInterval I`. Finally, sum up the `Value` for each of these `Load` elements. Furthermore, for each of these edges, get the amount of activations, during `TimeInterval I`, then the workload can be calculated as shown in Definition 1:

Definition 1.

Workload(v, t, I) =

$\sum_{e \in \text{incomingEdges}(v)}$ a1 x workload(e, t)

           where edgeActivation(e, I, a1)

- $\sum_{e \in \text{outgoingEdges}(v)}$ a2 x workload(e, t)

           where edgeActivation(e, I, a2)

Which entails summing up the workload caused by all incoming nodes, and subtracting from that the workloads distributed through the outgoing edges. The calculation of the overall workload of a node (for all tasks t that the node is concerned with) is simply summing up all separate workloads, as shown in Definition 2.

Definition 2.
workload(v, I) = $\sum_{t \in tasks}$ workload(v, t, I)

Example 3. Consider the organization as presented in Example 1 and 2. Imagine the following scenario (during an interval I): A Dakota airplane has crashed in the sea, the airport forwards this crash message to the coastguard (causing a load of 5), who in turn delegates the land operations to the alarm center (causing them a load of 1). Besides that, the press starts asking questions about the crash (causing a load of 1 each time), as they have observed the plane crashing in the sea. They request information 40 times, and the Coastguard replies the same number of times (causing the press a load of 0.8 each time). The workload calculation is as follows: workload(coastguard, rescue, I) = (1 * 5) – (1 * 1) = 4 man-hours during interval T for the rescue task workload(coastguard, inform, I) = (40 * 1) – (40 * 0.8)=8 man-hours during interval I for the inform task.

As the calculation for the workload has been explained, the workload of a node can be compared with the capacity of a node, this is referred to as the load of a node. Two different types of loads have been distinguished. First of all, the load for a specific task t can be calculated. To calculate this load, first remember that the capacities are defined for a list of tasks, let l be the list of which t is an element. As it is impossible to calculate loads for individual tasks, loads can only be calculated in terms of these lists of tasks, therefore the calculation of a load for a task t is done by means of calculating the load for the entire list l the task is part of. Let v be a node, t be a task and I be an interval and let *capacity(v, l, I)* be the capacity of the node v for task list l, during interval I. This can be derived from the labeled algebra as follows: Get the `capacity` for `TaskList L` in which task t is defined for node v during interval I: C = `capacityOf(L,v,I)`. Thereafter, look up the `Value` CV of this capacity: `capacity-Value(C,CV)`. Now the load is defined as shown in Definition 3.

Definition 3.
load(v, t, I) =
$(\sum_{task \in l}$ workload(v, task, I))/ capacity(v, l, I) where t∈l

---

This defines that the load for a task is calculated by summing up all workload within the task list l for which a capacity has been defined which includes task t as well (so for every task within l) and dividing it by the capacity defined for that list.

The load can also be calculated for the node as a whole, this is simply done by taking the workload of the node, and dividing it by the overall capacity, *capacity(v, I)*, which can be found using the algebra: CA = `overallCapacity(v,I)` after which the `Value` OCV can be looked up: `overallCapacityValue(CA,OCV)`. The load is now calculated as shown in Definition 4.

> **Definition 4.**
> **load(v, I)** = workload(v, I)/ capacity(v, I))

An example of an interesting type of information that can be derived from the load is the load distributions among the nodes in the graph. An organization with evenly balanced nodes is typically preferable over a very uneven distribution of loads.

Example 4. Picture the organization in case of an airplane crash in the North-Sea, the Netherlands again. Following the capacity example as given in Section 2.2 the coast-guard has a capacity of 8 man-hours during I for the rescue task, and a capacity of 2 man-hours for the inform task, during that same period. Another capacity that is part of this organization is that of the press. The capacity of the press (which is not shown in a formalization) is defined as being 50 during the time-interval I in which the incident management occurs. The load of the coastguard and the press nodes can be calculated: The general load for the coastguard is: load(coastguard, I) = (12 / 8) = 1.5. More specifically, for the task rescue the load is 0.5 and for the inform task the load is 4.0. For the press, the workload is only caused by the information coming from the coastguard, which cannot be distributed elsewhere. Therefore the workload of the press is 40 x 0.8 = 32. As they only have one task, the load of the press, load (press, I), is equal to 0.64. Based on this, it can be seen that the press has a relatively low load compared to the coastguard. By means of this information, a person that is analyzing an organization could suggest that the press should reduce the requests for information to the coastguard and try getting most of their information within the press organization, as they still have sufficient capacity.

3.2 Overloading

As the load for a node has been defined, the definition of a node being overloaded can be given. A certain role is overloaded in case one, or both of the following situations hold: (1) There exists a task t for which the load is greater than 1.0; (2) The load for the entire node, load(v, I) exceeds 1.0. A formal definition is presented below. Please note that due to the choice of representing the capacities by group restricted capacities it can occur that the loads for the individual group are not overloaded whereas the overall load is.

> **Definition 5:**
> **overloaded(v, I)** =
> $\exists$t:Task (load(v,t,I) > 1.0) $\vee$ (load(v,I) > 1.0)

Example 5. Following from example 4, it can be seen that the role of coastguard is heavily overloaded, for one of the tasks (inform) the load is 4.0, which means 4 times the capacity. The press however is not overloaded as it has a load value of 0.64.

4 Case-Study: Dakota Incident

This Section presents details regarding the implementation of the labeled graph approach into a software tool, and shows an empirical evaluation using a trace obtained from the domain of incident management.

4.1 Implementation

In order to be able to use the algebra and calculations for analyzing multi-agent organizations, a software tool has been created. First, the algebra presented in Section 2
has been implemented in PROLOG [5], including the calculations that are presented
in Section 3. For a comparative study of translating an algebraic specification into a
PROLOG program, see [6]. A specific interval can be specified over which the calculations of the organizational performance are done. Thereafter, in order to make the
calculations of the workloads and loads for the nodes more insightful for e.g. domain

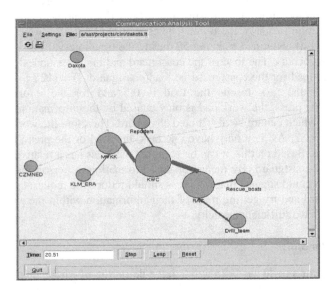

Fig. 2. Screenshot of the visualization tool

experts to evaluate, a visualization tool has been created that graphically shows how
much work is being transferred between different nodes within the graph, and represents the load for each of these nodes. Figure 2 shows a screen-shot of the visualization tool. The radius of a node is increased in case the load increases, so the bigger the
node the heavier the load on that specific node. Further, communication channels that
are intensively used (i.e. edges that are activated many times during a particular time
interval) are highlighted as well by turning red in case of a lot of activity (or purple in
case of a huge amount of activity).

4.2 Empirical Evaluation

In order to evaluate the functioning of the implementation and the approach itself, a
case study has been performed in the incident management domain. The case-study
itself is based upon reports of a plane crash which occurred in the Netherlands in
1996. A trace of the events that occurred during the rescue of the passengers on board
of the plane has been obtained from domain experts and logs that have been made of
the communications that took place during the incident management in 1996. The

examples used in Sections 2 and 3 include simplifications used for this case study. To enable an analysis, the organization, including the roles and the communications that took place, has been translated to a graph. Thereafter, a domain expert has labeled the graph with the values he thinks are appropriate values for workload caused by activation of a communication line (i.e. an edge). Furthermore, the expert has set capacities for the roles (i.e. nodes) within the incident management organization. According to the experts in the field (written down in incident management reports) the role of the coastguard (abbreviated in the figure to KWC) was heavily overloaded due to too many requests for information of the press, regional alarm center (RAC) and the military airport (MVKK). This indeed showed in the visualization, based on the capacities and workloads set in the graph. The coastguard has a large capacity for handling all the work, but is unable to handle all incoming requests. This shows that the analysis using the labeled graph approach is indeed in line with the manual expert evaluations.

5   Supporting Humans Within Organizations

Given that the load of the various organizations can now be specified, and measured, this approach can be used to support human functioning in an organization. For example, the coastguards in the scenario sketched above could be supported by informing them that the press is costing them a lot of time, and it would be better to delegate some of these tasks. Hereby, one can think of agents residing in the environment that support the humans, drawing inspiration from Ambient Intelligence [1] and Ubiquitous Computing [15]. In this section, an executable model for such an agent is described in the form of a number of properties that express its behaviors. In addition, simulation runs for the agent model are presented.

5.1   Agent Properties

The properties specified for the personal assistant agent have been formulated in the LEADSTO language (cf. [2]). LEADSTO is an executable sublanguage of the Temporal Trace Language (TTL, cf. [3]). The basic building blocks of this language are causal relations of the format $\alpha \twoheadrightarrow_{e, f, g, h} \beta$, which means:

If   state property α holds for a certain time interval with duration g,
then   after some delay (between e and f) state property β will hold
          for a certain time interval of length h.

where α and β are state properties of the form 'conjunction of literals' (where a literal is an atom or the negation of an atom), and e, f, g, h non-negative real numbers.

The following properties can be distinguished for the support agent. First of all, subtle warnings are given by the personal assistant agent in case a role is overloaded for a somewhat longer time (usually peaks can be handled for a short while, so there is no need for assistance in case the overload occurs for a very short period), but when the overload has not taken place for a very long time (< max_subtle_warning), then the personal assistant agent gives a subtle advice. This property is formulated in the rule below (note that in case the subscript below the LEADSTO arrow is omitted a standard delay of 0,0,1,1 for e,f,g, and h respectively is used):

overloaded_for(R, d) ∧
d > min_subtle_warning ∧ d < max_subtle_warning
→ subtle_advice_needed_for(R)

The subtle advice generated is based upon the tasks the role is currently overloaded for. In case the role is not overloaded for single tasks, but simply for the combination of tasks as a whole, the warning is given that the human should reduce the overall load:

subtle_advice_needed_for(R) ∧
load(R, T, L) ∧ L > 1
        → communication_from_to(PA, R, you_are_overloaded_for_task_try_to_reduce_load(T))
subtle_advice_needed_for(R) ∧
∀T:TASK [load(R, T, L) ∧ L ≤ 1]
        → communiation_from_to(PA, R, you_are_generally_overloaded_try_to_reduce_load)

Of course, the human playing the role might not respond to the warning of the agent. As a result, the agent can take more drastic measures, namely overriding task alloca-tion. First, the agent derives that the situation requires drastic measures:

overloaded_for(R, d) ∧
d ≥ max_subtle_warning
→ drastic_measures_needed_for(R)

These drastic measures include assigning the tasks for which the role is overloaded to other participants of the organization. The agent only does this in case it is allowed to reallocate the task:

drastic_measures_needed_for(R) ∧
load(R, T, L) ∧ L > 1 ∧
    pa_allowed_to_reallocate_task(T)
    → performed(pa, reallocation_of_load(R, T, L-1)) ∧
        communication_from_to(pa, R, reallocated_part_of_task(T))

How the agent precisely reallocates this task is outside of the scope of this paper, but the agent could take the overall load of other roles into account. If the role is not over-loaded for specific tasks, but in general, then complete tasks are reallocated. Hereby, it is assumed that the personal assistant agent knows what the best available candidate is to be reallocated. This can for example be based on the observed preferences for tasks of the fulfiller of the role.

drastic_measures_needed_for(R) ∧
∀T:TASK [load(R, T, L) ∧ L ≤ 1] ∧
best_candidate(T2) ∧
pa_allowed_to_reallocate_task(T2)
→ performed(pa, reallocation_of_load(R, T2, L)) ∧
    communication_from_to(pa, R, reallocated_task(T))

5.2   Simulation Results

Using the rules specified in Section 5.1, simulations have been performed. Hereby, the case of the coastguard has been taken as a basis. Figure 3 shows the first trace using the support agent. In the figure, the left side denotes a subset of the atoms that occur during the simulation run whereas the right hand side indicates a timeline where a black box indicates that an atom holds at the time point, and a grey box means that the atom is false.

In the Figure, it can be seen that in this case the personal assistant agent is allowed to reallocate tasks of the type Inform:

pa_allowed_to_reallocate_task(inform)

In addition, the workload observed by the personal assistant agent can be seen, which is identical to the values previously calculated in Example 5:

load(coastguard, rescue, 0.5)
load(coastguard, inform, 4)

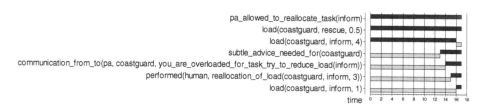

Fig. 3. Simulation trace of Support Agent: Case 1

Due to the overload, after the minimum duration before an advice is given (in this case 20 time points), the personal assistant agent derives that a subtle warning should be given:

subtle_advice_needed_for(coastguard)

As a result, a communication between the personal assistant agent and the role takes place:

communication_from_to(pa, coastguard,
                      you_are_overloaded_fror_task_try_to_reduce_load(inform))

In this case, the human playing the role decides to perform task reallocation itself due to the communication of the personal assistant agent:

performed(human, reallocation_of_load(coastguard, inform, 3))

Finally the overload situation disappears as a result of the reallocation of tasks:
load(coastguard, inform, 1)

In a second case study (shown in Figure 4), the scenario is again the coastguard scenario. However, the human does not listen to the initial advice of the agent. As a result, the agent derives that drastic measures should be taken:

drastic_measures_needed_for(coastguard)

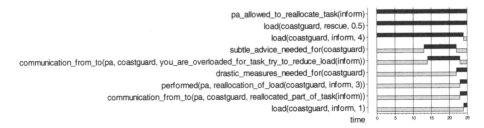

Fig. 4. Simulation trace of Support Agent: Case 2

Following this atom is the fact that the personal assistant reallocates the task to another human, including a communication to the role that this reallocation has taken place:

    performed(pa, reallocation_of_load(coastguard, inform, 3))
    communication_from_to(pa, coastguard, reallocated_part_of_task(inform))

This results in the same effect as the previous scenario: there is no longer an overload situation:

    load(coastguard, inform, 1)

6   Related Work

Operations research is a closely related field to the research presented in this paper, see e.g. [9]. Many theories have been developed in that field of research to enable a proper functioning of the organization as a whole, creating a planning for these operations, etc. The research presented in this paper is meant to monitor the performance of these organizations, not to design these operations within the organization.

Another related field is workflow management, in which tools exist that measure and analyze the execution of processes so that continuous improvements can be made. The approach in workflow management can be used as a support tool to analyze the execution, however workflow management systems constitute a huge system which is put into the organization to measure the performance, whereas the approach in this paper simply needs traces of the events and values for the capacities of nodes and workloads regarding tasks. This also enables the presented approach to be used for analyzing occurrences in the past and organizations in which introducing a workflow management system is not feasible.

There is a vast literature on designing multi-agent organizations. Zambonelli *et al.* develop a design methodology, GAIA [16]. GAIA identifies roles, organization rules, environment, and so on as necessary organizational abstractions. Using these constructs, GAIA methodology helps a system designer build its system in a systematic way. Padgham and Winikoff develop Prometheus, an agent-based software development methodology [11]. It consists of a system specification, architectural design, and detailed design phases. While these approaches are useful for designing multi-agent systems, they do not provide any mechanisms for analyzing executing organizations.

That is, these methodologies only care for the design phase, but are not targeted for analyzing the multi-agent system during execution, which is the case for the methodology presented in this paper.

Handley and Levis create a model to evaluate the effect of organizational adaptation by means of colored Petri nets [8]. The Petri nets are used to represent external interaction of decision makers as well as internal algorithms the decision maker must perform, and are equipped with labels. In this model the workload of the decision makers is monitored and is used as a performance indicator. The concept of entropy is used to measure the total activity value (which is linked to the workload) of a decision maker. When an overload of a decision maker occurs, the execution time of the internal algorithm has a delay of one additional time point. Decision makers can also base decisions on who to forward an output to on the total activity of the decision maker that can be chosen. Their approach differs from the approach in this paper in the sense that they specify the entire process within the organization, and use the Petri nets to actually simulate an organization. Therefore, their aim is more towards the decision process and the evaluation thereof whereas the approach presented here is more intended as a separate method for evaluating the performance of an organization from an external viewpoint.

Fink *et al.* develop a visualization system to help monitor the performance of businesses [7]. The focus of their work is on presenting a tool that can incorporate different performance metrics from different sources. The aim of the approach presented here is to analyze performance of a business automatically. In this sense, the work of Fink *et al.* is complementary to the work in this paper. Once certain properties are detected by the approach in this paper, they could be feed into a visualization tool to ease the exposure.

Regarding support possibilities for roles within an organization, other approaches have been developed as well. In [4] for example, an approach is introduced which reason about what task a human is performing at a certain time point, given a particular workflow. Such information could be used by the support agent proposed in this paper as well, for example for a more detailed analysis of task progress instead of the external approach taken now.

7   Conclusion and Future Work

This paper has presented a formal language for specifying organizations. The specification is based on a graph formalism. The nodes of the graph represent agents and the edges between the nodes are labeled to denote why those edges exist. This allows the representation of the interactions between the agents in an expressive way. It has been shown that using this organization structure properties of executing organizations can be detected, such as the cases where the organization hosts overloaded agents, successfully. This has been shown by means of an extensive case study in the incident management domain. Moreover, based on such an analysis, support can be provided to roles within the organization. In order to show the effectiveness of this support, simulation runs have been conducted whereby both obedient as well as non-obedient behaviors of the organizations have been addressed. In both cases eventually the overload situation was resolved.

The work presented in this paper is open for further improvements. Whereas this paper mainly deals with calculating the effect of an edge on its endpoints, it is also possible to calculate the effects of an edge on nodes that are not immediate endpoints. This can be regarded as calculating the cascading effects of interactions on third parties. Similarly, the representation can be made richer by adding capacities or work-flows for groups of agents to model the smaller units in an organization. Ideas developed in this paper can also be used to help agents model others and reason about others' workloads to manage their interactions more efficiently. Such reasoning could possibly even result in change of an organization in case the workload simply cannot be handled, see [10] for more extensive results on this. Furthermore, investigations on how well the approach scales up to large scale multi-agent systems will need to be performed in the future. One important possibility to note here is that of specifying such a system on multiple aggregation levels, whereby the analysis can take place at the highest level (e.g. the workload between departments) while at the lower level focus on parts of the organization (e.g. the workload within a department).

References

[1] Aarts, E., Harwig, R., Schuurmans, M.: Ambient Intelligence. In: Denning, P. (ed.) The Invisible Future, pp. 235–250. McGraw Hill, New York (2001)

[2] Bosse, T., Jonker, C.M., van der Meij, L., Treur, J.: A Language and Environment for Analysis of Dynamics by Simulation. International Journal of Artificial Intelligence Tools 16, 435–464 (2007)

[3] Bosse, T., Jonker, C.M., van der Meij, L., Sharpanskykh, A., Treur, J.: Specification and Verification of Dynamics in Agent Models. International Journal of Cooperative Information Systems (2008) (in press)

[4] Both, F., Hoogendoorn, M., Treur, J.: An Ambient Agent Model Exploiting Workflow-Based Reasoning to Recognize Task Progress. In: Aarts, E., Crowley, J.L., Ruyter, B., de, G.H., Pflaum, A., Schmidt, J., Wichert, R. (eds.) Ambient Intelligence, Proceedings of the Second European Conference on Ambient Intelligence, AmI 2008. LNCS, vol. 5355, pp. 222–239. Springer, Heidelberg (2008)

[5] Colmerauer, A., Kanoui, H., Pasero, R., Roussel, P.: Un Système de Communication Homme-Machine en Français. Groupe de Recherche en Intelligence Artificielle, Université d'Aix-Marseille, Lumini (1971)

[6] Drosten, K.: Translating algebraic specifications to Prolog programs: a comparative study. In: Grabowski, J., Lescanne, P., Wechler, W. (eds.) ALP 1988. LNCS, vol. 343, pp. 137–146. Springer, Heidelberg (1989)

[7] Fink, G., Krishnamoorthy, S., Kanade, A.: Naval Crew Workload Monitoring and Visualization. In: First Annual Conf. on Systems Integration, NJ (2003)

[8] Handley, H., Levis, A.: A Model to Evaluate the Effect of Organizational Adaptation. Computational & Mathematical Organization Theory 7(1), 5–44 (2001)

[9] Hillier, F.S., Lieberman, G.J.: Introduction to Operations Research. McCraw-Hill, SF (2002)

[10] Hoogendoorn, M.: Adaptation of Organizational Models for Multi-Agent Systems based on Max Flow Networks. In: Proceedings of the Twentieth International Joint Conference on Artificial Intelligence, pp. 1321–1326. AAAI Press, Menlo Park (2007)

[11] Padgham, L., Winikoff, M.: Prometheus: A Methodology for Developing Intelligent Agents. In: Giunchiglia, F., Odell, J.J., Weiss, G. (eds.) AOSE 2002. LNCS, vol. 2585, pp. 174–185. Springer, Heidelberg (2003)
[12] Russell, R.S., Taylor, B.W.: Operations Management. Prentice Hall, New Jersey (2003)
[13] Shehory, O., Sturm, A.: Evaluation of modeling techniques for agent-based systems. In: Proceedings of the Intl. Conf. on Autonomous Agents, pp. 624–631. ACM Press, New York (2001)
[14] Sudeikat, J., Braubach, L., Pokahr, A., Lamersdorf, W.: Evaluation of Agent Oriented Software Methodologies Examination of the Gap between Modeling and Platform. In: Odell, J.J., Giorgini, P., Müller, J.P. (eds.) AOSE 2004. LNCS, vol. 3382, pp. 126–141. Springer, Heidelberg (2005)
[15] Weiser, M.: Some computer science issues in ubiquitous computing. ACM SIGMOBILE Mobile Computing and Communications Review 3, 1559–1662 (1999)
[16] Zambonelli, F., Jennings, N.R., Wooldridge, M.J.: Developing Multiagent Systems: The Gaia Methodology. ACM Transactions on Software Engineering and Methodology 12(3) (September 2003)

Adding Organisations and Roles to JADE with JadeOrgs

Cristián Madrigal-Mora and Klaus Fischer

DFKI GmbH
Stuhlsatzenhausweg 3 (Building D 3-2),
D-66123 Saarbrücken, Germany
{Cristian.Madrigal,Klaus.Fischer}@dfki.de

Abstract. The use of organisational structures enables one to clearly scope the interactions between parties that collaborate toward a common goal. The representation of an agent organisation as a first class entity is a frequently missing feature in platforms for multiagent systems, and it is normally left as a result of the emergent behaviour of interacting agents. This is also the case for JADE, one of the most commonly used multiagent system middlewares. This paper presents JadeOrgs, an extension to JADE that introduces Organisations and Roles as first level entities available at runtime.

Keywords: JADE, model driven development, agents, organisations, JadeOrgs, roles.

1   Introduction

When a system has a large amount of jobs to be performed several times in coordination with several providers, it is inefficient to distribute the tasks among all the parties involved every single time. In this case, it makes better sense to establish this repeated coordination structure based on the previous successes. This provider grouping can be formalised by the concept of *Organisation*. Organisations are social structures that provide processes for conflict resolution, as a result from previously resolved problems or conflicts [1]. They institutionalise anticipated coordination, which is especially useful for medium and large-scale applications that require the delimitation of the agent communication behaviour.

Since the overall computation in Multiagent Systems (MAS) is obtained by the combination of the autonomous computation of every agent in the system and the communication among them [2], the coordination and communication among the agents is essential. Designing agents to act within an organisational structure can provide additional encapsulation, simplifying representation and design, and modularisation, enabling code reuse and incremental deployment.

Nevertheless, these coordination or organisational structures are not always explicitly supported by agent platforms, even when some agent metamodels and methodologies do present them. We consider that organisations and their corresponding role structure can reduce interoperability problems since they help

K. Fischer et al. (Eds.): ATOP 2005 and ATOP 2008, LNBIP 25, pp. 98–117, 2009.

specify the scope of interactions within and outside the organisation. Additionally, the evaluation of organisation members against a set of requirements, namely the role description, reduces the possibility that unfit parties/agents can join and also potentially enables them also to look for ways to comply with these requirements in order to take part of the interactions inside the organisation.

This paper presents JadeOrgs, an organisation-oriented extension for the JADE agent platform [3,4]. JADE is a FIPA [5] compliant multiagent system middleware which also serves as agent platform and provides basic services like directories and messaging. Its framework supports the implementation of ontologies for the contents of messages and knowledge of agents. JADE is also one of the preferred platforms to implement conversation protocols between autonomous agents, because it provides a library of behaviours for performing FIPA interaction protocols. New conversation protocols and their corresponding behaviours can be produced from scratch or by combining protocols. In spite of addressing the problem of composition of agent groups, it does not provide explicit features for groups apart of the emergent behaviour obtained by manifesting the behaviours of each agent.

The article is structured as follows: Section 2 presents related works; Section 3 presents the JadeOrgs metamodel, its implementation and a small example; Section 4 presents a comparison against other agent metamodels and discusses some of the benefits of using organisations; some open issues are addressed in Section 5 and Section 6 presents our last remarks and conclusion.

2   Related Work

This section presents a short overview of some related work in agent platforms, metamodels and methodologies with regard to agent organisations.

Regarding the analysis of organisations, the approach the we present on this paper falls under what [6] calls the perspective of computational organisation theory and artificial intelligence, in which the organisations are basically described at the role and group—composed of roles—levels. Under this perspective, we can also find works such as GAIA [7,8] and MOISE [9]. While other models, such as ISLANDER [10], define organisations as electronic institutions, in terms of norms and rules.

With respect to organisational structures, Holonic MAS [11] present particular pyramidal organisations where agents of a layer (having the same coordinator) are able to communicate and to negotiate directly between them [12]. This coordinator is also known as the holon's *head*. Any holon that is part of a whole is thought to contribute to achieving the goals of this superior whole. Apart from the head, each holon consist of a (possibly empty) set of other agents, called body agents. Holonic structures can be expressed quite naturally in terms of roles and groups, under the perspective described previously.

Besides our chosen agent platform, JADE, there are two other platforms that we consider relevant in this context. First, JACK Intelligent Agents [13] supports organisational structures through its Team Mode. In this mode, goals can be delegated to team member in order to achieve the team goals. JADEX [14,15] presents another interesting platform for the implementation of organisations. While JADEX does not currently have organisational structures, the approach presented here could be easily adapted to it, while gaining its BDI reasoning and the ability to do metareasoning on the organisation structures and behaviours.

Additionally, there has been previous work regarding organisations through agent middlewares, such as AMELI [16] and S-MOISE+ [17], while the support of these in the more broadly used agent platforms, like JADE, has been dependent on the way the platform deals with behaviour execution and message passing without enforcing policies and restrictions at the organisation level through run time computational entities.

From our study of the literature, the only other approach that we have found that addresses the issue of implementing organisations in JADE is powerJade [18]. The powerJade approach has various similarities with JadeOrgs with the biggest difference being in the implementation of roles. Roles in powerJade are implemented as agents since they are the ones in charge of performing powers and requesting requirements from the agents that play the roles: the players. When a player fails to meet a requirement, its role is deacted. Therefore, powerJade does not evaluate the role requirements when the players joins the organisation, like JadeOrgs does, but deacts the role if one of the requirements is not met during the execution of a Power. Some additional details how powerJade's roles implementation relates to JadeOrgs are discussed in Section 4.

3   Organisations and Roles in JadeOrgs

The definition of Organisation[1] that we propose to use in JADE is the *Agentified Group* in [19]: a set of agents that possesses all the features that any agent might possess. For example, just as an agent, it can send and receive messages directly and take on roles. For this purpose, the Organisation is a specialization of Agent.

An Organisation or a group in general is formed to attain new processes and results that were not available by individual members, therefore taking advantage of the synergies among them. Organisations may be established statically—at design time by the system designer—or dynamically—at runtime—as a collective task or goal arises. In order to perform this common task, the organisation distributes responsabilities to its members according to the *Roles* they play in the organisation.

3.1   Motivation

The JadeOrgs extension to JADE was designed to provide a Platform Specific Model (PSM) for JADE for the transformation of models define with the Platform Independent Modelling Language for Multiagent Systems (DSML4MAS)

---

[1] Capitalised terms refer to classes or relevant concepts.

[20]. The PIM4Agents metamodel [21] represents its abstract syntax, and its semantics and concrete syntax are presented in [20]. In this context, the JADEOrgs
metamodel was defined in the Eclipse Modeling Framework (EMF) [22] in order
to take advantage of the transformation tools available for Eclipse and to fit our
model driven approach, depicted in Figure 1. In this approach, a model defined
with the PIM4Agents is transformed to a model described with the JadeOrgs
metamodel, and finally the JadeOrgs model is serialised into Java source code.
Transforming a PIM4Agents model to a PSM level model in JadeOrgs allows,
if necessary, the refinement of the model with JADE/JadeOrgs concepts and
avoids the need of introducing platform specific concepts in the PIM4Agents.
The model to model transformations are specified in the Atlas Transformation
Language (ATL) [23] and the model to code serialisation is implemented using
MOFScript [24].

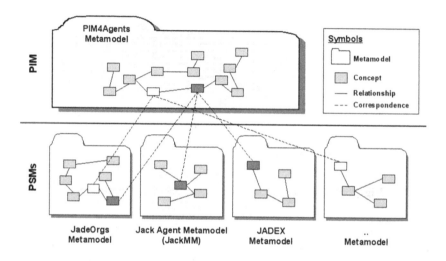

Fig. 1. Overview of the model driven approach with PIM4Agents

The metamodel started as an extraction of the JADE class model from JADE's
source code and documentation. However, when coming to the definition of the
transformations from PIM4Agents to the JADE PSM, we noticed that additional
flexibility and adaptability could be provided to JADE if we represented Organisations and Roles from the PIM4Agents as computational entities in JADE
instead of just mapping them directly in agents.

Therefore, we concentrate on the Organisation as a computational entity for
execution purposes and the Role as a description of the requirements the member
agents must fulfil. Although we use the analogy of social organisation, given the
parallelisms that exist with regard to the distribution of tasks and teamwork,
our Organisation and Role concepts are not intended, at this point, to address
directly the issues of implementing institutions, alliances or coalitions, although
our work could potentially aid the implementation of them in JADE.

3.2   The JadeOrgs Metamodel

The JadeOrgs metamodel is centred around three concepts/classes: *JadeOrgsAgent, Organisation* and *Role* (Figure 2). We should note that even-though we present the metamodel graphically using UML Class Diagrams, the metamodel is actually implemented in the Eclipse Modelling Framework Ecore language.

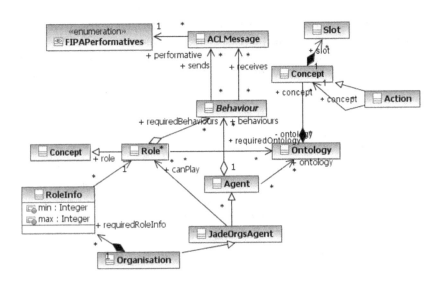

Fig. 2. Partial view of the core of the JadeOrgs metamodel

The JadeOrgsAgent is a specialisation of JADE's Agent class that provides the provides the data structures and methods necessary to manage the agent's membership information in whatever organisations it has joined, as well the list possible roles the JadeOrgsAgent can play. In the first implementation of JadeOrgs [25], we had intended to use JADE's Agent class directly and just provided with some auxiliary classes to manage this membership data, with the intention of allowing existing system implementations to add this functionality without changing their agent types hierarchy. However, it proved much practical to just provide this functionality in a specialisation of Agent.

The Organisation class contains references to all its members, as well as the Roles under which the membership relation is stated. The information about the required roles is represented by the association class RoleInfo, which provides the cardinality information with respect to the amount of role filler agents required. The Organisation class extends the Agent class, given that we want it to be able to perform tasks and communicate with its members and other agents. As such, the Organisation is itself an Agent and possesses its own set of behaviours. Additionally, Organisation also provides the functionality of registration and

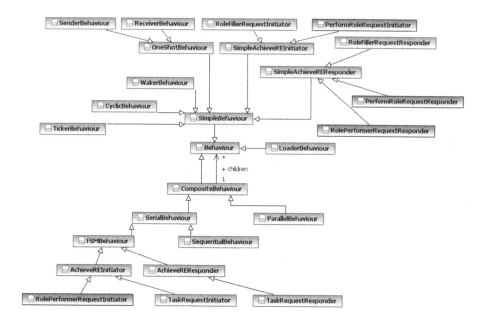

Fig. 3. Partial view of the core of the Behaviour hierarchy

deregistration of members as the Organisation changes over time. These tasks are performed using communication protocols that serve this purpose and that will be described in detail further on.

The Role class is implemented as an Ontology Concept, part of the *OrganisationOntology*. Among the properties of the Role class, we find required behaviours, required ontologies and message templates for sent and received messages. Each of these properties allow different requirements to be checked and depending on the evaluation strategy desired only some of them may be specified. For instance, the list of required behaviours can potentially be used (i) to verify that the agent is actually capable of performing the Role's tasks or (ii) to allow the Agent to acquire the Behaviours required to fulfil the role by adding them to its known behaviours, depending on the value of the Role's properties. In a similar fashion, the required ontologies allow evaluation on the knowledge available to the agent.

The Behaviour class, shown in Figure 2, represents merely the root of the Behaviour hierarchy that JADE provides. The complex behaviours allow the nesting of behaviours and permit different ways of executing them. JADE also provides an implementation of various FIPA protocols. For example, the SimpleAchieveREInitiator and SimpleAchieveREResponder are provided to implement all the FIPA-Request-like interaction protocols defined by FIPA [26] in which initiator sends a single message to the responder in order to verify if the RE (Rational Effect) of the communicative act has been achieved or not.

We have extended these behaviours for the organisation establishment. Figure 3 presents a partial view of this Behaviour hierarchy.

Since the Ecore language concentrates mainly on the representation of classes or types, it proves necessary to introduce some "auxiliary types" if one wants to represent instances of other classes/types. We therefore introduced the deployment aspect (see Figure 4) to allow the modelling of the organisation composition at design time. The AID class represents JADE's agent identifier. We extend the AID class into 2 types: AgentInstance to represent regular Jade agent instances and JadeOrgsInstance to represent instances of JadeOrgsAgents and Organisations. In this aspect MembershipInfo is the association class that binds the types together to express that a JadeOrgsInstance is member of an Organisation under a given Role. A diagram from this aspect will be used to present the example below.

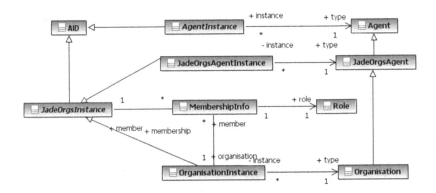

Fig. 4. The deployment aspect of JadeOrgs

3.3   JadeOrgs Protocols and Interactions

Publishing to the Directory Facilitator. The Organisation structure can be established at design time or at run time. For the ones setup in design time, the initialisation of the organisation structure is already set; however, for those that are determined until run time, a selection of role fillers needs to take place. JADE already provides a directory service called the Directory Facilitator (DF). Through the DF, an agent/organisation can search for other agents/organisations that possess a given set of features, such as the protocols supported or the ontologies it can access. For technical details on querying the DF Service, please see [27].

In order to take advantage of the DF Service, we extend the class used to describe agents, namely *DFAgentDescription*, which is part of JADE's *FIPAAgentManagementOntology*. As depicted in Figure 5, we first extend DFAgentDescription by adding a list of performed roles, creating the descriptor for Organisation members, *DFOrganisationMemberDescription*.

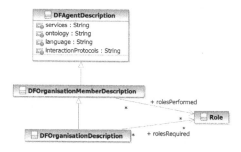

Fig. 5. Directory description class hierarchy of OrganisationOntology

Since the Organisation requires and, as the agent that it is, performs roles, we create the Organisation descriptor, *DFOrganisationDescription*, by extending DFOrganisationMemberDescription with a list of required roles.

Organisation Establishment. Once the descriptions for Organisations and members are published to the DF, the organisation establishment can take place on the run time case. As a first step, a search for suitable agents/organisations is performed by querying the DF Service. When the list of prospective DFOrganisationMemberDescriptions or DFOrganisationDescriptions is retrieved, the agent/organisation initiates the RoleFillerRequest protocol with the organisation it wants to join. The protocol is implemented by the RoleFillerRequestInitiator and RoleFillerRequestResponder behaviours. As described in Figure 6, the organisation takes the Responder role and a RoleRequest object is sent by the Requester as content of the ACL_request message. Once this request is received by the Responder, an ACL_refuse message is produced if the request is denied, or an ACL_inform message is produced if the request has been accepted. As it can be expected, the decision process for accepting/denying these requests is left to other internal behaviours of the agent/organisation. An analogous protocol can be applied for the organisation that wants to recruit a new member.

Depending on the design policies, the decision process may include, for example, a verification that the requesting agent possesses all the behaviours necessary to fulfil the requested role. Although we do not solve this issue completely, the Role description allows at least a couple of simple evaluation options that can be extended:

Type compatibility: The canPlay association between JadeOrgsAgent and Role permits a simple check through the type/class definition.

Required Behaviours: The list of required behaviours permits to check if the candidate role filler "knows" the behaviours that implements the desired protocols.

Message Templates: The message template mechanism that JADE provides allows to specify a basic list of messages that should be sent and received by the role filler as part of the protocols/interactions that the role requires.

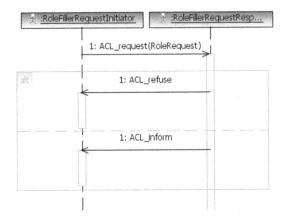

Fig. 6. RoleFillerRequest protocol

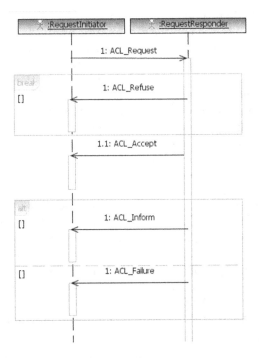

Fig. 7. TaskRequest protocol

This attribute of the role description is analogous to the *sends, posts* and *handles* attributes for roles in the JACK Intelligent Agents framework [13].

Task Distribution. In order to allow the organisation members to manage their own work load, the distribution of tasks is performed through the simple protocol presented in Figure 7. This protocol is basically a simplified version of the FIPA Request Protocol [26] which provides the RequestResponder with the option of refusing in case it is already busy.

The protocol is implemented through the *TaskRequestInitiator* and *TaskRequestResponder* behaviours previously shown in Figure 3. As part of the TaskRequestInitiator behaviour, the behaviour must implement a mechanism for choosing the desired role fillers for the task out of the set of available members under the role that should perform the task. For the coding of the mechanism, an interface called RoleFillerChooser has been provided.

3.4   Small Example: Product Sale With Loan

As a concrete example on how Organisations can help define the interaction context, we present a Product Sale scenario. The basic interaction in this scenario takes place between a *Buyer* and a *Seller* and it is depicted in Figure 8. The interaction is initiated by the Buyer making a query about a certain product. If the product is not in stock, the Seller sends an OutOfStock message and the interaction terminates. If the product is in stock, the Seller replies with the product price. The Buyer receives the price and considers if it has enough money to pay for it. If it does not, the Buyer cancels the transaction. If it does have the money, it sends the payment to the Seller and, correspondingly, the Seller ships the product.

Under this scenario, if the Buyer does not have enough money, it has to find the means to get the necessary money. One solution, would be to get a loan from a Bank. This situation could be modelled in JadeOrgs with the organisation, agent and roles types depicted in Figure 9. On the right side of the image,

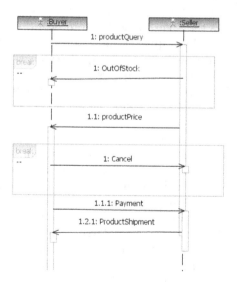

Fig. 8. View of the Product Sale Protocol

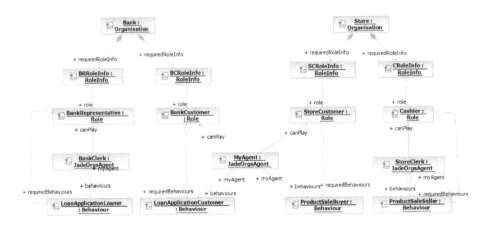

Fig. 9. Organisational structures for the sample scenario

the *Store* organisation is the one that contains the ProductSale interaction previously described. It has two roles *StoreCustomer* and *Cashier*, and they require the behaviours that implement the Buyer and Seller described in the protocol respectively. The Cashier role can be played by the *StoreClerk* agent type and the StoreCustomer role can be played by the *MyAgent* agent type.

On the left side of Figure 9, we find the *Bank* organisation, with its two roles: *BankRepresentative* and *BankCustomer*. The BankRepresentative role can be played by agents of the *BankClerk* type and requires the LoanApplicationLoaner behaviour. Correspondingly, the BankCustomer role requires the LoanApplicationCustomer behaviour and can be played by the MyAgent agent type. As can be deduced from the required behaviours, one of the possible interactions inside the Bank organisation is the LoanApplication protocol (Figure 10). In this protocol, a Customer sends a loan application to Loaner; the Loaner evaluates the application and determines if the Customer qualifies for a loan. If he does not, the interaction is over with a rejection message. But if he does, he receives a confirmation of the acceptance of his application and he must then sign the loan contract, after which the Loaner deposits the loaned amount in the Customers account.

Once the structures and interactions have been established, we proceed to describe the scenario with instances. In Figure 11, we can see the initial state of the scenario. The agent instance *John* is member of the *BargainElectronicStore* organisation instance under the StoreCustomer role. The BargainElectronicStore also has the agent instance *Marie* as a member playing the Cashier role. In this context, the previously described situation occurs: John want to buy a product but does not have enough money to pay Marie the required amount.

At this point, let's assume that agent John was provided with a behaviour that specifies ways to obtain money and determines that if there is a Bank organisation in the environment, it could apply for a loan since its canPlay property indicates that it can play the BankCustomer role. Therefore, John

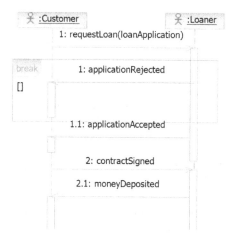

Fig. 10. Loan Application protocol

queries the DF to find any Bank organisations in the system and retrieves the description for *Bank123*, since Bank123's DFOrganisationDescription indicates that it requires the BankCustomer role. With Bank123's identifier, John initiates the RoleFillerRequest protocol and joins the organisation since it meets the requirements for role type and required behaviours.

Fig. 11. Instance distribution of the scenario (initial state)

As a BankCustomer of Bank123, it can initiate the LoanApplication protocol with a BankClerk. Bank123 assigns this task to BankClerk instance *Peter*. Since John provides a good credit history in the application, Peter approves the loan. Once John has received the loaned money, it activates its StoreCustomer role again in BargainElectronicStore and initiates the ProductSale protocol with Marie. This time around John succeeds and obtains the product.

We are aware that this is a very small example of a very trivial situation, however we consider that it does illustrate how the use of organisations and roles can help encapsulate and group functionalities and interactions in a clear and intuitive way, while still allowing some flexibility in the composition of the organisations at run time. It is important to note that since there is no centralised protocol description in JADE, only a projection of each role is implemented in a behaviour, it is hard to guarantee that any accepted candidate agent can fulfil a given role. Therefore, we have provided the three "weak" evaluation methods presented: type compatibility, required behaviours and message templates. We are looking at importing a protocol description for this evaluation, probably from the ones provided in PIM4Agents models that are transformed into JadeOrgs models.

4   Evaluation and Discussion

In this Section, we compare JadeOrgs (and Jade) to the metamodels of some known agent oriented methodologies and present a discussion on the possible pros and cons of applying organisational structures like the ones proposed in this work to JADE and MAS, in general.

4.1   Metamodel Comparison

In order to evaluate the concepts and properties that the JadeOrgs metamodel possesses, we have compared it to the metamodels of some agent methodologies using a subset of the features of the AOSE Methodology evaluation questionnaire from the Agentlink III AOSE TFG [29]. In this questionnaire, a set of methodologies was evaluated with respect to concepts/properties, notation, modelling and lifecycle coverage. At this stage, we have chosen to evaluate the coverage of the concepts and properties because, since our approach only provides a metamodel with runtime library and not a complete methodology, most of the questions of the notation, modelling and lifecycle sections did not apply to our approach. The evaluation results are presented in Table 1, the two rightmost columns present our answers to the questionnaire for JadeOrgs and JADE in order to provide a baseline and show how JadeOrgs has extended JADE. Because of space constraints, we do not present the result of all the methodologies presented in the AOSE TFG results presentation [28], but only a subset of the ones that presented society structures and role concepts, namely Gaia [8], Ingenias [30], PASSI [31] and TROPOS [32]. We are aware that a questionnaire provides very subjective results, as was also noted in [28], however at the current time, we consider it can provide an intuition of how JadeOrgs stands with regard to other agent languages.

It is visible in the comparison table that JadeOrgs has inherited certain weaknesses from JADE, namely with regard to proactiveness, situatedness and protocol support. These properties can, of course, be implemented in the agent code, but they should definitely be considered for the inclusion of additional first order concepts in JadeOrgs. For example, to improve in proactiveness, Goals (for Behaviours and Organisations) could be added as presented in Ingenias.

JadeOrgs improves on JADE with the addition of an explicit cooperation model—task delegation—and a society structure. Our approach to organisations with roles seems to be general enough to be able to express the society

Table 1. Concept/Property Comparison (partly taken from [28])

Concept/ Property	Gaia	Ingenias	PASSI (Creator/ PhD Stud./ Grad. Stud)	TROPOS	JADE	Jade-Orgs
Autonomy	H	H	H/H/M	L	H	H
Mental atti-tudes	N	H	L/L/M	M	L	L
Proactiveness	L	H	H/M/H	NN	L	L
Reactiveness	L	H	H/H/H	NN	H	H
Concurrency	M	H	H/H/M	L	H	H
Teamwork and roles	H	H	M/H/H	M	L	H
Cooperation model	Team-work	ALL	Task del., Team-work	Nego-tiation	NN	Task del.
Protocols sup-port	H	H	H/M/H	NN	NN (pro-jected be-haviours)	NN
Communication modes	Async	Direct, Indirect, Synch., Asynch.	Direct		Direct, Synch., Asynch.	same as JADE
Communication language	ACL like	Speech acts, Signals	Speech acts		ACL	ACL
Situatedness	H	H	H/M/M	H	L	L
(Main) Sup-ported agents		BDI (mainly)	Mainly: State-based, rational, reactive	BDI, Ra-tional	Reactive, Rational*	same as JADE
Society of agents mod-elling	SA	SA	A/-/-	A	D	SA
Society struc-ture	-	Organisa-tions, Groups	p2p, simple hierarchies, holons	Agent Society Pattern, such as Broker, Mediated, Match-maker	-	Organisa-tions

NN: None, M: Medium, L: Low, NA: Not Applicable
SD: Strongly Disagree, D: Disagree, N: Neutral, A: Agree, SA: Strongly Agree

structures that other approaches use: hierarchies, holons, groups. For example, organisations in Ingenias are composed by groups that perform certain tasks or achieve certain goals. The same structure can be represented in JadeOrgs by creating a suborganisation in place of the Ingenias subgroup.

4.2 Further Remarks on Organisations

Organisations can be used easily to delegate tasks and simplify the modelling of interactions. For instance, in order to make interaction protocols more stable, some include interactions for validating features of their participants and control aspects. Through the use of clearly identified and properly managed organisations that take over these certification/authentication aspects, these tasks can be delegated. This way, agents do not have to start normal interactions by passing this evaluation/validation processes, instead they identify themselves as member of a "trusted certifying organisation" proving that they fulfil the requirements.

Additionally, the predictability, reliability, and stability of MAS can be improved through the use of agent groupings [19], such as Organisations. The use of these groupings of agents allows the scoping of interactions, tasks and information accesses, therefore making each sub-organisation a specialist for a given scope and allowing the design, implementation, and testing of each scope in an incremental way, starting from the agents and their tasks/behaviours, up to the Organisation's behaviours and interactions.

In some cases, the gain of structure, provided by Organisations, can potentially come with a loss of autonomy to the individual agents. In one extreme case, the Organisation performs all the interaction with external parties, analogous to the the head of a holon, and the agent members lose part of their autonomy because of the restrictions and tasks that are imposed by the Organisation. In the other extreme case, an Organisation merely groups agents and provides the means to interact with them as one entity, so that any messages that the Organisation receives are merely forwarded to all members or to the designated handler of the given message, but the agents are not restricted from interacting directly with other parties. Our approach is generic enough to allow both extremes and cases in between, of course. It is only necessary to provide the adequate behaviours to the Organisation, so that it can enforce/perform the policies and interaction patters desired.

As stated previously, modelled organisation structures are usually realised as part of the internal knowledge representation of the agent and not as first level entities at runtime. We consider that while the existence of these runtime entities may not be an advantage in all scenarios, they can potentially reduce the communication costs to keep members updated of changes in the organisation structure in scenarios where this structure is dynamic. Without runtime organisations, a broadcast mechanism is necessary to keep inform members about agents joining or leaving the organisation. With a runtime organisation, the organisation realises the change and, in the case of a departure, informs only the parties that are currently interacting with the leaving agent.

One drawback of having runtime organisations is the increase in computational resources necessary for the overall MAS, since the number of agents in the system will increase. This increase depends directly on how the relation between organisations and role players are implemented. To illustrate this, let us take the example depicted in Figure 12 to compare how this relation is implemented in JadeOrgs and powerJade. As previously mentioned, roles in

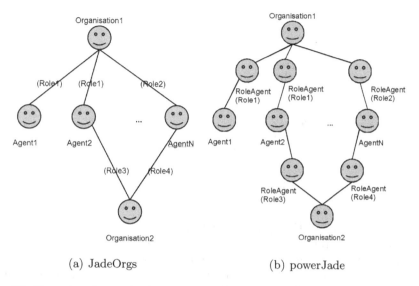

(a) JadeOrgs   (b) powerJade

Fig. 12. Example of organisation structure instances: 2 Organisations bound to N Agents through 4 roles

JadeOrgs are a piece of knowledge that the agent/organisation describing the requirements for the role players. In powerJade, the roles are represented in two ways: a description of the requirements for the role players—as in JadeOrgs— and a role agent that manages the status of the role player for each role that the role player assumes. The total number of agent instances in the system A for JadeOrgs is $A_{JadeOrgs} = m + n$ where n is the number of role player agent instances and m is the number of organisation instances. For powerJade, $A_{powerJade} = m + n + \sum_{i=0}^{n} r_i$ where r_i is the number of "role agent instances" linked to each role player. The powerJade implementation of roles can be ad- vantageous in the sense that the role player has less concerns about interacting with the organisation, for instance it is not required to know the organisation's ontology/language since the role agent can serve as a proxy. However, this is not the case in all scenarios. In JadeOrgs, the management of the role player status is done by the organisation directly and if such a proxy was necessary, it could be implemented as an additional role or a suborganisation could be created to group the proxy with the represented agent.

5   Future Work

The concept of Organisation is currently being applied in the design of the pro- totypes for a supply chain management system for the steel industry, which are an extension to the work presented in [33]. In this context, there are several ag- gregates/devices in different factory locations that form a group to produce a

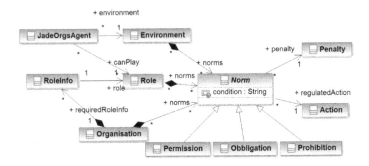

Fig. 13. Normative Aspect for JadeOrgs

specific customer order. Using the concepts provided in the present work, a customer order can be represented as an Organisation of aggregates required for its production. This order-agents actively keep track of their progress by interacting with their member aggregate-agents, which at the same time go in and out of groups to represent the frequent changes in the production of an order.

Organisations, as described in this paper, serve also as behaviour containers for the behaviours required for each role. Agents entering an organisation can fetch the set of behaviours that define their role. It is of crucial importance to study and compare how behaviours can be defined, how detailed they are required to be, which aspects are they expected to cover, how dependent they are of the definition mechanisms of each possible participating agent, and where is the most suitable place for the interface between the behaviour and the agents proper implementation.

In order to support better design and easier management of organisations, the relationship between a conversation protocol and its corresponding role-behaviours has to be improved. This improvement could also impact the overall results significantly if the conversion could be automated or the relation made at least more straightforward. Better proposals of definition that encompass both behaviours and global views of protocol would serve this purpose better.

As a complement to these protocol descriptions, we are currently looking at introducing norms as part of the role and organisation descriptions. From the approaches studied, the DynaCROM ontology [34] fits particularly well with the way the organisations are structured in the JadeOrgs metamodel. In DynaCROM, different norms are set at the organisation, role and environment levels and agents can determine the set of norms they should follow according to the role they play, the organisation they play it in and the environment they are located in. Such a Normative Aspect could look as depicted in Figure 13. The enforcement of the norms could be performed by each organisation in its internal interactions. Another possibility to study is the transfer of business rules from the application domain to norms that the agents should abide by.

6 Conclusion

The representation of an Organisation using a first level entity is a feature missing frequently in multiagent system platforms, as it is normally left as a result of the emergent behaviour of interacting agents. This is also the case for JADE, one of the most used multiagent system platform. The concept of an organisation is proposed for this platform as a specific kind of agent. The fact that it is represented by an agent and not left as a virtual manifestation result of individual behaviours opens new options for collaborations modelling. Interaction protocols can be more easily modularised and, by scoping the aspects in complex interactions, the predictability, reliability, and scalability of such distributed systems are increased.

We have also discussed how there can be different types of organisations with respect to how much the group representation can intervene and how strict the protocols that rule the group are. Having a concrete representation entity for an organisation also facilitates the definition of the policies, by making them explicit instead of implicit. Organisations provide not only advantage for design time, but also for enabling dynamic establishment of organisations at run time.

References

1. Gasser, L.: Social Conceptions of Knowledge and Action: DAI Foundations and Open Systems Semantics. Artificial Intelligence 47(1-3), 107–138 (1991)
2. Schillo, M., Fischer, K.: Holonic multiagent systems. KI 17(4), 54–55 (2003)
3. Bellifemine, F., Poggi, A., Rimassa, G.: JADE - a FIPA-compliant agent framework. In: Proceedings of the Practical Applications of Intelligent Agents (1999)
4. JADE: Java Agent Development Framework (2001), http://jade.tilab.com
5. Foundation for Intelligent Physical Agents: FIPA Abstract Architecture Specification. Document number SC00001L (2002),
   http://www.fipa.org/specs/fipa00001/SC00001L.html
6. van den Broek, E.L., Jonker, C.M., Sharpanskykh, A., Treur, J., Yolum, P.: Formal modeling and analysis of organizations. In: AAMAS Workshops, pp. 18–34 (2005)
7. Zambonelli, F., Jennings, N.R., Wooldridge, M.: Developing Multiagent Systems: The Gaia Methodology. ACM Transactions on Software Engineering and Methodology 12(3), 317–370 (2003)
8. Wooldridge, M., Jennings, N., Kinny, D.: The Gaia methodology for agent-oriented analysis and design. JAAMAS 3(3), 285–312 (2000)
9. Hannoun, M., Boissier, O., Sichman, J.S., Sayettat, C.: MOISE: An Organizational Model for Multi-agent Systems. In: IBERAMIA-SBIA, pp. 156–165 (2000)
10. Esteva, M., de la Cruz, D., Sierra, C.: ISLANDER: an electronic institutions editor. In: AAMAS, pp. 1045–1052. ACM, New York (2002)
11. Schillo, M., Fischer, K.: A taxonomy of autonomy in multiagent organisation. In: Nickles, M., Rovatsos, M., Weiss, G. (eds.) AUTONOMY 2003. LNCS, vol. 2969, pp. 68–82. Springer, Heidelberg (2004)
12. Adam, E., Mandiau, R.: Roles and Hierarchy in Multi-agent Organizations. In: Pěchouček, M., Petta, P., Varga, L.Z. (eds.) CEEMAS 2005. LNCS, vol. 3690, pp. 539–542. Springer, Heidelberg (2005)

13. AOS: JACK Intelligent Agents, The Agent Oriented Software Group (AOS) (2006), http://www.agent-software.com/shared/home/
14. Pokahr, A., Braubach, L., Lamersdorf, W.: Jadex: Implementing a bdi-infrastructure for jade agents. EXP 3(3), 76–85 (2003)
15. Braubach, L., Pokahr, A., Lamersdorf, W.: Jadex: A short overview. In: Main Conference Net.ObjectDays 2004, pp. 195–207 (2004)
16. Esteva, M., Rosell, B., Rodrguez-Aguilar, J.A., Arcos, J.L.: AMELI: An Agent-Based Middleware for Electronic Institutions. AAMAS 1, 236–243 (2004)
17. Hübner, J.F., Sichman, J.S., Boissier, O.: S-MOISE+: A Middleware for Developing Organised Multi-agent Systems. In: Boissier, O., Padget, J., Dignum, V., Lindemann, G., Matson, E., Ossowski, S., Sichman, J.S., Vázquez-Salceda, J. (eds.) ANIREM 2005 and OOOP 2005. LNCS, vol. 3913, pp. 64–78. Springer, Heidelberg (2006)
18. Baldoni, M., Boella, G., Genovese, V., Grenna, R., van der Torre, L.: How to Program Organizations and Roles in the JADE Framework. In: Bergmann, R., Lindemann, G., Kirn, S., Pěchouček, M. (eds.) MATES 2008. LNCS, vol. 5244, pp. 25–36. Springer, Heidelberg (2008)
19. Odell, J., Nodine, M.H., Levy, R.: A metamodel for agents, roles, and groups. In: Odell, J.J., Giorgini, P., Müller, J.P. (eds.) AOSE 2004. LNCS, vol. 3382, pp. 78–92. Springer, Heidelberg (2005)
20. Warwas, S., Hahn, C.: The Platform Independent Modeling Language for Multiagent Systems. In: Fischer, K., et al. (eds.) ATOP 2005 and ATOP 2008. LNBIP, vol. 25, pp. 129–153. Springer, Heidelberg (2009)
21. Hahn, C., Madrigal-Mora, C., Fischer, K.: A platform-independent metamodel for multiagent systems. Autonomous Agents and Multi-Agent Systems 18(2), 239–266 (2009)
22. Budinsky, F., Steinberg, D., Merks, E., Ellersick, R., Grose, T.: Eclipse Modeling Framework. Addison Wesley Professional, Reading (2003)
23. ATLAS Group, INRIA & LINA, University of Nantes: INRIA, ATL - The Atlas Transformation Language Home Page (2006), http://www.sciences.univ-nantes.fr/lina/atl/
24. SINTEF ICT: MOFScript (2006), http://www.eclipse.org/gmt/mofscript
25. Madrigal-Mora, C., León-Soto, E., Fischer, K.: Implementing Organisations in JADE. In: Bergmann, R., Lindemann, G., Kirn, S., Pěchouček, M. (eds.) MATES 2008. LNCS, vol. 5244, pp. 135–146. Springer, Heidelberg (2008)
26. Foundation for Intelligent Physical Agents: FIPA Request Interaction Protocol Specification. Document number SC00026H (2002), http://www.fipa.org/specs/fipa00026/SC00026H.html
27. Bellifemine, F., Caire, G., Trucco, T., Rimassa, G.: JADE PROGRAMMER'S GUIDE, http://jade.tilab.com/doc/programmersguide.pdf
28. Agentlink III AOSE Technical Forum Group: Methodologies evaluation (2005), http://www.pa.icar.cnr.it/cossentino/al3tf3/docs/aose-evaluation.ppt (accesssed, March 2009)
29. Cossentino, M.: Methodology evaluation questionnaire (2005), http://www.pa.icar.cnr.it/cossentino/al3tf3/docs/questionnaire.doc (accesssed, March 2009)
30. Pavón, J., Gómez-Sanz, J.J.: Agent oriented software engineering with ingenias. In: Mařík, V., Müller, J.P., Pěchouček, M. (eds.) CEEMAS 2003. LNCS, vol. 2691, pp. 394–403. Springer, Heidelberg (2003)

31. Cossentino, M.: From requirements to code with the PASSI methodology. In: Henderson-Sellers, B., Giorgini, P. (eds.) Agent-Oriented Methodologies. Idea Group Inc., USA (2005)
32. Bresciani, P., Perini, A., Giorgini, P., Giunchiglia, F., Mylopoulos, J.: TROPOS: An Agent-Oriented Software Development Methodology. Journal of Autonomous Agents and Multiagent Systems 8(3) (2004)
33. Jacobi, S., León-Soto, E., Madrigal-Mora, C., Fischer, K.: Masdispo: A multiagent decision support system for steel production and control. In: AAAI, pp. 1707–1714 (2007)
34. Felicíssimo, C., Choren, R., Briot, J.P., Lucena, C.: Informing Regulatory Dynamics in Open MASs. In: Noriega, P., Vázquez-Salceda, J., Boella, G., Boissier, O., Dignum, V., Fornara, N., Matson, E. (eds.) COIN 2006. LNCS, vol. 4386, pp. 147–162. Springer, Heidelberg (2007)

Interoperability with Goal Oriented Teams (GORITE)

Ralph Rönnquist[1] and Dennis Jarvis[2]

[1] Intendico Pty Ltd
Suite 40, 85 Grattan Street, Carlton, Victoria 3053, Australia
ralph.ronnquist@intendico.com
[2] Centre for Intelligent and Networked Systems, CQUniversity
Rockhampton, Queensland 4702, Australia
d.jarvis@cqu.edu.au

Abstract. We look at interoperability with Goal Oriented Teams modelling, which includes an outsourcing paradigm as the means by which to link separate Business Processes. Although the framework proposes the Team Programming perspective for Business Process modelling, it also supports the notion that a role filler achieves its goals by outsourcing to an external Business Process model. The core capability, Remote-Coaching, provides the required separation between the Business Process model at intentional level and the interfacing technology that facilitates the actual connection to the external Business Process model. Following the Service Oriented Architecture (SOA) principles, the outsourcing sub system is generalised to avoid practical constraints on the remote technology base, i.e., the remote Business Process model might be another Goal Oriented Teams (GORITE) model, or based on some other framework.

Keywords: Enterprise modelling, Business Process Model Interactions, Team Programming, BDI, GORITE.

1 Introduction

The IEEE [10] has defined interoperability as "the ability of two or more systems or components to exchange information and to use the information that has been exchanged". This definition identifies two key processes – information exchange and information use – that are required for interoperability of systems. However, it does not specify what constitutes information, exchange or use. In the knowledge management literature, information is normally contrasted with data and knowledge. According to Tuomi [17], data constitutes simple facts; information then arises from the combination of data into meaningful structures. Finally, when information is situated within a particular context, we have knowledge. Knowledge transfer is currently outside the scope of mainstream interoperability solutions and is an area of active research, particularly within the multi-agent systems community. The key problem is that knowledge is dynamic - it requires

K. Fischer et al. (Eds.): ATOP 2005 and ATOP 2008, LNBIP 25, pp. 118–128, 2009.

interpretation, via appropriate procedures, of information that is situated within a particular context. For example, a control system for an Unmanned Air Vehicle (UAV) needs to determine (procedures) whether the aircraft it has identified (information) from its on board sensors (data) are hostile (knowledge). In general, knowledge generation is an activity that requires sophisticated reasoning, as evidenced by activities such as medical diagnosis, patient planning and in the business domain, model based accounting. At present, there is no consensus on how knowledge should be generated for particular domains, let alone shared between applications. WSDL [18] provides a starting point, but the the specification of services is only a part of the problem. One also needs service ontologies with agreed upon semantics for particular domains of application. This is a much more challenging problem than developing data ontologies.

The problem of interoperability is further exacerbated from a business perspective because it generally starts with the basic principles used for modelling the organisation in terms of its Business Processes, rather than the development of ontologies to describe the data and information that will be subsequently employed by these processes. We would argue that by focusing on processes, such modelling efforts are more naturally grounded on the knowledge, rather than information side of the interoperability fence. Another critical modelling concern is the question of whether the organisation is conceived as a single business, or whether it is seen as an aggregation of businesses that pursue their own objectives under the umbrella of the organisation. Although this may seem like a rather abstract question, the answer has a significant impact on the technology used for interlinking architectural components. When the whole organisation is seen as a single business, one needs a technology that covers all parts of the business within a single Business Process model, whereas the more amorphous view allows for multiple Business Process models and a technology that provides connectivity between separate models.

One may argue, of course, that the term "interoperability" already implies an amorphous view, by imagining an organisation consisting of separate sub organisations. However this is primarily an engineering perspective of the physical reality, where the networked organisation physically consists of multiple, separated sites. In respect of Business Process modelling, the organisation can be seen as a single business recursively divided into business units, that all operate with respect to a common business objective. Alternatively, the organisation may be modelled as comprised of multiple, separate businesses that pursue separate business objectives whilst providing services for each other. By the latter concept, we perceive the organisation with SOA shades, and define the organisational parts on the basis of functional capabilities. Strictly speaking, there is no single Business Process model of the organisation, but rather a collection of models of the separate businesses, which includes their service based interfaces against each other.

Just for simplicity, we use the terms "singular" and "plural" to label the two modelling perspectives. By the Singular perspective, we would make a single Business Process model across the whole organisation, and every business (unit) involved would be harnessed by the role or roles it must fill within the organisational intent. By the Plural perspective, we would model businesses (units) with respect to their own objectives, and present them through their service interfaces, which other businesses may choose to use based on dynamic considerations relating to the current situation when the need for a presented service arises.

From a technology perspective, we talk about the concept of inter-operation at the intent level between separate organisational models. This is well "above" the connectivity level, which generally speaking is well understood. At the intent level, the concern is to, within the one Business Process model, utilise the services of a "foreign" business as a means for a business unit to achieve its goals. Technically, the question is whether the modelling framework includes the concept of "foreign" business as something different from the unit-to-unit interactions within the Business Process model, or not. It is easy to see that a notion like that is required in order for a modelling framework to support the Plural perspective; without a notion of "foreign" business, a modeller has to settle for using the Singular perspective.

What is required in the plural case is a modelling framework that supports the concept of outsourcing and presents that concept to the organisational models in terms of goals. Goal directed programming has been realised predominantly through implementations of the BDI model of agency [4] that are based on the execution model formalised by Rao and Gerogeff [15]. In these implementations (as exemplified by PRS [6], dMARS [9] and most recently JACK [2]), goal achievement is represented in terms of dynamically constructed plan networks, with subgoals procedurally embedded within the plans providing the linkages. In the case of team behaviours, such as outsourcing and team formation, a network (and more importantly, the logic for its construction and operation) spans multiple agents; this is undesirable from both a software engineering and a modelling perspective. Formal models of teamwork have been developed (e.g. [5] and [8]) and implemented (e.g. STEAM [16] and MIST [12]). Still, as with the BDI approaches, teamwork arises through the reasoned (but formalised) interaction of individual entities.

JACK Teams [1] introduced the concept of a team as a separate entity with its own beliefs, desires and intentions and provided support for the specification and execution of team behaviours within the conventional BDI execution model. However, while outsourcing models such as LAP [13] could be constructed with JACK Teams, the goal decomposition for outsourcing (which is the key modelling artefact) would be procedurally distributed over multiple plans in multiple teams.

In the remainder of this paper, we present the outsourcing paradigm of the Goal Oriented Teams (GORITE) framework [7], with an illustration of the modelling involved.

2   The GORITE Framework

The Goal Oriented Teams (GORITE) framework is a technology for Business Process modelling based on goal oriented articulation, and reflecting organisational structure by a Team Oriented Paradigm. Each unit, or team, is attributed with the models that define how it achieves its goals, either by orchestrating the activities of its sub teams, or as an actual performer, performs the intended tasks. In addition, a performer may have the RemoteCoaching capability and by that achieve its goals by outsourcing to a remote performer, which it then monitors.

Within the business process modelling community, it is recognised that a business process model must result in the realisation of business goals. Still, this relationship is not central to the modelling approaches currently employed. Rather, the field has focused on process dynamics at the expense of goal achievement, as indicated by [3], where four different process modelling approaches are identified:

- Input/output flows - passive participants that are being consumed, produced or changed by activities
- Workflows - (partial) time ordering of activities performed by active participants
- Agent-related workflows - agent cooperation, i.e. the order in which active participants get and perform their part of work
- State-flows - changes produced by activities executed in the frame of a given process instance

By adopting a process focus, one requires multiple perspectives, each with their own modelling approach, notation and support tools. For example, BPMN [19] supports a workflow approach.

A goal focus as in GORITE brings the potential of a modelling approach that can accommodate all the above perspectives within a single modelling framework. Furthermore, GORITE provides an integrated framework for modelling organisational structure, which is largely absent from the above approaches.

The GORITE emphasis is that of developing a software system with complex behaviour by using the analogy to human organisation as a design technique, and thus form a software architecture that in concept is based on autonomous organisational units. But in the software, as opposed to a human organisation, autonomous reasoning is represented and carried out at all levels. Through this, the system behaviour is designed at all levels, and although the behaviour may be too complex to predict, it is engineered behaviour with a high degree of repeatability, which brings significant gains in terms of performance, simplicity and maintainability of the software.

The Team Oriented Programming side of GORITE is based on the notion that a software system is conceived as an organisation of cooperating agents, or recursively, as a team of sub teams, which operate together so as to provide the system function. In the Team Oriented design, the behaviour of organisational units are defined separately from the behaviour of their sub units. Unit behaviour is expressed as an orchestration of the services that sub units provide. A team is an organisational unit, which operates autonomously according to its defined business processes in order to fill its function as sub unit of a larger team. In other words, a team is a performer for the larger team (or teams) it belongs to, while its own behaviour typically is defined as a coordination of the performer it consists of. The team concept is recursive in this way; that a team consists of sub teams. From the "above", the team is seen as a performer in itself, and from "below" it has members that are performers.

The outsourcing paradigm makes for an explicit transition from the one Business Process model to another. This allows the coaching performer and the coached performer to ascribe to the objectives of their separate organisations. The Business Process model for the coached performer would include the presentation of services, which the coaching performer makes use of to achieve its goals.

The process modelling of GORITE is Goal Oriented, which means that processing is casted in terms of achieving goals. Thus, the process models for a team are like statements or paragraphs that explain how the team achieves its goals by means of achieving sub goals and performing tasks. At some points in the goal hierarchy, sub goals are deferred to team members, which deploy their own processes to achieve these goals. The team level process is primarily concerned with the coordination of member activity rather than how the detailed tasks are performed.

The GORITE execution model (see [7] and [11]) is a BDI execution model, but quite different to the traditional BDI execution model of Rao and Georgeff [15], as a reflection of the GORITE perspective on how complex system behaviours arise. In GORITE, Goal objects are used to specify the ways that are available to achieve a goal. At execution, separate Instance objects are created to represent the intentions of achieving (or performing) goals. The execution infrastructure dynamically generates instance objects from the goal objects in the selected plan and adds them to the intention tree. The structure of an intention in the intention tree mirrors that of its corresponding plan through the Instance objects created when intending the plan's sub goals.

Thus, the abstract concept is of a single intention tree, which grows by progressing the goal instances that are the nodes of the tree. One might also think of the intention tree as evolving in time from left to right. At the left are the completed goal instances, which are either *passed* or *failed*. The middle part is the currently active part (and the actually realised portion) of goal instances still in progress. In this part, one can identify the execution top-level points, which are the root of the intention tree, plus any sub tree in a "Todo group". When the main execution reaches a goal instance that is in a "Todo group", it immediately returns the state of that instance, which remains *blocked* until the "Todo group" execution of the sub tree completes. The right-hand part of the intention tree is the part still in the future.

GORITE goal processing involves both a lexical belief context and a dynamic data context. The latter is a data structure created specifically for the individual goal execution, to support a business process modelling perspective. The lexical belief context supports an agent perspective on goal processing, allowing goals to use and update beliefs of more long-term persistence. The dynamic data context is shared along an intention, but is split up to provide local data contexts for parallel intentions. When parallel intentions join, their local data contexts are joined into the parent context. The introduction of a dynamic data context is novel - in the traditional BDI model, beliefs correspond to a lexical belief context only. In terms of interoperability, the provision of the dynamic perspective is critical to providing interoperability at the knowledge level, as it provides the context in which an individual agent will decide what procedures to execute in order to achieve the current goal.

For example, consider the following goal hierarchy, which implements a contract net auction:

```
// In: RFQ, bidder*, Out: winner
addGoal( new Goal( "hold auction", Sequence, new Goal [] {
    new Goal( "bidder", "request bid" ), // In: RFQ, bidder*, Out: bid*
    new Goal( "select winner", BDI ),   // In: bid*, Out: winner
    new Goal( "bidder", "tell winner" ) // In: bidder*, winner, Out:
} ) );
```

In the code snippet above, the data used and produced by the goals are noted as comments. The incoming data context for the "hold action" goal has an "RFQ" data element with a value describing what is auctioned, and role "bidder" established with multiple fillers. The asterisk, "*", is used to indicate a multi-valued data item.

With multiple fillers for the "bidder" role, the first goal, "request bid", causes parallel intentions for each "bidder" to perform the "request bid" goal, each in their own way. A "bidder" eventually makes a response by means of defining a "bid" data element in the dynamic context. When all "bidder" intentions have completed, the parallel "bid" values are aggregated into a multi-valued "bid" data element, which is available to the next goal, "select winner". The "select winner" goal is a BDI goal to be achieved by the team entity holding the auction, and its outcome is a setting of the "winner" data element. This is followed by the third goal, "tell winner", which is directed to the "bidder" role and again gets repeated for each "bidder" role filler in parallel.

2.1 Comparison With Other BDI Frameworks

It was noted in [14] that all major BDI architectures have employed the execution model proposed by Rao and Georgeff [15]. In this model, while the current goal drives plan selection, goals are procedurally embedded in plans. Thus, agent behaviour is represented in terms of interlinked plans, which is not desirable from either a software engineering or a modelling viewpoint. Furthermore, plans are executed directly and so intentions are not explicitly captured. GORITE overcomes these shortcomings through its explicit goal modelling, separation of goals and actions, and projecting intentions onto data. GORITE further includes, similarly to JACK, a tuple-based belief model, and a use of logic programming for belief reflection.

The team modelling notions are syntactically similar to JACK Teams, but there are significant semantic differences. GORITE provides a richer and more flexible organisational model through:

- the task team modelling being separated from process modelling
- the team - sub team relationship being separated from role filling in task teams
- the execution machinery recognising and dealing with multi-filled roles
- the inclusion of role filling capabilities, which allows for models that super-impose role filler performer behaviour within the team belief context
- the dynamic nature of model construction, including team structures and performer capabilities, which allows for both individual and categorical definitions of teams and performers

From an interoperability perspective, GORITE represents a significant advance, as it allows for the specification (and linkage) of both organisational models and goal models.

3   Outsourcing Illustration

The following is an outline of how the outsourcing paradigm may look in actual GORITE code. We imagine a company "Widget Enterprises[1]", which produces widgets that include the three parts P_1, P_2 and P_3. Widget Enterprises produce P_1 parts themselves, while they have business agreements with "XYZZY Manufacturing" for both P_2 and P_3 parts and also "ACME Engineering" for P_3 parts only.

The Widget Enterprises' software model for this would firstly include definitions of the connectivity adaptors, which implement the particulars of connectivity between the companies involved. There is place for generic technology to deal with connectivity, but sometimes the practical situation warrants more specific solutions. For our example, we imagine the software to include the special purpose classes XYZZYLink and ACMELink, both implementing the RemoteCoaching.Connector interface defined in GORITE, as illustrated by the following outline:

```
public class XYZZYLink implements RemoteCoaching.Connector {
    public RemoteCoaching.Connection perform(String goal, ... ) {
        // ...
    }
}
public class ACMELink implements RemoteCoaching.Connector {
    public RemoteCoaching.Connection perform(String goal, ...) {
        // ...
    }
}
```

Both of the classes would provide their appropriate connectivity level implementation in order to forward a service request to the remote side. Following

---

[1] All the company names are totally fictitious, and made up on the spot, just to make the example more readable.

GORITE's execution principle, the service is casted as achieving a goal. Data transfer is embedded within the input to and output from the service. When a request is made, the adaptor creates a link object for the meta-level monitoring of the request's progress. The local side may then use the link object for checking the current state of the request processing, or cancelling its request.

The Widget Enterprises model would include instantiations of the adaptors. Normally there would be a single adaptor for any one remote, with plurality in requests being handled by creating link objects. However, the connectivity level has quite a few variations, although these to a large extent are irrelevant at the intentional level. It simply means that the intentional level framework needs to be flexible in regards to the connectivity level.

The following is an outline of a Widget Enterprises model in respect of presenting how the outsourcing paradigm is reflected in code. First it defines the task team required for making an assembly, and the Widget Enterprises team is augmented with the method of producing a P_1 part.

```
Team widget_enterprises = new Team( "Widget Enterprises" ) {{
    addTaskTeam( "assemble widget", new TaskTeam() {{
        new Role( "P1 producer", new String [] { "Make a P1", ... } );
        new Role( "P2 producer", new String [] { "Make a P2", ... } );
        new Role( "P3 producer", new String [] { "Make a P3", ... } );
    }} );
    addGoal( new Goal( "Produce a P1", ... ) );
}};
```

The code snippet above creates a Team entity to model the structure and reasoning of a "Widget Enterprises" unit in respect of assembling widgets; it highlights an internal task team structure for this, and identifies three different roles for parts producers. One may think of the Role object as a socket or seat that needs to be filled by a performer. The Role object models the intentional interface required of a role filling performer, and it provides a symbolic entity to refer to within the orchestration plans of the team.

Next, the model is extended by adding a coaching performer that is capable of coaching XYZZY Manufacturing, who can produce both P_2 and P_3 parts, as follows:

```
widget_enterprises.addPerformer(
    new Performer( "Coach XYZZY" ) {{
        addCapability(
            new RemoteCoaching( new XYZZYLink() ) {{
                addGoal( new RemoteGoal( "Produce a P2", ... ) );
                addGoal( new RemoteGoal( "Produce a P3", ... ) );
        }} );
    }} );
```

Each RemoteGoal includes, in the "..." part above, a declaration of the data items to be passed on to and returned from the remote service. When the goal is processed, the data items to pass on will be collated and passed to the "perform" method of the attached connection interface, and when the goal processing finishes, the returned data items are picked up and placed into the dynamic data context. In that way the remote service is treated as a task in the intent level model, with the particulars of service connection delegated to the connection level.

We note that the code snippet above only highlights the outsourcing interface, and omits the additional capabilities that are needed to handle the goals "Make a P2" and "Make a P3", and translate them into the required coaching protocols around the remote goals "Produce a P2" and "Produce a P3".

The Widget Enterprises model is similarly extended with a coaching performer for ACME Engineering, as follows:

```
widget_enterprises.addPerformer(
    new Performer( "Coach ACME" ) {{
        addCapability( new RemoteCoaching( new ACMELink() ) {{
            addGoal( new RemoteGoal( "Produce a P3", ... ) );
        }} );
    }} );
```

As always, there are a number of different ways to set up a model, and we have chosen one of them. In particular, there is a choice of producer for P_3, and that choice can be made upfront or dynamically. For instance, the parts producers may be chosen through a contract net negotiation at the time when parts are needed (just-in-time). In that case, the producers would include bidding goal as well as production goal.

3.1   Incoming Interface

The remote business model might also be a GORITE model, in which case incoming services would be modelled as *percepts* for a performer. The framework includes a Perceptor class for defining an incoming connection that creates percepts and raises goals to handle them. The outline setup will involve three parts, where the first is a performer capable of handling percepts. The second part is to create the Perceptor for that performer, and at the same time get a handle to that object at the connection level. It is the connection level code that will create the percept data, and, which is the third step, present that to the Perceptor.

Perceptor objects may be added to both teams and performers, and generally it is a modelling choice where to place them in a team structure, e.g. it would not be uncommon to receive service requests at the top level team.

4   Conclusion

In this paper, we have discussed interoperability at the intent level, with the magnifying glass on the inter-business relationship. We have noted that most frameworks only support *singular* intent level modelling, which puts all businesses conceptually within a single model. We have illustrated how the Goal Oriented Teams (GORITE) framework includes supporting modelling elements to make "outsourcing" an explicit part of a model. This renders a *plural* intent level modelling, which properly distinguishes between internal and external businesses, avoids a mixing of objectives of the separate businesses, and streamlines the transition from the intent level to the connectivity level technology.

References

1. Agent Oriented Software Pty. Ltd, JACK Intelligent Agents JACK Teams Manual (2005a), http://www.agent-software.com
2. Agent Oriented Software Pty. Ltd, JACK Intelligent Agents JACK Manual (2005b), http://www.agent-software.com
3. Andersson, B., Bider, I., Johannesson, P., Perjons, E.: Towards a Formal Definition of Goal-Oriented Business Process Patterns. Business Process Management Journal 11(6) (2005), http://www.ibissoft.com/publications/Patterns.pdf
4. Bratman, M.E.: Intention, Plans and Practical Reasoning. Harvard University Press, Cambridge (1987)
5. Cohen, P., Levesque, H.: Teamwork. Nous 25(4), 487–512 (1991)
6. Georgeff, M.P., Lansky, A.L.: Procedural knowledge. In: Proceedings of the IEEE Special Issue on Knowledge Representation, pp. 1383–1398 (1986)
7. Goal Oriented Teams (GORITE) home page, http://www.intendico.com/gorite
8. Grosz, B., Kraus, S.: Collaborative Plans for Complex Group Action. Artificial Intelligence 86, 269–357 (1996)
9. d'Inverno, M., Kinny, D., Luck, M., Wooldridge, M.: A formal specification of dMARS. In: Rao, A., Singh, M.P., Wooldridge, M.J. (eds.) ATAL 1997. LNCS (LNAI), vol. 1365, pp. 155–176. Springer, Heidelberg (1998)
10. IEEE, IEEE Standard Computer Dictionary: A Compilation of IEEE Standard Computer Glossaries. IEEE Press, New York (1990)
11. Jarvis, J., Jarvis, D., Rnnquist, R., Jain, L.: Holonic Manufacturing Systems: A BDI Approach. Springer, Heidelberg (2008)
12. Nguyen, M.H., Wobcke, W.R.: A Flexible Framework for SharedPlans. In: Sattar, A., Kang, B.-H. (eds.) AI 2006. LNCS, vol. 4304, pp. 393–402. Springer, Heidelberg (2006)
13. Perugini, D., Jarvis, D., Reschke, S., Gossink, D.: Distributed Deliberative Planning with Partial Observability: Heuristic Approaches. In: Lawton, J., Patel, J., Tate, A. (eds.) Proceedings of the Fourth International Conference on Knowledge Systems for Coalition Operations (KSCO 2007), Waltham, MA, USA, May 1-2, 2007, pp. 43–48 (2007)
14. Pokahr, A., Braubach, L., Lamersdorf, W.: A Flexible BDI Archi-tecture Supporting Extensibility. In: Proceedings of the 2005 IEEE/WIC/ACM International Conference on Intelligent Agent Technology, IAT 2005 (2005a)
15. Rao, A., Georgeff, M.: BDI Agents: from theory to practice. In: Proceedings of the 1st Int. Conf. on MAS, ICMAS 1995 (1995)

16. Tambe, M.: Towards Flexible Teamwork. Journal of Artificial Intelligence Research 7, 83–124 (1997)
17. Tuomi, I.: Data is more than knowledge: implications of the reversed knowledge hierarchy for knowledge management and organizational memory, in HICSS-32. In: Proceedings of the 32nd Annual Hawaii International Conference on System Sciences (1999)
18. W3C, Web Services Description Language (WSDL) Version 2.0 Part 1: Core Language (2007), http://www.w3.org/TR/wsdl20
19. White, S.A.: Introduction to BPMN (2004), http://www.bpmn.org

The Platform Independent Modeling Language for Multiagent Systems

Stefan Warwas and Christian Hahn

DFKI GmbH
Stuhlsatzenhausweg 3
66123 Saarbrücken
{Stefan.Warwas,Christian.Hahn}@dfki.de

Abstract. This article presents the language features of the platform independent modeling language for multiagent systems (DSML4MAS). This language bases on the principles of language-driven development and provides tool support for designing, validating, testing and executing the generated design artifacts. In this article, we particularly present how we used the Object Constraint Language to specify the static semantics of DSML4MAS and use it for model validation at design time.

Keywords: multiagent systems, platform independent, modeling language, model-driven development, PIM4Agents, AOSE.

1 Introduction

Associated with the increasing acceptance of agent-based computing as a novel software engineering paradigm, a lot of research addresses the identification and definition of suitable models and techniques to support the development of complex software systems with respect to agent-based computing. Agent-Oriented Software Engineering (AOSE) as a new programming paradigm has mainly evolved itself from Object Oriented Software Engineering (OOSE), where AOSE has placed greater emphasis on the autonomy, interaction, intelligence, and proactiveness of agents.

However, as stated in [1] agent technology still faces many challenges in being adopted by the industry and possibly taking over from objects technology as the dominant software development technology. Especially, the development of industrial-strength applications requires the availability of software engineering methodologies that should typically consist of a set of methods, models, and techniques that facilitate a systematic software development process, resulting in increased quality of the software product. Even though many agent-oriented methodologies have been proposed, few are mature or described in sufficient detail to be of real use. None of them is in fact complete (in the sense of covering all of the necessary activities involved in software engineering) and is able to fully support the industrial needs of agent-based system development [2]. This is also confirmed in [3] stating that up to now, developing multiagent systems (MASs)

K. Fischer et al. (Eds.): ATOP 2005 and ATOP 2008, LNBIP 25, pp. 129–153, 2009.

currently involves higher costs than using conventional paradigms due to the lack of supporting methods and tools [3].

From our point of view, several obstacles hamper the break through of agent-based computing like the insufficient tool support, the gap between design and implementation or an adequate formal semantics that support testing, validation, and code generation issues. Even if agent-based modeling has become popular, the generated artifacts are rarely complete with respect to the requirements that are needed for code generation as well as for the automatic execution. A formal semantics could increase the domain experts' understanding on how to model correctly in terms of ensuring that all requirements are met for the automatic code generation. Even when agent-based code is generated, full testing and validation is usually required, which consumes a significant chunk of development effort. This effort can be decreased if the validation and testing facilities base on a formal semantics that can already be used during design time to test and validate the generated design.

Moreover, only little research has been done with respect to the development of adequate tools to support the design of agent-based systems. In particular, integrated development environment support for developing agent systems is rather weak, and existing agent tools do not offer the same level of usability as state-of-the art object oriented IDEs [3]. Beside a graphical visualization, we think that adequate tool support should also provide facilities to support the domain experts with respect to testing, evaluation, and execution of the designed artifacts.

Furthermore, real world systems usually have heterogeneous infrastructure. Thus, agent-based systems never exist in isolation. Interoperability between agents and other technologies like Service Oriented Architectures (SOA) is crucial for the successfully application of agent technology in real world systems.

Recently, we developed the domain specific modeling language for MAS called DSML4MAS (cf. Section 3) aiming at increasing the industrial acceptance of MASs. Therefore, DSML4MAS provides (i) a clear platform independent vocabulary, (ii) a formal semantics, as well as (iii) code generation facilities. The corresponding DSML4MAS Development Environment[1] (DDE) [4] allows us to specify MASs with DSML4MAS and to transform the created models to agent execution platforms like Jack Intelligent Agents [5] and Jade (Java Agent DEvelopment Framework) [6]. This volume contains a related article that provides more details on the platform specific model of Jade [7]. Moreover, our model-driven approach allows integrating various technologies at a platform independent layer.

In this article, we particularly present parts of the static semantics of DSML-4MAS specified with the Object Constraint Language (OCL). These OCL constraints have been manually derived from the formal Object-Z specification of DSML4MAS presented in [8]. The benefit provided by OCL is that we can directly make use of it in DDE. So, we can utilize these OCL constraints for model validation during design time.

Throughout this paper, we want to use the development of an agent-based conference management system (CMS) as example. The scenario is aligned to

---

[1] http://dsml4mas.sourceforge.net

[9]. For our purposes, the committee of a conference consists of the program committee chair, the program committee members, the reviewers, and the authors. The program chair sends a call for papers to researchers that might be interested. After the authors submitted their papers (before the submission deadline elapses), the program chair partitions the papers and assigns them to the program committee members. The program committee members choose reviewers and assign papers to them. The result of the reviews is collected by the programm committee members and is sent back to the program committee chair. Finally, the results are sent by the program committee chair to the authors. Authors of accepted papers have to submit the camera ready version before the final deadline elapses.

This article is structured as follows: Section 2 provides an overview of the related work. DSML4MAS is introduced in Section 3. The succeeding sections introduce the agent view (Section 4), the role view (Section 5), the organization view (Section 6), the interaction view (Section 7), the behavior view (Section 8), and the deployment view (Section 9) of DSML4MAS. For each of the views we describe (i) the abstract syntax, (ii) the concrete syntax, and (iii) the static semantics. Finally, Section 10 summarizes this article.

2   Related Work

There exist several tool-supported agent-oriented methodologies for developing MASs. Some examples are PASSI with the PASSI Tool Kit (PTK) [10] and ROADMAP with REBEL [11]. The available methodologies differ in their scope, tool support, and maturity. In this section we want to discuss three tool supported agent-based methodologies that are the closest to our approach.

In accordance to [12], Tropos is a software development methodology founded on the key concepts of agent-oriented software development. The Tropos methodology bases on the Tropos metamodel (see [13] for a detailed discussion) and covers the development phases requirements analysis, design, and implementation. Tools for goal analysis (GR-Tool, see [14]) and model checking (T-Tool, see [15]) have been separately implemented. The eCAT tool is used for automated testing. The modeling tool of the Tropos methodology is called TAOM4e and provides code generation for Jade and Jadex. The focus of Tropos lies on requirements analysis, design, and on model checking.

In accordance to [16], Prometheus is an agent-oriented software engineering methodology. Prometheus supports the whole agent-oriented software development process from analysis to implementation. The Prometheus Design Tool (PDT) [17] offers diagrams for the high-level analysis of a system, the refinement with interaction diagrams with Agent UML (AUML, [18]), and the specification of processes. PDT contains a cross checking tool that covers problems like inconsistency checking, identification of dangling model elements, type checking, etc. Moreover, PDT provides code generation for Jack.

According to [19], INGENIAS is a methodology for specifying MASs on a platform independent level. The INGENIAS metamodel covers aspects such as

organizations of agents, agent interactions, and environments of MASs. The IN-
GENIAS methodology is supported by the INGENIAS Development Kit (IDK)
[20] which is a graphical modeling tool. INGENIAS provides code generation for
Jade. Moreover, the INGENIAS Code Uploader extension supports refactoring
of Jade code. INGENIAS belongs to the few approaches that also focus on code
generation and implementation.

Instead of focusing on methodologies, our goal is to specify an expressive language that can be used to generate most parts of a MAS implementation. For this
purpose, we use the Object Constraint Language (OCL[2]) to specify the static
semantics of DSML4MAS. Most of the other approaches focus mainly on agent-
oriented analysis and design phases. Code generation and the involved problems
like synchronization between code and design are often neglected. In our point
of view, these aspects are critical for the practical application of agent-oriented
software engineering. Our contribution consists of an expressive platform independent modeling language and adequate tool support that supports the user
designing and implementing MAS.

3   Domain-Specific Modeling Language for Multiagent Systems

For designing MASs, we developed a platform-independent domain specific modeling language for MAS called DSML4MAS [21] in accordance to the language-
driven initiative [22]. Like any other language, DSML4MAS consists of an abstract
syntax, formal semantics, and concrete syntax:

- The abstract syntax of DSML4MAS is defined by a platform independent
  metamodel for MAS called PIM4AGENTS defining the vocabulary in terms
  of concepts and their relationships. The details of PIM4AGENTS are briefly
  discussed in more detail in the remainder of this paper.
- The formal semantics is expressed using the specification language Object-
  Z [23] which is a stated-based and object-oriented specification language.
  Object-Z is specialized on formalizing object-oriented specifications and
  bases on mathematical concepts (like sets, functions, and first-order predi-
  cate logic) that permits rigorous analysis and reasoning about the specifications. The denotational semantics of DSML4MAS are defined by introducing
  additional variables, which are used to define the semantics and invariants in
  Object-Z classes. Operational semantics in Object-Z are specified in terms
  of class operations and invariants restricting the operation sequences. For a
  detail discussion on the semantics of DSML4MAS, we refer to [8].
- The concrete syntax is defined as set of notations facilitating the presentation and construction of DSML4MAS. It is specified using the Graphical
  Modeling Framework[3] (GMF) that provides the fundamental infrastructure
  and components for developing visual design and modeling surfaces in Eclipse

---

[2] http://www.omg.org/docs/ptc/03-10-14.pdf

[3] http://www.eclipse.org/gmf/

and is thus an adequate framework for implementing domain specific modeling languages [24].

To close the gap between design and implementation, we provide generic model transformations from DSML4MAS on the platform independent level to two underlying execution platforms (i.e. Jack or Jade on the platform specific level).

However, in this paper we mainly focus on the different language features and illustrate how to make use of the formal semantics defined with Object-Z in the graphical editor to support validating and testing at design time. For this purpose, we manually transform the static semantics defined by the Object-Z specification into OCL statements that can be validated by the GMF environment at design time. How this is done in principle is described in [25]. This allows us to provide tool support for testing, evaluation, and execution of the designed artifacts. Furthermore, GMF provides different error levels and validation modes that further improves the mechanisms for testing and validating the design artifacts.

– **Error Levels:** For every rule in GMF it is possible to specify an error message and an error level. There are three levels: ERROR, WARNING, and INFO. The according messages are displayed in the "Problems View" of Eclipse. Moreover, icons are displayed in the editor to highlight the elements that violate a constraint.
– **Validation Mode:** There exist different validation modes for constraints. Live validation means that the constraints are always evaluated if something changes in a model. Manual validation means that the user has to manually invoke the validation procedure.

4   Agent View

The agent view defines how to model single autonomous entities, the capabilities they have to solve tasks and the roles they play within the MAS. Moreover, the agent view defines to which resources an agent has access to and which kind of behaviors it can use to solve tasks.

Section 4.1 explains the abstract syntax of the agent view. Parts of the OCL constraints that have been derived from the formal Object-Z specifications to specify the static semantics of DSML4MAS are discussed in Section 4.2. Finally, Section 4.3 shows how to model the agents of the CMS example.

4.1   Abstract Syntax

The agent view (cf. Fig. 1) is centered on the concept of *Agent*, the autonomous entity capable of acting in the system. An *Agent* has access to a set of *Resources* which may include any kind of *Object* (e.g. Service) situated in the surrounding *Environment* that can be accessed by the *Agent*. Furthermore, the *Agent* can perform particular *DomainRoles* that define in which specific context the *Agent*

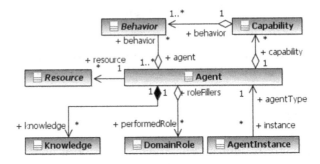

Fig. 1. Agent metamodel

Listing 1. Partial semantics of the agent view

```
context PIM4Agents :: Agent :: Agent inv :
  self.behavior
    -> union( self.capability
       -> collect(c | c.behavior))
    -> union( self.performedRole
       -> collect(r | r.providesCapability
          -> collect(c | c.behavior)))
    -> size() > 0
```

is acting and *Behaviors* defining how particular tasks can be achieved by the *Agent*. These *Behaviors* may be grouped together into *Capabilities* the *Agent* may have available. Beside the *Capabilities* to achieve certain goals, the *Agent* may have additional *Knowledge* about the current state of the world which serves as input for *Behaviors* or *Capabilities*.

4.2   Static Semantics

In this section, we want to present parts of the static semantics of the agent view. The constraint depicted in Listing 1 requires every agent to possess at least one behavior. An agent without any behavior could neither act autonomously nor could react to its environment.

4.3   Concrete Syntax

In the CMS use case we distinguish two agent types, namely Researcher and SeniorResearcher. Researchers, in contrast to senior researchers, cannot be the chair of a conference and cannot be member of a conference committee.

Fig. 2 shows the described agent types. We modeled the different roles of the CMS as domain roles that are performed by the agents. For example, the

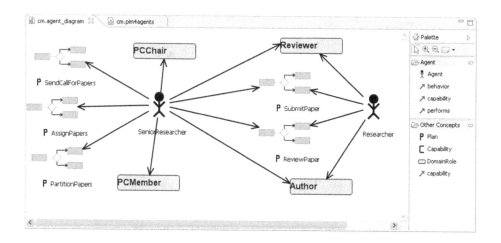

Fig. 2. Agent diagram

Researcher agent is permitted to the Reviewer and Author domain roles, whereas the SeniorResearcher can additionally perform the PCChair and PCMember roles.

The behavior that is required by an agent to perform a domain role is specified by a plan. For example, the SubmitPaper plan specifies what an agent has to do to submit a paper to a conference. Plans are discussed in detail in Section 8.

5   Role View

The role view covers the abstract representations of functional positions of autonomous entities within an organization or other social relationships. In general, a role in DSML4MAS can be considered as set of features defined over a collection of entities participating in a particular context. The features of a role can include (but not be limited to) activities, permissions, responsibilities, and protocols. A role is a part that is played by an entity and can as such be specified in interactive contexts like collaborations.

5.1   Abstract Syntax

The role view (cf. Fig. 3) mainly deals with the different forms of roles and which kind of functionalities they should provide or support. A *Role* is an abstraction of the social behavior of the *Agent* in a given social context, usually an *Organization*. The *Role* specifies the responsibilities of the *Agent* in that social context. It refers to (i) a set of *Capabilities* that define the set of *Behaviors* it can possess and (ii) a set of *Resources* the *Role* has access to. Role hierarchies can be defined through the *specializationOf* relationship which defines which kinds of *Roles* are specializations of a super role.

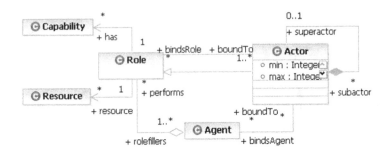

Fig. 3. Role metamodel

Listing 2. Parts of the static semantics of the role view

```
context PIM4Agents::Role::Role inv:
   self -> closure(parts) -> excludes(self)

context PIM4Agents::Role::Role inv:
   self -> closure(partOf) -> excludes(self)

context PIM4Agents::Role::Role inv:
   self -> closure(parts)
       -> intersection(self->closure(partOf))
       -> isEmpty()
```

An *Actor* is a kind of interaction role. The *Actor* inherits from the *Role* and thus can have access to particular *Capabilities* and *Resources* that are necessary for exchanging messages. An *Actor* can be further partitioned in terms of a certain position within a *Protocol* through the subactor reference.

The reason why to distinguish between subactors will be getting more clear in Section 7 focusing on the graphical design of the SubmitPaper protocol.

In contrast to an *Actor*, a *DomainRole* represents a certain functionality within a particular domain. These kinds of *Roles* are normally used in the context of *Organizations* in order to express which kinds of positions need to be filled.

5.2   Static Semantics

The partial static semantics of a role is depicted in Listing 2. The first invariant states that a role should not be part of the role' *parts* transitive closure[4].

---

[4] The `closure` operation is not part of the OCL 2.0 specification. It has been added by the MDT OCL implementation.

In the same tenor, a role should not be part of its *partOf* transitive closure which is defined by the second invariant and both transitive closures should be disjunct.

5.3   Concrete Syntax

Fig. 4 shows the domain roles of the CMS scenario. We specified that the roles PCChair and PCMember are disjoint. This means, no agent instance is allowed to perform more than one of these roles at the same time regarding one organization instance. Author and Reviewer are not disjoint regarding one organization instance. Instead they are disjoint regarding a certain paper. This is the reason why they are not disjoint in this diagram.

6   Organization View

The organization view defines how single autonomous agents are arranged to more complex organizations. Organizations in DSML4MAS can be either an autonomous acting entity like an agent, or simple groups that are formed to take advantage of the synergies of its members, resulting in an entity that enables products and processes that are not possible for any single individual.

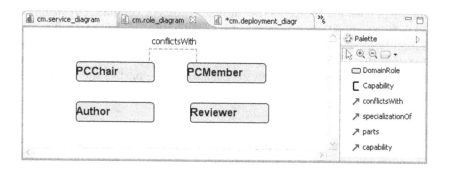

Fig. 4. Role diagram

The organization view consists of two parts. Section 6.1 introduces the concept of *Organization* of DSML4MAS. The internals of an organization, for example how domain roles are bound to actors in protocols, is specified by the concept of *Collaboration* which is introduced in Section 6.2.

6.1   Organizations

Abstract Syntax. The organization view (cf. Fig. 5) describes how single autonomous entities cooperate within the MAS and how complex social structures can be defined. The *Organization* is a special kind of *Agent* and can therefore perform *DomainRoles* and have *Capabilities*. In addition to the *Agent* properties,

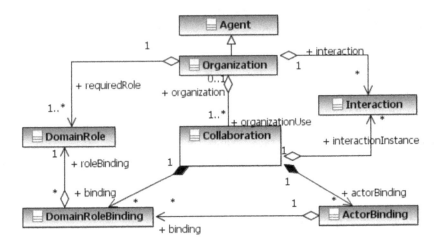

Fig. 5. Organization metamodel

an *Organization* may require certain *DomainRoles* performed by its members and may have its own internal *Protocols* specifying (i) how the *Organization* communicates with other *Agents* (i.e. atomic *Agents* or complex *Organizations*) and (ii) how organizational members are coordinated. Which particular forms of collaboration inside an *Organization* exists is expressed by the concept of a *Collaboration* that defines how specific *Interactions* are used in terms of binding *Actors*—part of the *Interaction*—to *DomainRoles*—part of the *Organization* (see Section 6.2).

Static Semantics. An organization specifies the domain roles and protocols that are utilized by the cooperating agents. A collaboration specifies a subset of roles of an organization that are involved in an interaction. Bindings are used to express which domain role is bound to which actor.

The first constraint in Listing 3 enforces that for every interaction protocol an organization uses, there has to be a collaboration that specifies the details how the protocol is used. The same protocol might be used in several contexts inside the same organization.

The second constraint enforces that every required role of an organization has to be bound by at least one domain role binding of a collaboration that is part of that organization. This prevents dangling domain roles.

Concrete Syntax. Fig. 6 depicts the ConferenceOrganization which is a generic organization type for conferences. It requires the domain roles representing the program committee chair (PCChair), program committee members (PCMember), Author, and Reviewer. The three protocols PaperSubmission, PaperAssignment, and PaperPartition specify the communication protocols that are used by the

Listing 3. Parts of the static semantics of the organization view

```
context PIM4Agents::Organization::Organization inv:
   let ui : Set(PIM4Agents::Interaction::Interaction) =
      self.organizationUse.interactionInstance
         -> flatten()
         -> asSet() in

   self.interaction
      -> forAll(d | ui ->includes(d))

context PIM4Agents::Organization::Organization inv:
   let ur : Set(PIM4Agents::Role::DomainRole) =
      self.organizationUse.binding.roleBinding
         -> flatten()
         -> asSet() in

   self.requiredRole
      -> forAll(d | ur ->includes(d))
```

organization. The binding between domain roles of organizations and actors of protocols is specified by collaborations (see Section 6.2).

Fig. 6 demonstrates the scalability of the concrete syntax of DSML4MAS. In the center, we can see the organization diagram which is described in this section. The upper part shows the collaboration diagram (see Section 6.2) that specifies the internals of the ConferenceOrganization. The lower part depicts the details of the PaperSubmission protocol which specifies the message exchange inside the ConferenceOrganization regarding the submission of papers (see Section 7). The sub-diagrams can be opened by double-clicking the compact representations in the organization diagram. This enables the user to focus in each view on the core aspects and abstract from details that are not relevant in this stage.

6.2   Collaborations

A collaboration specifies the interaction between a subset of the roles of an organization. For example, it defines which domain roles of an organization are involved in the collaboration and how these domain roles are bound to actors of the utilized protocol(s).

Static Semantics. Listing 4 depicts the partial static semantics of a collaboration. As a collaboration clearly defines how to make use of an interaction within this social context, it must be ensured that the organization's collaborations only refer to interactions that are used within this particular organization. The corresponding invariant is defined by the first OCL statement in Listing 4. Moreover, in the same tenor, it is ensured by the second invariant that the domain roles

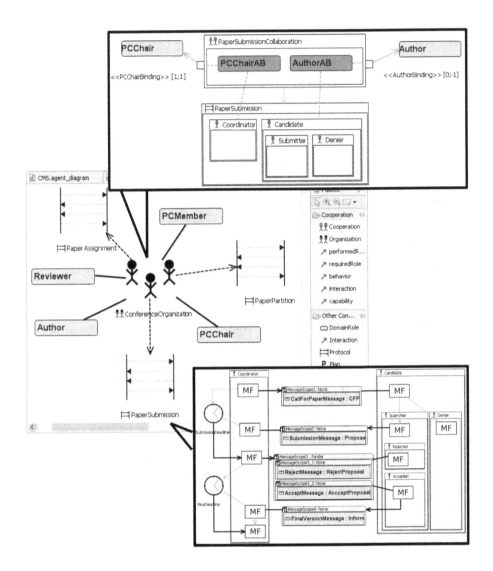

Fig. 6. Organization diagram

that are referred by the domain role binding of a collaboration are required by
the organization this collaboration belongs to.

Concrete Syntax. Fig. 7 shows the details of the PaperSubmissionCollaboration.
The collaboration specifies the bindings between the domain roles PCChair and
Author, and the Coordinator and Candidate actor of the PaperSubmission protocol.

The domain role binding PCChairAB binds the PCChair domain role to the
Coordinator actor in the PaperSubmission protocol. Likewise, the AuthorAB binds

Listing 4. Partial semantics of a collboration

```
context PIM4Agents::Organization::Collaboration inv:
   self.interactionInstance
      -> forAll(ii | self.organization.interaction
         -> includes(ii)

context PIM4Agents::Interaction::DomainRoleBinding inv:
   let col : PIM4Agents::Organization::Collaboration =
      PIM4Agents::Organization::Collaboration.allInstances()
         -> select(d | d.binding
            -> includes(self))
         -> asSequence()
         -> first() in

   col.organization.requiredRole
      -> union(col.organization.performedRole)
      -> includes(self.roleBinding)
```

the Author domain role to the Candidate actor of the PaperSubmission protocol. Domain role bindings specify maximum and minimum constraints for the number of role fillers that can be assigned at run-time. For example, the PCChairBinding defines that the ConferenceOrganization requires exactly one role filler for the PCChair domain role.

One domain role can be bound to several actors of different protocols within the same collaboration. For example, actor bindings can be utilized to specify that one domain role is bound to an actor in the first protocol and to another actor in a second protocol. This implies whoever performs the domain role of that organization has to play the according actors in the bound protocols.

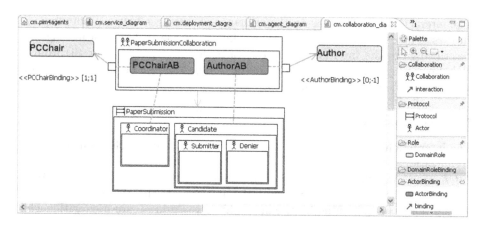

Fig. 7. Collaboration diagram

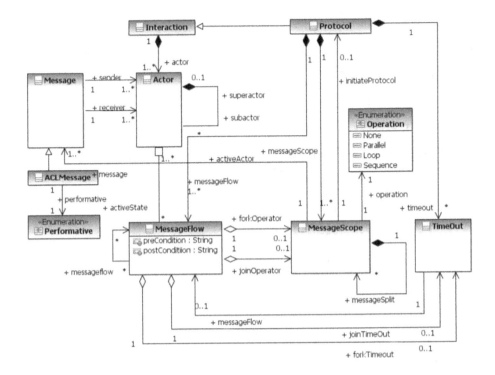

Fig. 8. Interaction metamodel

7   Interaction View

The interaction view focuses on the exchange of messages between autonomous entities. Thereby, two opportunities are offered: (i) the exchange of messages is described from the internal perspective of each entity involved, or (ii) from a global perspective in terms of agent interaction protocols focusing on the global exchange of messages between entities.

7.1   Abstract Syntax

The interaction view of DSML4MAS (cf. Fig. 8) defines in which manner agents, organizations, or roles interact. A *Protocol* is considered as a special form of an *Interaction*. Accordingly, the main concepts of a *Protocol* are *Actor*, *ACLMessage*, *MessageFlow*, *MessageScope*, and *TimeOut*. In the collaboration view, furthermore, the system designer can specify how *Protocols* are used within *Organizations*. This is done through the concept of a *Collaboration* that defines how *DomainRoles* of an *Organization* are bound to *Actors* of *Protocols*. An *Actor* is a named set of role fillers at design time. The role fillers are introduced in the deployment view (see Section 9) or at run-time.

Actors as specialization of *Role* can have subactors, where an *AgentInstance* bound to the parent actor must be bound to exactly one subactor. The actor *subactor* relationship is discussed in more detail in Section 7.3. Furthermore, *Actors* require and provide certain *Capabilities* and *Resources* defined in the role view of DSML4MAS.

Messages are an essential mean for the communication between agents in MASs. In DSML4MAS, we distinguish between two sorts of messages, i.e. *Message* and *ACLMessage* which further includes the idea of *Performatives*. Messages have a content and may refer to an *Ontology* that can be used by the participating agents to interpret the *Message* and its content. A *MessageFlow* defines the states of the protocol in which an *Actor* could be active. The main function of the *MessageFlow* is firstly to send and receive *ACLMessages* which is done through the concept of a *MessageScope* and secondly to specify time constraints (i.e. the latest point in time) in which these *ACLMessages* need to be sent and received through the *TimeOut* concept. A *TimeOut* defines the time constraints for sending and receiving messages and how to continue in the case of a *TimeOut* through the *messageFlow* reference.

A *MessageScope* defines the *ACLMessages* and the order how these are sent and received. In particular this is achieved by connecting *ACLMessages* to *Operations*. Beside *ACLMessages* sent and received, a *MessageScope* may also refer to *Protocols* that are initiated at some specific point in time in the parent *Protocol*. This particular feature allows modeling of nested protocols. The order in which *ACLMessages* are exchanged is defined by a so-called *Operation* featuring the alternatives *Sequence*, *Parallel*, *Loop*, and *None*.

A combination of these *Operations* can easily be achieved by the *MessageScope's* *messageSplit* reference which allows to nest *Operations*. Beside *Operations*, further branching can be defined by specifying transitions between *MessageFlows* using their *messageflow* reference. A *preCondition* and *postCondition* can be specified in order to define in which case the transition is triggered.

7.2   Static Semantics

Listing 5 illustrates the partial static semantics of interaction view related concepts. The first invariant states that a protocol describes the interaction of at least two actors. As a message flow can be considered as state of a particular entity within an interaction, it should be clear that one of the two protocol-specific actions (i.e. send or receive) should be performed. This is expressed in the second invariant through the message scope reference (i.e. *forkOperator* responsible for sending, *joinOperator* responsible for receiving messages).

7.3   Concrete Syntax

Fig. 9 shows the PaperSubmission protocol of the CMS example. The Coordinator actor represents the program committee chair and the Candidate actor the potential authors. The protocol starts by sending the CallForPaperMessage (performative *CFP*) to the set of all candidates.

Listing 5. Partial static semantics of interaction-related concepts

```
context PIM4Agents :: Interaction :: Protocol inv:
    self.actors -> size() >= 2

context PIM4Agents :: Interaction :: MessageFlow inv:
    not self.forkOperator -> isEmpty() or
    not self.joinOperator -> isEmpty()
```

There exist candidates that send a submission (covered by Submitter actor) and candidates that do not submit (covered by the Denier actor). The protocol terminates for all role fillers of the Denier actor.

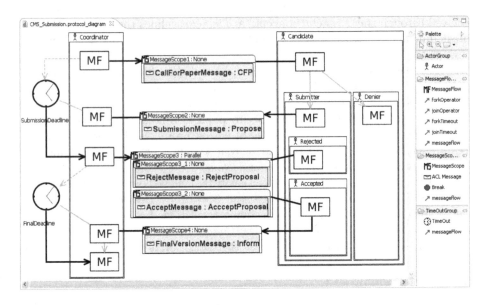

Fig. 9. Protocol diagram

The SubmissionDeadline is the timeout between sending the cfp message and receiving the submissions. If the timer elapses, the Coordinator sends a RejectMessage to all submitters that were rejected (covered by the Rejected actor) and a AcceptMessage to all role fillers that were accepted (covered by the Accepted actor). All role fillers that receive an acceptance notification have to submit the camera ready version before the FinalDeadline elapses.

8   Behavior View

The behavior view describes the vocabulary available for specifying the internal behavior of intelligent entities. The vocabulary can be defined in terms of

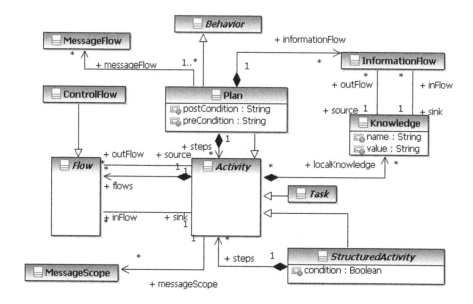

Fig. 10. Behavior metamodel

combining simple actions to more complex control structures or plans that are used for achieving predefined objectives or goals.

8.1   Abstract Syntax

The behavioral view describes how plans are composed by complex control structures and simple atomic tasks and how those constructs are linked by *Flows*. The core concepts of the behavioral view are depicted in Fig. 10. A *Behavior* represents the super class connecting the agent viewpoint with the behavioral viewpoint, where a *Plan* can be considered as a specialization of the abstract *Behavior* to specify an agent's internal processes. A *Plan* contains a set of *Activities* that are linked with *Flows*. A *Flow* is either of the type *ControlFlow* or *InformationFlow*.

Furthermore, a *Plan* refers to a set of *MessageFlows* to ensure that the message exchange (defined by the *Protocol*) is implemented by the particular *Plan* in an adequate manner.

The body of a *Plan* is mainly represented by the specializations of an *Activity*. A *StructuredActivity* (see Fig. 11) is an abstract class that introduces more complex control structures into the behavioral view. It inherits from *Activity*, but additionally owns a set of *Activities* and *Flows*.

A *Sequence* as a specialization of a *StructuredActivity* denotes a list of *Activities* to be executed in a sequential manner as defined by contained *ControlFlows* through their *sink* and *source* attributes. Beside using the concept of *Sequence*, a sequence of *Activities* can additionally be directly described by linking the

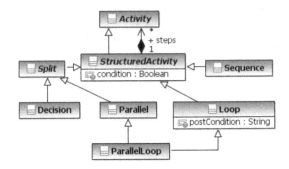

Fig. 11. Structured activities in DSML4MAS

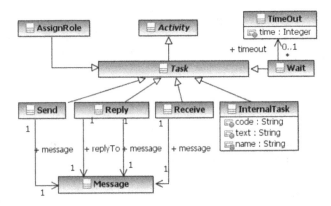

Fig. 12. Tasks in DSML4MAS

particular *Activities* through *ControlFlows*. However, the concept of *Sequence* allows hiding the concrete trace which might be important when designing complex *Plans* as scalability is improved. A *Split* is an abstract class that defines a point in a *Plan* where a single thread of control splits into multiple threads of control. We distinguish between *Parallel* and *Decision* as specializations. A *Parallel* is a point in a *Plan*, where a single thread of control splits into multiple threads of control which are executed in parallel. Thus a *Parallel* allows *Activities* to be executed simultaneously or in any order. How the different threads are synchronized is defined by a *SynchronizationMode*. Feasible options are XOR (i.e. exactly one path is synchronized), AND (i.e. all paths are synchronized), and NofM (i.e. n of m paths are synchronized).

In contrast to a *Parallel*, a *Decision* in DSML4MAS is a point in a *Plan* where, based on a *Condition*, at least one *Activity* of a number of branching *Activities* must be chosen. A *Decision* can either be executed in an XOR or OR manner. In contrast, a *Loop* is a point in a *Plan* where a set of *Activities* are executed repeatedly until a certain pre-defined *Condition* evaluates to false. It allows looping

Listing 6. Parts of the static semantics of plan-related concepts

```
context PIM4Agents::Behavior::Activity inv:
   self.activities
      -> select(d | d.oclIsTypeOf(Begin))
      -> size() = 1

context PIM4Agents::Behavior::Activity inv:
   self.activities
      -> select(d | d.oclIsTypeOf(End))
      -> size() = 1

context PIM4Agents::Behavior::ControlFlow inv:
   let sc : Activity <- Plan.allInstances()
      -> union(StructuredActivity.allInstances())
      -> select(p | p.steps
         -> includes(self.source))
      -> first() in

   let tc : Activity <- Plan.allInstances()
      -> union(StructuredActivity.allInstances())
      -> select(p | p.steps
         -> includes(self.target))
      -> first() in

   sc = tc;

context PIM4Agents::Behavior::Flow inv:
   self.sink <> self.source
```

that is block structured, i.e. patterns allow exactly one entry and exit point. A *ParallelLoop* as a specialization of *Loop* and *Parallel* allows specifying iterations in the form that each trace is executed in parallel.

Like a *StructuredActivity*, a *Task* (depicted in Fig. 12) is an abstract class that inherits from *Activity*. Unlike a *StructuredActivity*, a *Task* mainly focuses on atomic activities and thus does not contain any *Activities* or *Flows*. Fig. 12 depicts the partial metamodel of *Task*-related concepts. A *Send* activity specifies that the referred *Message* is sent, whereas the *Receive* activity denotes that the particular *Message* is received. Moreover, the *AssignRole* activity allows to assign *AgentInstances* to *Roles* (i.e. *Actors*). Finally, an *InternalTask* can be used to define code.

8.2   Static Semantics

Listing 6 depicts the partial static semantics of plan-related concepts. Any plan or structured activity contains exactly one begin and one end task. Moreover, the sink and source activities of a control flow belong to the same plan or structured activity. Consequently, no control flow is defined across two plans/activities.

Finally, the source and sink activities of a flow are different, i.e. no flow can point to its source activity.

8.3   Concrete Syntax

Fig. 13 depicts the SubmitPaper plan. It implements the behavior of the Candidate actor and its sub-actors of the PaperSubmission protocol from Fig. 9. The plan starts with the ReceiveCallForPaper task which receives an incoming CFPMessage. The lower part of Fig. 13 shows the properties view of the ReceiveCallForPaper task. We can see that the task refers to the CFPMessage.

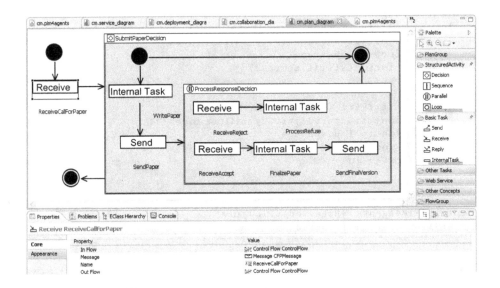

Fig. 13. Behavior diagram of the SubmitPaper behavior

DSML4MAS distinguishes between *ACLMessages* that are used to specify the message sequences of a protocol and the actual *Messages* that are sent by plans. As protocols are reusable components, *ACLMessages* do not specify the resources that are transmitted by them. If a message shall be sent by a plan (e.g. the CFPMessage from Fig. 13), we have to introduce a new *Message* that refers to an *ACLMessage* of a protocol (here the CallForPaperMessage) and assign some application specific resources to it. In the CMS example, the program committee chair sends information about the conference, the deadlines, etc.

The internal task WritePaper is a kind of black box behavior that is not further refined at the model level. The behavior has to be implemented after generating the source code. For example, one could open a dialog box for the researcher to select the paper he wants to submit to the conference.

Either the author submits a paper or the plan terminates. If the author submits a paper, he has to wait for either a RejectMessage or an AcceptMessage

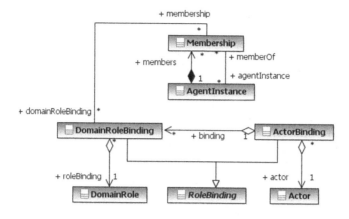

Fig. 14. Deployment metamodel

from the program committee chair. The ReceiveReject and ReceiveAccept tasks are executed in parallel with XOR semantics which can be set in the properties view of the parallel task. If the author receives an AcceptMessage, he has to finalize the paper (FinalizePaper task) and send it to the program committee chair (SendFinalVersion task).

9 Deployment View

The deployment view describes the run-time agent instances involved in the system and how these are assigned to the organization's roles.

9.1 Abstract Syntax

The deployment view of DSML4MAS (cf. Fig. 14) deals with the kind of *AgentInstances* that exist in the running systems and how these instances are bound to the particular *DomainRoles* through the concept *Membership*. Even if using the deployment view is optional, i.e. the instances of agents could also be introduced on the particular agent platform selected to execute the design, for closed MASs it might already make sense to define the agent instance during design time.

An *AgentInstance* refers to its agent type, which is either *Agent* or *Organization*. Moreover, *AgentInstances* are linked through the *Membership* concept to one or more *AgentInstances* of type *Organization*. The *Membership* concept references one or more *DomainRoleBindings* of the *Organization* type. The *DomainRoleBinding* exactly specifies which *DomainRole* is performed by the agent instance and to which *Actors* of the utilized protocols the member is bound to (in a certain organization instance).

9.2 Static Semantics

The deployment view and its concepts are optional, i.e. concepts like *AgentInstances* do not need to be defined for executing the model transformations.

Listing 7. Partial static semantics of the deployment view

```
context PIM4Agents :: Deployment :: AgentInstance inv:
    self.agentType.oclIsTypeOf(PIM4Agents :: Agent :: Agent)
        implies (self.members -> size() = 0)

context PIM4Agents :: Deployment :: AgentInstance inv:
    self.agentType.performedRole
        -> includesAll(
            self.memberOf.domainRoleBinding
                -> collect(d | d.roleBinding )
                -> flatten())
```

However, there might be situations where the number of run-time instance is already known at design time in which case these instances can directly be defined using DSML4MAS.

Listing 7 depicts some OCL constraints further defining the static semantics of the deployment view. The first invariant ensures that if an agent instance refers to an agent as type, the agent instance itself has not any member. Furthermore, the second invariant guarantees that an agent instance can only be bound through the domain role binding to domain roles its agent type is able to perform.

9.3   Concrete Syntax

Fig. 15 shows the deployment diagram of the CMS example. We modeled an instance of the ConferenceOrganization, called ExampleCon'09. Furthermore, there are three agent instances: Alice and Bob are of type Researcher and Peter is of type SeniorResearcher.

The domain role an agent instance performs in an organization instance is specified by the membership concept which is visualized as a link. In the lower part of Fig. 15, we can see that the selected membership relation refers to the PCChairBinding of the SubmitPaperCollaboration. Therefore, it is clear that Peter performs the PCChair domain role of the ExampleCon'09 and plays in the same context the Coordinator actor of the PaperSubmission protocol (see also Fig. 7).

The icon at the membership relation of Alice visualizes a validation error. The error is caused by Alice who is of type Researcher and is assigned to the PCMember role in the ExampleCon'09. This is invalid since the Researcher agent type is not permitted to perform the PCMember role. If the validation mode is set to live validation, DDE already prevents the creation of an invalid relation.

10   Summary

One of the main problems that prevent AOSE from a broad application in main stream software development is the lack of methodologies and suitable tool support. In this paper we presented the language features of the domain specific

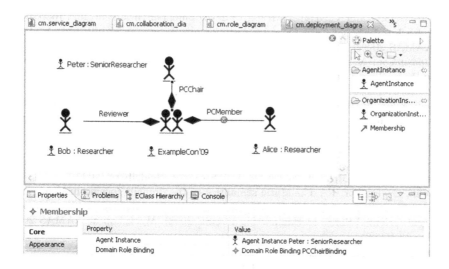

Fig. 15. Deployment diagram

modeling language for multiagent systems (DSML4MAS). Therefore, for each of the different views on MASs we presented (i) the abstract syntax specified by a metamodel, (ii) static semantics specified with OCL constraints, and (iii) the concrete syntax illustrated by the well-known conference management systems example.

The OCL invariants cover the static semantics and were manually derived from the formal semantics expressed by the specification language Object-Z. This allows the user to test and validate the generated design artifacts and ensures that the model transformations to Jack and Jade produces reasonable code.

Our future work will comprise the extension of the language features towards an agent-based methodology that supports the user in the stepwise refinement of the generated design. For this purpose, we will follow a model-driven approach that generates most of the design artifacts that finally need to be manually refined.

References

1. Odell, J.: Objects and agents compared. Journal of Object Technology 1, 41–53 (2002)
2. Dam, K.H., Winikoff, M.: Comparing agent-oriented methodologies. In: Giorgini, P., Henderson-Sellers, B., Winikoff, M. (eds.) AOIS 2003. LNCS, vol. 3030, pp. 78–93. Springer, Heidelberg (2004)
3. Luck, M., McBurney, P., Gonzalez-Palacios, J.: Agent-based computing and programming of agent systems. In: Bordini, R.H., Dastani, M., Dix, J., El Fallah Seghrouchni, A. (eds.) PROMAS 2005. LNCS, vol. 3862, pp. 23–37. Springer, Heidelberg (2006)

4. Warwas, S., Hahn, C.: The DSML4MAS development environment. In: Proceedings of 8th International Conference on Autonomous Agents and Multiagent Systems (AAMAS 2009). ACM, New York (2009) (accepted as demo paper)
5. Papasimeon, M., Heinze, C.: Extending the UML for designing JACK agents. In: Proceedings of the Australian Software Engineering Conference, ASWEC 2001 (2001)
6. Bellifemine, F., Bergenti, F., Caire, G., Poggi, A.: 5. In: JADE - a Java agent development framework. Multiagent Systems, Artificial Societies, and Simulated Organizations, vol. 15, pp. 125–147. Springer, Berlin (2005)
7. Madrigal-Mora, C., Fischer, K.: Adding organisations and roles to JADE with JadeOrgs. In: Fischer, K., et al. (eds.) Category Theory Applied to Computation and Control. LNBIP, vol. 25, pp. 98–117. Springer, Heidelberg (2009)
8. Hahn, C., Fischer, K.: The static semantics of the domain specific modeling language for multiagent systems. In: Proceedings of the 9th International Workshop on Agent-Oriented Software Engineering (AOSE 2008). Workshop at AAMAS 2008, May 13 (2008)
9. Zambonelli, F., Jennings, N.R., Wooldridge, M.: Organisational rules as an abstraction for the analysis and design of multi-agent systems. International Journal of Software Engineering and Knowledge Engineering 11, 303–328 (2001)
10. Cossentino, M., Potts, C.: A case tool supported methodology for the design of multi-agent systems. In: Proceedings of the International Conference on Software Engineering Research and Practice, SERP (2002)
11. Juan, T., Pearce, A., Sterling, L.: Roadmap: Extending the Gaia methodology for complex open systems. In: Proceedings of the First International Joint Conference on Autonomous Agents and Multiagent Systems (AAMAS), pp. 3–10. ACM, New York (2002)
12. Bresciani, P., Giorgini, P., Giunchiglia, F., Mylopoulos, J., Perini, A.: Tropos: An agent-oriented software development methodology. Journal of Autonomous Agents and Multi-Agent Systems 8, 203–236 (2004)
13. Susi, A., Perini, A., Mylopoulos, J., Giorgini, P.: The Tropos metamodel and its use. Informatica 29 (Slovenia) 29, 401–408 (2005)
14. Giorgini, P., Mylopoulos, J., Sebastiani, R.: Goal-oriented requirements analysis and reasoning in the Tropos methodology. Engineering Applications of Artificial Intelligence 18, 159–171 (2005)
15. Fuxman, A., Pistore, M., Mylopoulos, J., Traverso, P.: Model checking early requirements specifications in Tropos. In: Proceedings of the Fifth IEEE International Symposium on Requirements Engineering (RE 2001), Washington, DC, USA, pp. 174–181. IEEE Computer Society, Los Alamitos (2001)
16. Padgham, L., Winikoff, M.: Prometheus: A methodology for developing intelligent agents. In: Proceedings of the Third International Workshop on AgentOriented Software Engineering, at AAMAS, pp. 37–38. ACM, New York (2002)
17. Thangarajah, J., Padgham, L., Winikoff, M.: Prometheus design tool. In: Proceedings of the Fourth International Joint Conference on Autonomous Agents and Multiagent Systems (AAMAS), pp. 127–128. ACM, New York (2005)
18. Bauer, B., Müller, J., Odell, J.: Agent UML: A formalism for specifying multiagent interaction. In: Ciancarini, P., Wooldridge, M.J. (eds.) AOSE 2000. LNCS, vol. 1957, pp. 91–103. Springer, Heidelberg (2001)
19. Jorge, F.R.: Agent oriented software engineering with INGENIAS. In: Mařík, V., Müller, J.P., Pěchouček, M. (eds.) CEEMAS 2003. LNCS, vol. 2691, pp. 394–403. Springer, Heidelberg (2003)

20. Gomez-Sanz, J.J., Fuentes, R., Pavón, J.: García-Magariño, I.: INGENIAS development kit: a visual multi-agent system development environment. In: AAMAS 2008: Proceedings of the 7th international joint conference on Autonomous agents and multiagent systems, Richland, SC, International Foundation for Autonomous Agents and Multiagent Systems, pp. 1675–1676 (2008)
21. Hahn, C.: A platform independent agent-based modeling language. In: Proceedings of the Seventh International Conference on Autonomous Agents and Multiagent Systems (AAMAS), pp. 233–240 (2008)
22. Cook, S., Jones, G., Kent, S., Wills, A.C.: Domain-Specific Development with Visual Studio DSL Tools, 1st edn. Addison-Wesley Professional, Reading (2007)
23. Smith, G.: The Object-Z Specification Language. Advances in Formal Methods, vol. 1. Kluwer Academic Publishers, Dordrecht (2000)
24. Warwas, S., Hahn, C.: The contrete syntax of the platform independent modeling language for multiagent systems. In: Proceedings of the Agent-based Technologies and applications for enterprise interOPerability (ATOP 2008) at AAMAS 2008 (2008)
25. Roe, D., Broda, K., Russo, A.: Mapping UML models incorporating OCL constraints into Object-Z. Technical Report 2003/9, Imperial College, 180 Queen's Gate, London (2002)

Enhancing UML to Formalize the FIPA Agent Interaction Protocol

Øystein Haugen[1,2] and Ragnhild Kobro Runde[2]

[1] SINTEF, Oslo, Norway
[2] University of Oslo, Department of Informatics, Oslo, Norway

Abstract. The FIPA Contract Net Interaction Protocol cannot be described properly with UML 2.1 Sequence Diagrams. The ability to multicast messages is an important feature that is lacking. We show how minor enhancements of UML will make it more suited to express agent protocols. We also explain why the earlier enhancements proposed by the Agent UML are not quite satisfactory. We show how the protocol exceptions can be defined. Finally a formal semantics is given to the enhancements.

Keywords: UML modeling, Contract Net Interaction Protocol, STAIRS, multicast, sequence diagram.

1 Introduction

The FIPA protocol for negotiations between agents [1] applies a variant of sequence diagrams to express the protocol together with natural language text. At the time when the FIPA standard was created, UML was still in its version 1. Since then the OMG has standardized as available technology UML 2 [2]. In this paper we investigate whether the FIPA protocol can be described by means of UML 2. We consider the FIPA protocol to represent interaction that is typical for the needs in the realm of agents. We conclude that UML 2 cannot fully cope properly with the FIPA protocol, and therefore suggest a few enhancements that will make UML more capable of defining the FIPA protocol and thereby more suitable for the needs of the agent community.

The FIPA contract net interaction protocol describes how an initiator sends out a number of calls for proposal to a set of participants. Some of these participants will refuse the call, while others may come up with a proposal. The initiator will then consider the proposals and decide for each one whether it should be accepted or rejected. For those that are accepted, there are three different final results that may be sent back to the initiator. The FIPA protocol is depicted in Fig. 1.

The FIPA protocol is not a valid UML 2 diagram. It is described in a dialect of sequence diagrams using extensions to UML 1 known as "Agent UML" described in [3]. Some improvements to the notation were suggested by [4]. The key concept to express the multicasting is the multiplicity on the message ends to show how many message instances the diagram really describes. This approach functions

K. Fischer et al. (Eds.): ATOP 2005 and ATOP 2008, LNBIP 25, pp. 154–173, 2009.

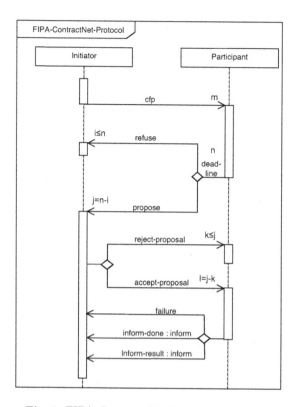

Fig. 1. FIPA Contract Net Interaction Protocol

well on an informal level, but is not sufficient if we want to describe what happens with every participant. The FIPA diagram says nothing about which participants are involved in which sequence of messages. E.g. there is nothing in the diagram that expresses that the reject-proposal messages are sent only to participants that earlier sent proposals back to the initiator. This is obvious to the human reader, but is nowhere defined. The problem in general is that multiplicity on messages is not sufficient to express the subsets of senders or receivers. We show in this paper means to express subsets of agents through annotations on the lifelines and/or on the messages.

In the sequel we shall look at how an experienced UML designer would attempt to express the FIPA protocol. Some of what we show here is similar to what was shown in [5] for how to use UML 2 concepts to express agents. We emphasize the precise interpretation of the diagrams and the fact that there are differences between approaches that all may serve the purpose of expressing agent interactions. We highlight mechanisms that exist in UML, but that have been rarely used and introduce a mechanism for multicasting that suits our purposes. We go on to show how exceptions of the protocol can be defined through existing and new concepts, and finally provide a formal definition of our enhancement based on the STAIRS semantics of sequence diagrams [6,7,8].

2   The Single Participant Approach

A common starting point when applying sequence diagrams to a complex situation is to simplify the scenario down to a situation having only one of each kind
of object. In our case this would mean defining a context where there are one
initiator and one participant even though we know that the protocol actually

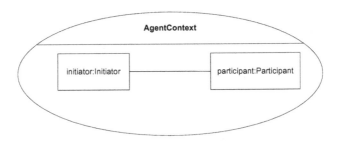

Fig. 2. Agent Context for the single general participant

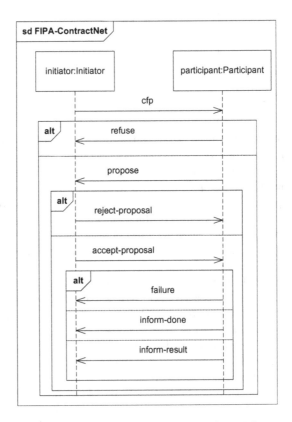

Fig. 3. FIPA protocol for the general participant

has little meaning if there is not more than one participant. In UML we define such a context by a collaboration (Fig. 2) where there are one initiator and one participant. That participant has all the abilities of any participant, but of course for one single case, the participant is only one agent.

The UML 2 sequence diagram in Fig. 3 defines the different options that are open to the participant by applying nested alt-fragments. Thus we are able to express that for a participant that refuses the call for proposal there will be no continuation of the protocol, and that the initiator will be informed of the final result only from participants whose proposals were accepted. Our diagram here is similar to that of [5], except from their use of multiplicities on messages that we shall return to shortly.

The diagram shown in Fig. 3 is more precise than the original FIPA illustration. However, we still have the problem that the approach misses the point that the initiator sends calls to many potential participants and that he in fact must cope with many replies. The diagram shows a very limited view, the situation as seen from a participant rather than the initiator.

3   The Approach of Typical Participants

Recognizing that our aim should be to describe more than one participant, our next attempt expresses that there are different participants with different situations relative to the initiative described in the protocol. Rather than defining one participant that is fully general, we now describe one participant for each distinct situation. In our context collaboration (Fig. 4) we define a set of participants with multiplicity.

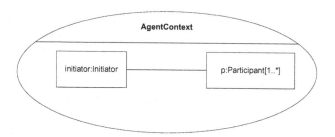

Fig. 4. Agent context with set of participants

In the sequence diagram in Fig 5, we apply the standard notation in the lifeline header to pick one object from a set by the use of a selector. The selector in this case is only a symbolic name serving as an index indicating what situation that given participant object is representing. We recognize the refused, the rejected, and the accepted situations.

In Fig. 5 we have one lifeline for each of these typical situations that a participant may be in. In this way we visualize more directly that there are several

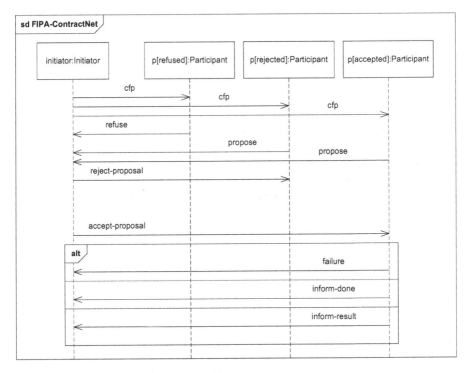

Fig. 5. FIPA protocol for typical participants

participants that the initiator must relate to. We are not able, however, to describe the multiplicities of each of the subgroups because each of the lifelines represents only one participant.

This approach fails to give the impression that the initiator has the same original approach to all participants in the first place. It also shows a situation where the initiator handles the different typical participants in strict sequence. This is by no means illegal as this diagram is not necessarily intended to define all possible traces of the protocol. Sequence diagrams show possible runs, but seldom all possible runs. Still we may want to express that there is nothing that prevents the initiator from receiving the return from an accepting participant before the return from a refusing participant. To express the possibility of such advanced orderings can to a certain extent be done by introducing parallel constructs, the par combined fragments, but this will quickly clutter the diagram defying the purpose of the description.

4 Introducing Configurations With Subsets

The main problem with the approach of typical participants in the previous section was that the sets from which these typical lifelines were selected, were not properly described. Their multiplicities and internal relationships were not defined.

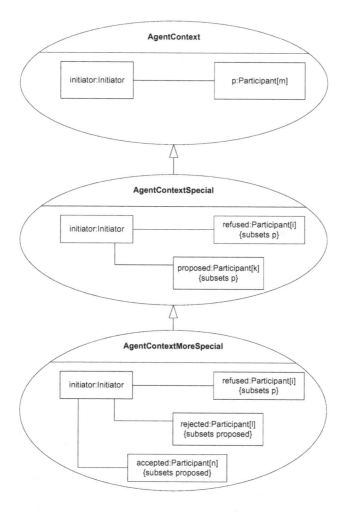

Fig. 6. Agent Context with specialization

We remedy this by introducing configurations with subsets. In fact this is available in UML 2 already, and extensively used in the class diagrams of the UML 2 metamodel (i.e. the model describing UML itself), but it is seldom used in modeling with composite structures. Subsets are constraints on a class property indicating that the defined property is a subset of some other property defined in a superclass of the encloser. An example (Fig. 6) will make this clearer.

In AgentContext we define one total set of participants p with multiplicity m. AgentContextSpecial is a specialization of the general AgentContext where we have defined two subsets of p and these subsets are given new names refused, and proposed. What this does is to keep the information that all objects of these sets are still contained in the original set p, but that they may have added capabilities or situations. In the FIPA context it is natural to have also third layer

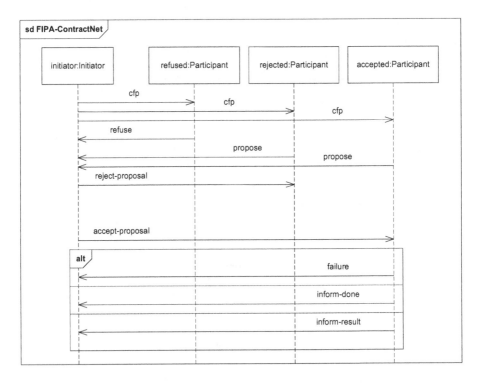

Fig. 7. FIPA protocol with subsets

of specialization as shown in `AgentContextMoreSpecial`. Here, the `proposed` subset from `AgentContextSpecial` is further divided into the subsets `rejected` and `accepted`.

The behavior definition given in Fig. 7 is structurally equivalent to that of Fig. 5, but the names of the lifelines now refer to the subsets that are actually UML properties. In Fig. 5 the names are symbolic selectors. One advantage of the subset approach is that we now have a way to express multiplicities for the different subsets. Within each of the subsets we apply the single lifeline approach assuming that every object within the subset exhibits the same behavior.

Notice that we have still only applied constructs that are already inside UML 2, but we have in this latest approach applied a description technique that is not very common. The technique has been presented with additions by Haugen and Møller-Pedersen in [9].

5 Introducing Subset Notation on Messages

We have found that the subset construct that can be effectively applied to composite structures as shown in Fig. 6 are useful also as identifiers in sequence diagrams as shown in Fig. 7. But the latter still fails to capture properly the distinction

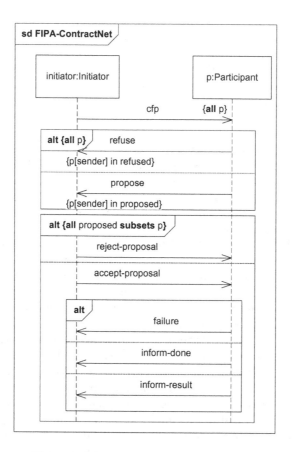

Fig. 8. FIPA protocol with subset notation

between showing one typical instance of the set (as depicted first in Fig. 5) and expressing that the interaction actually holds for every instance of the set.

Applying multiplicities to the messages as suggested by the FIPA protocol standard (Fig. 1) does not quite express this precisely as this is not a matter of numbers only, but rather a matter of subsets. That is why we suggest introducing a subset notation for messages that will make the diagram look very similar to the FIPA protocol standard. Still our notation will ensure unambiguous and precise meaning.

The notation is simple. Attached to one (or both) ends of a message there is a constraint that has the keyword **all** followed by a part name. That part must be a subset of the part represented by the lifeline on the message end with the **all** constraint. In Fig. 8 we have that `refused` and `proposed` are subsets of **p**.

Informally the meaning of this notation is the same as described by the FIPA protocol. Take e.g. the `cfp` message from `initiator` lifeline to **p** where the receiving end has attached the constraint "{**all p**}". This obviously is intended to mean that there is one message from the `initiator` to every member of the **p** set.

We also need one more construct. It is not sufficient only to be able to define multicasting of messages to or from a given subset. The problem is not to define how to send or receive a number of messages, the problem lies in defining how to handle the various responses that will return from that multicast. In Fig. 8 we see how the `refuse` and `propose` messages are possible responses to the initial `cfp`. We define a combined **alt**-fragment with an iterator-clause. The "**alt** {all p}" fragment iterates over all participants meaning that every participant has the choice between sending back `refuse` or `propose`.

Likewise the "**alt** {all proposed subsets p}" fragment iterates over the subset of all participants of the proposed subset meaning that for each participant sending a proposal, the initiator has the choice between rejecting and accepting the proposal. The constraint "{p[sender] in proposed}" in the first **alt**-fragment ensures that all participants sending a proposal will indeed be considered a member of the subset `proposed`.

When we say that the combined fragment is iterated over the participants in the subset, we mean that there is one such combined fragment for each participant in the subset and that these combined fragments are combined by an enclosing parallel construct. This means that the different participants' combined fragments are independent and can be merged together in any way. This will be explained again more formally below.

Notice that we have reached the same compactness in our description that we had with our first approach with the general participant in Fig. 3. However the p lifeline no longer represents only one participant object, but the whole set of participants. This in fact means that if the diagram contains one such multicasting or iteration construct, every construct on that lifeline must be multicast or iterated. This is in fact a static requirement on the sequence diagram.

The diagram in Figure 8 assumes that the initiator waits for the `refuse` and `propose` responses from *all* of the participants before starting to reject or accept the proposals. The FIPA protocol in [1] describes that the initiator should wait only until a given deadline, and that proposals received after the deadline should be rejected. In Section 7, we will come back to how this may be described in our approach.

6   The Semantics of the Multicasting and the Iterator-Clause

We define the semantics of our proposed constructs as shorthands for standard UML 2 sequence diagram constructs.

The different uses of the **all**-notation introduced in the previous section are all special variants of the same **all**-construct with the general format {all s subsets p} d where p is a part with multiplicity greater than one, s is a subset of p, and d is the (sub-)diagram for which the **all**-construct applies. As a syntactical constraint, we assume that for all messages in d, both the sending and the receiving ends of the message are included in d.

The **all**-construct is then defined by:

$$\{\text{all s subsets p}\}\ d \overset{\text{def}}{=} \underset{p'\in s}{\textbf{par}}\ d[p'/p] \tag{1}$$

where d[p'/p] is the diagram d with the lifeline p' substituted for the lifeline p. The **par**-fragment is defined in UML 2 as a parallel merge operator that will merge in all possible ways the sequences of the operands.

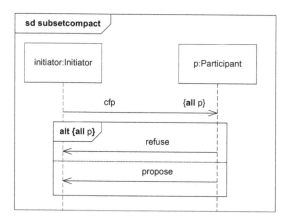

Fig. 9. Subsetcompact — multicasting and iterator

To illustrate how the definition works, consider the simplified sequence diagram in Fig. 9 which shows only the initial calls for proposal and the replies. Assuming that the set p only contains two participants, the semantics of Fig. 9 equals the semantics of the sequence diagram in Fig. 10.

In the FIPA protocol, the subsets (e.g. **refused** and **proposed** in Fig. 8) are fixed for each single execution of the protocol, but a participant refusing to participate the first time, may very well reply with a proposal to a later call, meaning that the subsets may be different for successive executions of the protocol. This is not captured by definition (1).

Instead, this is handled in the semantics by the notion of partitions. A partition of the set p is an indexed set of subsets $p_1, \ldots, p_n$ such that the union of the subsets equals p, and the subsets are pairwise disjoint. We allow for one or more of the subsets to be empty (e.g. in the case where none of the participants refuses the call). Formally, we let $\mathcal{P}(p, n)$ be the set of all possible partitions of p into n subsets.

The possible subsets of a part with multiplicity greater than one should be declared as a list $\langle p : L \rangle$ in the top-level diagram/fragment for which they are supposed to be fixed, e.g. FIPA-ContractNet $\langle p : [\text{refused}, \text{proposed}] \rangle$ for the example in Fig. 8. The semantics of such a diagram is then given by:

$$d\ \langle p : L \rangle \overset{\text{def}}{=} \underset{x \in \mathcal{P}(p, \#L)}{\textbf{alt}}\ d[x/L] \tag{2}$$

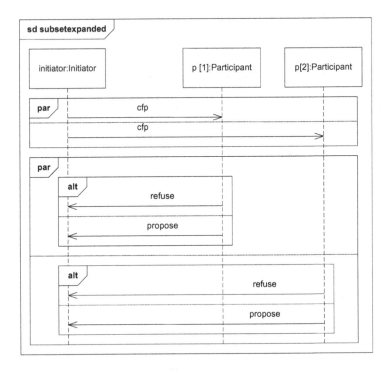

Fig. 10. The expanded sequence diagram

where #L is the number of elements in the list L and d[x/L] is the diagram d with x[1] (the first subset in the partition x) substituted for L[1] (the first element in the list of subsets L), x[2] substituted for L[2] and so on.[1]

In the case of nested subsets, such as in Fig. 6, the partitioning is performed with respect to the lowest level (i.e. `AgentContextMoreSpecial` in Fig. 6), while subsets higher in the hierarchy is given as the union of its corresponding subsets (i.e. `proposed` = `rejected` ∪ `accepted` in Fig. 6).

The fact that we have defined our new constructs as shorthands that may be transformed into standard sequence diagrams means that we have not introduced anything that obstructs the good semantic properties of sequence diagrams such as compositionality. By compositionality we mean that the sequence diagrams can be refined piecewise and we can be certain that the result when putting these pieces back together is a refinement of the original. Using the STAIRS approach [6,7,8] we formalize this by a trace semantics where we can show that sequence diagrams are monotonic with respect to refinement for most of the standard operators such as **alt**, **seq**, **loop**, and **par** [10].

---

[1] In our protocol, only one of the parts has multiplicity greater than one. However, definition (2) may easily be generalized to the case with two or more such parts.

7   Exceptions in the FIPA Protocol

The FIPA protocol describes two exceptions to the interaction protocol flow depicted in Fig. 1. The first of these states that at any point in time, one of the participating agents may inform the initiator that it did not understand what was communicated by sending a `not-understood` message.

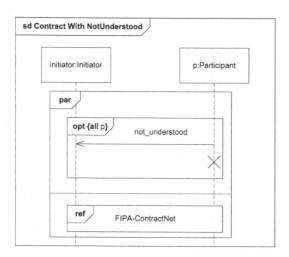

Fig. 11. FIPA protocol with the message `not-understood`

We interpret this to mean that the participants may send the `not-understood` message at *any* point in time, not only as a possible response to a message from the initiator. The sequence diagram for this is shown in Fig. 11. The diagram uses the **opt**-operator which is a shorthand for an **alt** with the empty diagram as its second operand, meaning that the sequence inside the **opt**-construct may or may not happen.

In Fig. 11, the combined "**opt** {**all p**}"-fragment describes that each individual participant has the option of sending the `not-understood` message, but it may also choose not to. The **par**-fragment then states that the optional sending of `not-understood` happens in parallel with (i.e. at any time during) the normal protocol flow from Fig. 8.

The FIPA protocol description in [1] does not provide a detailed description of what the initiator should do when receiving a `not-understood` message, except that it may result in termination of the interaction and that terminating the entire protocol might not be appropriate when there are other participants that may be continuing with their sub-protocols. In Fig. 11, we have described the case where the communication terminates only for those participants sending the `not-understood` message. It is possible to imagine also other possible actions, such as the initiator sending a clarifying message, or a `not-understood` message having cascade effects on other participants. Describing such alternatives poses no difficulties for our approach, but we have not included it here as it is not part of the protocol description in [1].

In Fig. 11, the cross after the **not-understood** message on the participant lifeline is the UML 2 termination symbol, representing the fact that the lifeline no longer takes part in the communication. In this diagram, the termination symbol occurs inside one of the operands of a **par**-fragment. In this case, the sequences of the two operands should be merged as described earlier, but without communication to or from a lifeline that has been terminated earlier in the sequence. This is formally defined in Appendix A.

When the lifeline with the termination symbol represents a part which may have many instances, the nearest enclosing **all**-clause defines what subset the termination applies to. In the case of Fig. 11, this is the "{**all p**}"-clause given in the **opt**-fragment, meaning that the communication terminates only for those participants who have sent **not-understood**, while the rest of the participants continue as before.

The FIPA protocol also describes another exception where the initiator at any time may cancel the protocol. We have interpreted this to mean that the initiator can select any participant to cancel at any time, and that the initiator does not need to cancel the whole negotiation or perform other compensating actions towards other participants. The cancellation is slightly more complicated than the not-understood exception, and the isolated behavior for cancellation between the initiator and one participant is described in the style of the general participant in Fig. 12.

To define this exception applied to the normal FIPA protocol situation, we use the same technique as Fig. 11. The resulting diagram is shown in Fig. 13.

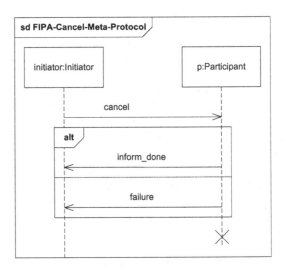

Fig. 12. FIPA Cancel Meta-Protocol

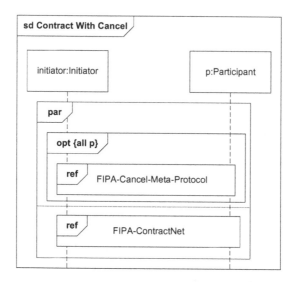

Fig. 13. The whole Cancel situation for all participants

Whenever the targeted participant receives a `cancel` signal, the participant will return either a `failure` or an `inform-done` signal. Then the targeted participant will terminate its protocol. Every participant is handled independently.

As a final example, we describe how the time constraints of UML 2.1 and the exception mechanisms introduced in this section may be used to express the FIPA requirement that the initiator should wait for `refuse/propose` responses only until a given deadline, and that proposals received after the deadline should be rejected automatically.

As a first step, Fig. 14 extends the basic protocol in Fig. 8 with the appropriate time constraints. A formalization of time constraints in the setting of STAIRS may be found in [11]. In Fig. 14, `@t` is a time observation making `t` a reference to the time when the `cfp` message is sent. We assume that the sending of a multicast message has no duration as such. We let `d` be the deadline duration relative to `t`, and the two constraints $\{t..t+d\}$ then describe that the `refuse` and `propose` messages should be received by the initiator some time in the interval between `t` and `t+d`, i.e. no later than `d` time units after the `cfp`. Similarly, the two constraints $\{t+d..\infty\}$ ensure that the initiator waits at least until the given deadline before rejecting and accepting proposals. The FIPA protocol does not state any requirements about how soon the initiator should respond to proposals. It if did give such a requirement we would substitute the infinity by some given time.

Another difference from Fig. 8, is that in Fig. 14, the set `p` is now assumed to be partitioned into the three subsets `refused`, `proposed`, and `notResponded`. The last subset, `notResponded`, consists of those participants for which the initiator has not received any response within the deadline, i.e. there is no communication

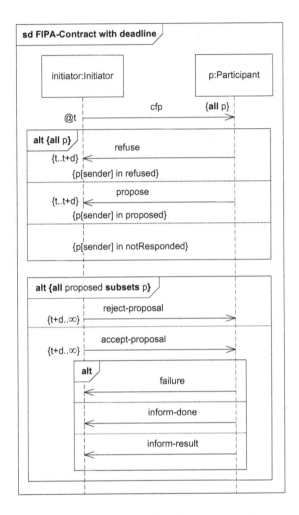

Fig. 14. FIPA protocol with time constraints

back from these participants as described in the third alternative of the first **alt**-construct of Fig. 14.

The isolated behavior for a single response received after the deadline is described for a general participant in Fig. 15. A late **refuse** message needs no further treatment by the initiator, while a **propose** message received after the deadline should result in the initiator rejecting the proposal.

Finally, Fig. 16 combines the handling of late responses from Fig. 15 with the normal protocol execution from Fig. 14. Fig. 16 follows the same pattern as that of Fig. 13, with the difference that in this case, the exceptional behavior (i.e. late responses) may occur for participants with no previous response, i.e. from participants in the set **notResponded**.

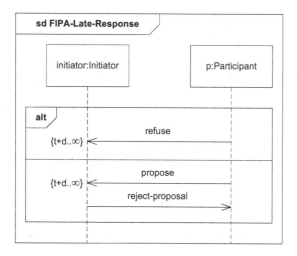

Fig. 15. Late responses

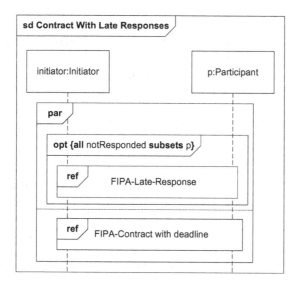

Fig. 16. FIPA protocol with time constraints and the handling of late responses

8 Related Work

In the literature on defining communication in multi-agent systems, most of the focus has been on being able to analyze the specification rather than on the precision of the original description itself. Since few tools have been made to handle FIPA ACL [1] or the AUML [3,5], the ambiguity of the notations has not been much considered.

El Fallah-Seghrouchni et al. [12] use colored petri nets to model multi-agent systems, but they do not claim that the colored petri nets notation can serve the same purpose as the sequence diagrams of AUML. In [13], Ayed and Siala show how Event B can be used to define the semantics of AUML. Their translation between AUML and Event B is expressed in structured text and it is not clear if the translation is defined formally in a tool. Most probably they perform the translation manually and take the decisions on ambiguity implicitly. Again their concern is more the analysis possibilities than the expressiveness of the original language.

Other contributions, such as [14] and [15], give some overview of languages and methods. In [14], Walton distinguishes between agent communication language and protocol language. For the latter Walton shows examples of Lightweight Coordination Calculus (LCC). The LCC appears as a way to define the complete semantics for the agent system and Walton claims that FIPA ACL can be coded in LCC. In fact this would mean that also the FIPA ACL can be seen as a partial protocol language.

Poslad [15] compares briefly a number of different standards for specifying multi-agent systems interaction and claims that the semantics of the FIPA interaction process models is weak and based on the Agent UML graphs. This corresponds well with our criticism of the suggested language constructs as their main problem is that they may be ambiguously interpreted. Our main goal has been to clarify the notation and corresponding semantics.

Our definition of multicast is not the first attempt to define multicasting in the area of sequence diagrams. Helouet made a definition in [16] which was combined with the ITU version Z.120 where he defined multicast groups that in some way resemble our subsets. Another definition was given by Gherbi and Khendek [17] using OCL for defining the transformations. Event Studio (http://eventhelix.com/) claims to have included a multicast feature in their sequence diagram tool.

In [18], Whittle extended UML 2 sequence diagrams with an all-operator for sending messages to and from a lifeline with multiple instances. He also defined an exist-operator, for describing that the operand applies to at least one of the instances. However, subsets, which are important in our specification of the FIPA protocol, is not captured in [18], neither is the ability to define that the different instances may send/receive alternative messages (i.e. our combined "**alt all**"-fragments).

9   Conclusions

We have shown how UML 2 can be used to express the FIPA Contract Net Interaction Protocol. We have gone through a series of approaches with varying capabilities with regards to precisions, completeness, and compactness. Finally we suggested two improvements to the sequence diagram notation to define multicast messages and combined-fragment iterators over subsets. We have also shown how these construct may be used to describe precisely the exceptional behavior of the FIPA protocol.

The clue to these new constructs is to apply the already existing UML construct of subsets of properties. The new constructs are defined as shorthands that may be transformed into standard sequence diagrams. This preserves the positive characteristics of sequence diagrams such as compositionality. Furthermore we believe that it preserves the intents of the FIPA protocol designers and that it is more accurate than the earlier proposals to use multiplicities.

Acknowledgements. We thank the participants at ATOP 2008 for useful comments on a previous version of this paper. The work presented here has partly been developed within the MoSiS project ITEA2-ip06035. MoSiS is a project within the ITEA 2 - Eureka framework [19].

References

1. Foundation for Intelligent Pysical Agents: FIPA Contract Net Interaction Protocol Specification (2002)
2. OMG: Unified Modeling Language 2.1 (2006)
3. Odell, J., Parunak, H.V.D., Bauer, B.: Extending UML for agents. In: AOIS Workshop at AAAI 2000 (2000)
4. Huget, M.P.: Extending agent UML sequence diagrams. In: Giunchiglia, F., Odell, J.J., Weiss, G. (eds.) AOSE 2002. LNCS, vol. 2585, pp. 150–161. Springer, Heidelberg (2003)
5. Bauer, B., Odell, J.: UML 2.0 and agents: how to build agent-based systems with the new UML standard. Journal of Engineering Applications of Artificaial Intelligence 18, 141–157 (2005)
6. Haugen, Ø., Stølen, K.: STAIRS — Steps to analyze interactions with refinement semantics. In: Stevens, P., Whittle, J., Booch, G. (eds.) UML 2003. LNCS, vol. 2863, pp. 388–402. Springer, Heidelberg (2003)
7. Haugen, Ø., Husa, K.E., Runde, R.K., Stølen, K.: STAIRS towards formal design with sequence diagrams. Journal of Software and Systems Modeling 4, 349–458 (2005)
8. Runde, R.K., Haugen, Ø., Stølen, K.: The pragmatics of STAIRS. In: de Boer, F.S., Bonsangue, M.M., Graf, S., de Roever, W.-P. (eds.) FMCO 2005. LNCS, vol. 4111, pp. 88–114. Springer, Heidelberg (2006)
9. Haugen, Ø., Møller-Pedersen, B.: Configurations by UML. In: Gruhn, V., Oquendo, F. (eds.) EWSA 2006. LNCS, vol. 4344, pp. 98–112. Springer, Heidelberg (2006)
10. Runde, R.K.: STAIRS — Understanding and Developing Specifications Expressed as UML Interaction Diagrams. Ph.D thesis, University of Oslo (2007)
11. Haugen, Ø., Husa, K.E., Runde, R.K., Stølen, K.: Why timed sequence diagrams require three-event semantics. In: Leue, S., Systä, T.J. (eds.) Scenarios: Models, Transformations and Tools. LNCS, vol. 3466, pp. 1–25. Springer, Heidelberg (2005)
12. Fallah-Seghrouchni, A.E., Haddad, S., Mazouzi, H.: A formal study of interactions in multi-agent systems. I. J. Comput. Appl. 8 (2001)
13. Ayed, L.J.B., Siala, F.: Specification and verification of multi-agent systems interaction protocols using a combination of AUML and event B. In: Graham, T.C.N., Palanque, P. (eds.) DSV-IS 2008. LNCS, vol. 5136, pp. 102–107. Springer, Heidelberg (2008)
14. Walton, C.: Agency and the Semantic Web. Oxford University Press, Oxford (2006)

15. Poslad, S.: Specifying protocols for multi-agent systems interaction. TAAS 2 (2007)
16. Hélouët, L.: Distributed system requirement modeling with message sequence charts: the case of the RMTP2 protocol. Information & Software Technology 45, 701–714 (2003)
17. Gherbi, A., Khendek, F.: Distributed real-time behavioral requirements modeling using extended UML/SPT. In: Gotzhein, R., Reed, R. (eds.) SAM 2006. LNCS, vol. 4320, pp. 34–48. Springer, Heidelberg (2006)
18. Whittle, J.: Precise specification of use case scenarios. In: Dwyer, M.B., Lopes, A. (eds.) FASE 2007. LNCS, vol. 4422, pp. 170–184. Springer, Heidelberg (2007)
19. Dahle, H.P.: Model-driven development offers high level approach (2007), http://www.itea2.org/public/project_leaflets/MOSIS_profile_oct-07.pdf
20. Broy, M., Stølen, K.: Specification and Development of Interactive Systems: Focus on Streams, Interfaces, and Refinement. Springer, Heidelberg (2001)

A   Formal Definitions

In STAIRS [6,7,8], the sequences described by a sequence diagram is formally defined using traces of events (e.g. the sending or receiving of a message). For the example diagrams given in the paper, all of the traces will be finite. However, in general, traces may also be infinite. In this appendix, we extend the definition of parallel composition to apply also to traces which may contain the termination symbol.

The parallel composition (i.e. merge) of two traces h_1 and h_2 is defined in [7] by:

$$h_1 \parallel h_2 \stackrel{\text{def}}{=} \{h \in \mathcal{H} \mid \exists p \in \{1,2\}^\infty : \tag{3}$$
$$\pi_2((\{1\} \times \mathcal{E}) \textcircled{T} (p,h)) = h_1 \wedge$$
$$\pi_2((\{2\} \times \mathcal{E}) \textcircled{T} (p,h)) = h_2\}$$

This definition makes use of an oracle, the infinite sequence p, to resolve the order in which the events from the two traces h_1 and h_2 are merged. $\mathcal{E}$ is the set of all events, while $\mathcal{H}$ is the set of all well-formed traces (where the sending of a message occurs before the corresponding reception). π_2 is a projection operator returning the second element of a pair, while $\textcircled{T}$ is a filtering function filtering pairs of traces with respect to pairs of elements such that for instance

$$\{(1, e_1), (1, e_2)\} \textcircled{T} (\langle 1,1,2,1,2 \rangle, \langle e_1, e_1, e_1, e_2, e_2 \rangle)$$
$$= (\langle 1,1,1 \rangle, \langle e_1, e_1, e_2 \rangle)$$

For a formal definition of $\textcircled{T}$, see [20].

We now extend definition (3) to also take the termination symbol into account. The termination symbol itself is represented in the trace as the special event X_l, where l is the name of the terminated lifeline.

The parallel composition of two traces h_1 and h_2 which may contain one or more termination symbols, may be calculated by first using definition (3) and then removing all events involving a lifeline terminated earlier in the trace.

Formally, we first define the function $remove(l, h)$ which removes all events involving the lifeline l from the trace h:

$$remove(l, h) \stackrel{def}{=} \begin{cases} \varepsilon & \text{if } h = \varepsilon \\ remove(l, h') & \text{if } h = \langle e \rangle \frown h' \wedge (tr.e = l \vee re.e = l) \\ \langle e \rangle \frown remove(l, h') & \text{if } h = \langle e \rangle \frown h' \wedge tr.e \neq l \wedge re.e \neq l \end{cases} \quad (4)$$

where ε denotes the empty trace, $\frown$ is concatenation of two traces and $tr.e$ and $re.e$ is the transmitter (i.e. sender) and receiver of the event e, respectively.

We also define the function $filter(h)$ which takes a trace and uses $remove$ to return the trace where all events on a lifeline who has been terminated earlier in the trace are removed:

$$filter(h) \stackrel{def}{=} \begin{cases} \langle e \rangle \frown filter(remove(l, h')) & \text{if } h = \langle e \rangle \frown h' \wedge e = X_l \\ \langle e \rangle \frown filter(h') & \text{if } h = \langle e \rangle \frown h' \wedge e \neq X_l \end{cases} \quad (5)$$

Finally, parallel composition of traces which may contain the termination symbol is defined by:

$$h_1 \parallel' h_2 \stackrel{def}{=} \{ h \in \mathcal{H} \mid \exists h' \in h_1 \parallel h_2 : h = filter(h') \} \quad (6)$$

Modeling Interaction Protocols as Modular and Reusable 1st Class Objects

Esteban León-Soto

German Research Center for Artificial Intelligence, DFKI GmbH
Multi-agents and Simulated Reality Department,
Campus. D3.2, 66123 Saarbrücken, Germany
esteban.leon@dfki.de

Abstract. Interoperability involves solutions at different levels, from concrete data representation to coordination of actions. These solutions are even more difficult to handle when the systems being integrated expect to remain autonomous. This is frequently the case in business processes between different organizations. In order to work together several technical and organizational issues have to be solved. One of the most important aspects is coordination and efficient communication. Interaction protocols have been introduced as conversation contracts between participants in order to solve this. Interaction protocols are very difficult to develop and maintain. The present work provides a consolidating model that enables modularity for interaction protocols design and reuse of solutions by composing them to fit the different scenarios.

Keywords: Interaction Protocols, Interoperability, Service Contracts, Business Process Modeling, Modularity.

1 Introduction

Interoperability requires that organizations that desire to cooperate in a distributed process solve problems at different levels. Among concrete problems like data grounding is the issue of participants coordination in order to achieve a goal. This is the objective for interaction protocols. Experience has shown[1] that during the development process, these protocols can become very complex and difficult to manage. The present work is focused on this concrete problem: how to specify interaction protocols from a global perspective in a way that is easy and practical to recombine and reuse them.

In this document, a model for representing interaction protocols will be presented. This model is based on several proposals and contributions of the multi-agent community. One of the intentions is to consolidate these concepts in a single model and at the same time enable a mechanism for modularity and composition of protocols. Interaction protocols are seen as a finite state machine (FSM), where states are the different situations a conversation can have and the transitions are the different actions that the participants can perform. For each possible state a set of possible actions will be specified, which are the possible

K. Fischer et al. (Eds.): ATOP 2005 and ATOP 2008, LNBIP 25, pp. 174–196, 2009.

actions in the specific situation that connect the state of the conversation to the resulting state if the action is performed.

These protocols are intended to be used in complex scenarios, like business processes, as contracts, stipulating how the participants are expected to behave, similar to rules in a game, in order to be interoperable. To make conversations more predictable and consequently easier to handle, interaction protocols are introduced. In principle, these narrow down the variability of a conversation to only those sequences of messages that work towards achieving the goal of the conversation. For that reason, conversation protocols are a very important component in interoperability, in which a simple way of coordinating participants to achieve a certain objective is desired. A conversation protocol is vital, in order to keep complexity demanded from the participants' behaviors low.

Reuse demands to have different levels of abstraction, in order to use solutions in different kinds of concrete cases. The present work will provide a model that can be used at all levels of abstraction, and treats protocols as first-class objects, which represent concepts from the global point of view and can be used by designers, but also by sophisticated software agents, in case they are being used, to reason about protocols.

First, in Section 2 a model of the state-action space will be defined, followed by Section 3 which will discuss some specific aspects of propositions in this model. Based on that, in Section 4 the model of conversation protocols is defined. Section 5 specifies how composition of protocols is to be done. Finally the present work is discussed in Section 6 and concludes in Section 7.

2   Definition of an State-Action Space Model

2.1   Model of State Space and State Descriptions

A model of the state space of a conversation will be defined. Since these states tend to be rather large and repetitive, a practical mechanism to refer to a group of states that share properties in common will also be introduced.

Definition 1. *Propositions Set P: The finite set of all different atomic propositions used to describe states in a conversation:*

$$P = \{p_1, p_2, p_3, \ldots, p_n\}$$

with the property

$$the p_i \in P \wedge p_j \in P \wedge i \neq j \Rightarrow p_i \neq p_j \tag{1}$$

It is important to remark, that all propositions are completely distinct from each other. There are no two propositions in the set P about the same fact.

Definition 2. *State σ: a specific truth value assignation to each proposition that is part of a Conversation description (to all $p_i \in P$). The set of all States is Σ. A state σ is a set of elements of the relation T:*

$$T = P \rightarrow \{true, false\}$$

a state σ is defined as:

$$\sigma = \{\langle p_i, t\rangle | \langle p_i, t\rangle \in T, i = 1, 2, \ldots, n\} \tag{2}$$

where:
All propositions have a truth value assigned in each state

$$\forall p_i \in P, \exists \langle p_i, t\rangle \in \sigma, \ \forall \sigma \in \Sigma \tag{3}$$

A state cannot have a proposition associated with a truth value and at the same time the same proposition with the opposite truth value.

$$\langle p_i, t\rangle \in \sigma \Rightarrow \langle p_i, \neg t\rangle \notin \sigma, \ \forall \sigma \in \Sigma \tag{4}$$

Two states $\sigma \in \Sigma$ are equal if for each of propositions $p_i \in P$ they have the exact same truth value assigned:

$$\sigma_1 = \sigma_2 \Leftrightarrow \forall \langle p_i, t_i\rangle \in \sigma_1 \land \forall \langle p_i, t_i'\rangle \in \sigma_2 : t_i = t_i' \tag{5}$$

A state is for instance:

$$\sigma_1 = \{\langle p_1, true\rangle, \langle p_2, false\rangle, \ldots, \langle p_n, false\rangle\}$$

Since different states having differences irrelevant in the context may have the same meaning or properties from a certain perspective, a way for referring to such groups of states will be defined.

Definition 3. *A state description s is an association of a set of truth value assignations to some or all propositions of P, that serve as constraints, and a set of all states that fulfill these constraints. The set of all state descriptions is called S^1.*

$$S : \mathcal{P}(T) \rightarrow \mathcal{P}(\Sigma) \tag{6}$$

elements $s \in S$ are defined as:

$$s(\langle p_a, t_a\rangle, \ldots, \langle p_b, t_b\rangle) = \tag{7}$$
$$\{\sigma \in \Sigma | \langle p_a, t_a\rangle \in \sigma, \ldots, \langle p_b, t_b\rangle \in \sigma\}$$

for some arbitrary propositions p_x in $[p_a, \ldots, p_b]$ where:

$$a \geq 1 \land b \leq |P|$$

$$p_x \in P$$

$$t_x \in \{true, false\}$$

In this case it is important again to remark that state descriptions cannot have contradicting arguments, such state descriptions are empty:

---

[1] $\mathcal{P}(X)$ is the power set of set X.

Lemma 1. *All state descriptions with contradicting proposition truth value assignations are empty:*

$$s(\ldots, \langle p_p, t_p \rangle, \ldots, \langle p_p, \neg t_p \rangle, \ldots) = \emptyset \qquad (8)$$

Proof 1. *From (4) we know, there are no states with two contradicting propositions.*   □

From now on, for brevity, when there is no chance for confusion, mentioning a proposition will be synonym to assigning true to that proposition. At the same time, if the proposition is mentioned prefixed with the $\neg$ *negation* operator, the value assigned to the proposition is false:

$$\begin{aligned} p_i &= \langle p_i, true \rangle \\ \neg p_i &= \langle p_i, false \rangle \end{aligned} \qquad (9)$$

For example, the state

$$\sigma_1 = \{ \langle p_1, true \rangle, \langle p_2, false \rangle, \langle p_3, true \rangle, \ldots, \langle p_7, false \rangle, \ldots \}$$

can be written as:

$$\sigma_1 = \{ p_1, \neg p_2, p_3, \ldots, \neg p_7, \ldots \}$$

Also, for instance, *state description* $s(p_1, \neg p_2, \neg p_7)$ can contain, among others, the following states:

- $\sigma_1 = \{ p_1, \neg p_2, p_3, \ldots, \neg p_7, \ldots \}$
- $\sigma_2 = \{ p_1, \neg p_2, \neg p_3, \ldots, \neg p_7, \ldots \}$
- $\sigma_3 = \{ p_1, \neg p_2, \ldots, \neg p_7, \ldots, p_9, \ldots \}$
- $\sigma_4 = \{ p_1, \neg p_2, \ldots, \neg p_7, \ldots, \neg p_9, \ldots \}$

But it cannot contain for instance the following states:

- $\sigma_5 = \{ p_1, p_2, p_3, \ldots, \neg p_7, \ldots \}$
- $\sigma_6 = \{ \neg p_1, \neg p_2, p_3, \ldots, \neg p_7, \ldots \}$
- $\sigma_7 = \{ \neg p_1, p_2, \ldots, \neg p_7, \ldots, p_9, \ldots \}$
- $\sigma_8 = \{ p_1, \neg p_2, \ldots, p_7, \ldots, \neg p_9, \ldots \}$

2.2   Model of Actions in a State Space

In a finite state machine (FSM) and similar transition systems, the evolution of a system during run-time is modeled as transition over different states of the state space. The change of one state to another is performed by actions. For each state in the state space there are only some possible actions. Based on the model of state space previously defined, a model of actions using the state descriptions will be defined:

Definition 4. *A micro-operation m on a state is an association of a state σ, an operator of the set* $\{+, -\}$, *a proposition p and a resulting state as follows:*

$$\Omega : \Sigma \times \{+, -\} \times P \times \Sigma$$

The set of all micro-operations M is:

$$M = \{\langle \sigma, \omega, p_o, \sigma' \rangle \in \Omega |$$
$$\forall \langle p_i, t_i \rangle \in (\sigma \setminus \langle p_o, t_o \rangle) : \exists \langle p_i, t_i' \rangle \in \sigma' : t_i = t_i' \wedge \qquad (10)$$
$$\langle p_o, t_o \rangle \in \sigma'\}$$

where

$$t_o = \begin{cases} true & if \ \omega = + \\ false & if \ \omega = - \end{cases}$$

For a micro-operation $m = \langle \sigma, \omega, p, \sigma' \rangle$ the first operand σ is referred to as the starting state and σ' the target state. The target state is identical to the starting state with the exception of the element with the proposition p_o, which has a value dictated by the operand ω.

A micro-operation is the representation of the concept of bringing about a fact, making a proposition true, or removing the proposition, making it false. It can be possible that σ has already the proposition p in true, in such a case applying the operation will not produce any change and σ' would be exactly like σ.

Using the definition of a state description, an operation is defined as a set of micro-operations over the set of states defined by the state description:

Definition 5. *An operation o is an association of a state description s, a member of* $\{+, -\}$, *a proposition p and a set of micro-operations M' that have initial states belonging to the state description s:*
The set of all operations is called O.

$$O : S \times \{+, -\} \times P \to M' \subseteq M$$

$$o_{s, \pm p} = \{\langle \sigma, \pm, p, \sigma' \rangle \in M' | \sigma \in s\} \qquad (11)$$

where
$\pm$: is a place holder for a member of the set $\{+, -\}$.
Moreover, the specific state σ' targeted by the operation o, if a specific initial state σ is provided, is obtained by getting the micro-operation m member of o that has as starting state σ:

$$o_{s, \pm p}(\sigma) = \sigma' \qquad (12)$$

where

$$\langle \sigma, \pm, p, \sigma' \rangle \in o_{s, \pm p}$$

This allows to specify a single operation that applies to several states and with the operation $o_{s, \pm p}(\sigma)$ it is possible to know specific cases.

Operations applying to different propositions can be composed in a single one.

Definition 6. *A composed operation c_s is a set of different operations which all refer to the same state description s and to different propositions:*

$$c_s \subseteq O$$

where

$$o_{s\pm p} \in c_s \Rightarrow \nexists o_{s\pm p'} \in c_s : p = p' \tag{13}$$

$$i = 1, \ldots, |c_s|$$

Similarly to simple operations, the specific state targeted by the composed operation can be found using following definition:

$$c_s(\sigma) = \{\langle p_i, t'_i \rangle | \; (o_{sw_i p_i} \in c_s \Rightarrow \langle p_i, t'_i \rangle = w_i p_i) \quad \vee \\ (o_{sw_i p_i} \notin c_s \Rightarrow \langle p_i, t'_i \rangle = \langle p_i, t_i \rangle) \quad \} \tag{14}$$

where

$$\langle p_i, t_i \rangle \in \sigma$$

$$w_i \in \{+, -\}$$

$$i = 1, \ldots, |c_s|$$

$$w_i p_i = \begin{cases} \langle p_i, true \rangle \; if \; w_i = + \\ \langle p_i, false \rangle \; if \; w_i = - \end{cases}$$

The resulting state of applying the composed operation is a state which has all its corresponding propositions unchanged, except those for which an operation could be found in the composed operation, in which case, the value specified by the operation will be used.

Since all operations in a composed operation refer to the same starting state description, an abbreviated form of writing an action is:

$$c_s = \{o_{1 \; s,\pm p_1}, o_{2 \; s,\pm p_2}, o_{3 \; s,\pm p_3}, \ldots, o_{m \; s,\pm p_m}\} = \\ \{\pm p_1, \pm p_2, \pm p_3, \ldots, \pm p_m\} \tag{15}$$

For instance, the composed operation $c_{s_1} = \{+p_1, -p_3\}$ for any state in $s_1 = s(\neg p_2, p_4)$: performing it will change the current state of the system to another identical one with exception of p_1 which will be definitely true and p_3 which will be definitely false after the applying the composed operation.

$$\sigma_1 = \{p_1, \neg p_2, p_3 \, p_4\} \in s(\neg p_2, p_4)$$

$$c_{s_1}(\sigma_1) = \{p_1, \neg p_2, \neg p_3, p_4\}$$

also:

$$\sigma_2 = \{\neg p_1, \neg p_2, p_3 \, p_4\} \in s(\neg p_2, p_4)$$

$$c_{s1}(\sigma_2) = \{p_1, \neg p_2, \neg p_3, p_4\}$$

In the specific state σ_1 applying the operation c_{s1} will produce the state $\{p_1, \neg p_2, \neg p_3 \ p_4\}$ since all propositions not mentioned in c_{s1} (p_2 and p_4) remain the same, p_1 also remains as previously, since it was already true an the operation specifies $+p_1$, the opposite case happens with σ_2, where p_1 was negative and turns positive. p_3 is the only one changing in both, since in σ_1 and σ_2 it was true and the operation says $-p_3$, therefore it will be set to false. In other words, in σ_1 the composed operation c_{s1} brings about only p_3, since p_1 is already valid and in σ_2 the composed operation c_{s1} brings about both, p_1 and p_3.

Definition 7. *The state description that describes all states targeted by the composed operation c_s can be found using the function $S(c_s)$:*

$$S(c_s) = s(\langle p, t \rangle |\ (+p \in c_s \wedge t = true) \vee (-p \in c_s \wedge t = false) \vee \\ (\pm p \notin c_s \wedge \langle p, t \rangle \in s)) \tag{16}$$

The targeted state description s' can be calculated by setting all the propositions as specified in c_s and keeping all other propositions not mentioned in c_s as they were in s. Note that in this situation being $\pm p \notin c_s$ part of a conjunction, it is also interpreted as a conjunctional abbreviation meaning that neither of both cases of $\pm p$ are elements of c_s.

Lemma 2. *All calculated states from the state s using the composed operation c_s are in the state description calculated by the function $S(c_s)$:*

$$c_s(\sigma) \in S(c_s) \ \forall \sigma \in s \tag{17}$$

Proof 2. *That all states obtained by applying c_s on a state in s are part of the state description $S(c_s)$ can be proved by contradiction:*

$$\exists \sigma \in s : \quad c_s(\sigma) \notin S(c_s)$$
$$\Leftrightarrow \exists \langle p, t \rangle \in c_s(\sigma) : \neg \big((+p \in c_s \wedge t = true) \ \vee \\ (-p \in c_s \wedge t = false) \vee \\ (\pm p \notin c_s \wedge \langle p, t \rangle \in s) \ \big)$$
$$\Leftrightarrow \exists \langle p, t \rangle \in c_s(\sigma) : \ \neg (+p \in c_s \wedge t = true) \ \wedge \\ \neg (-p \in c_s \wedge t = false) \wedge \\ \neg (\pm p \notin c_s \wedge \langle p, t \rangle \in s)$$

$+p$ and $-p$ can be rewritten as o_{swp} using (15) summarizing the first two operands of the conjunction to one that expresses both cases at the same time with the same format as done in (14):

$$\Leftrightarrow \exists \langle p, t \rangle \in c_s(\sigma) : \neg (o_{s,w,p} \in c_s \wedge \langle p, t \rangle = wp) \ \wedge \\ \neg (\pm p \notin c_s \wedge \langle p, t \rangle \in s)$$

which is clearly the contradiction of Definition 6 for targeted states $c_s(\sigma)$ of a composed operation(14). □

In order to model the application of a sequence of composed operations, the following operator over composed operations will be defined:

Definition 8. *The binary operator "chain" represented by "$\rightarrow$" is defined as the association of 2 composed operations ($c1_s$, $c2_{s'}$) and a third resulting one ($c3_s$) such that:*

- *All states resulting of the application of the first composed operation are part of the state description s' of the second composed operation*
- *The third (resulting) composed operation $c3_s$ is the set of operations of the first composed operation overridden by the operations of the second composed operation: all operations of the second set of operations $c2_{s'}$ are part of the result together with all those of the first set $c1_s$ that refer to propositions not mentioned in $c2_{s'}$*

$$
\begin{aligned}
c1_s \rightarrow c2_{s'} = c3_s \quad & s.t: \\
S(c1_s) &= s' \\
c3_s = \{o_{sw_ip_i} \in c1_s | o_{s'w_jp_i} &\notin c2_{s'}\} \bigcup c2_{s'} \\
where \\
\omega_x \in \{+, -\}, \; x &= 1, \dots
\end{aligned}
\tag{18}
$$

Lemma 3. *The specific state targeted by a chain operation is the same as the state targeted by the second operand of the state targeted by the first operand of the chain operation:*

$$(c1_s \rightarrow c2_{s'})(\sigma) = c2_{s'}(c1_s(\sigma)) \tag{19}$$

Proof 3. *By applying recursively (14) we obtain:*

$$c2_{s'}(c1_s(\sigma)) = \sigma'' :$$

$$
\forall \langle p_i, t_i'' \rangle \in \sigma'' :
\begin{cases}
o_{s'\omega_i'p_i} \in c2_{s'} \Rightarrow \langle p_i, t_i'' \rangle = \omega_i'p_i \\
o_{s'\omega_i'p_i} \notin c2_{s'} \Rightarrow
\begin{cases}
o_{sw_ip_i} \in c1_s \Rightarrow \langle p_i, t_i'' \rangle = \omega_ip_i \\
o_{sw_ip_i} \notin c1_s \Rightarrow \langle p_i, t_i'' \rangle = \langle p_i, t_i \rangle
\end{cases}
\end{cases}
$$

which can be rewritten as:

$$
\forall \langle p_i, t_i'' \rangle \in \sigma'' :
\begin{cases}
o_{s'\omega_i'p_i} \in c2_{s'} \Rightarrow \langle p_i, t_i'' \rangle = \omega_i'p_i \\
o_{s'\omega_i'p_i} \notin c2_{s'} \wedge \\
\quad o_{sw_ip_i} \in c1_s \Rightarrow \langle p_i, t_i'' \rangle = \omega_ip_i \\
o_{s'\omega_i'p_i} \notin c2_{s'} \wedge \\
\quad o_{sw_ip_i} \notin c1_s \Rightarrow \langle p_i, t_i'' \rangle = \langle p_i, t_i \rangle
\end{cases}
$$

which can be rewritten as:

$$
\forall \langle p_i, t_i'' \rangle \in \sigma'' :
\begin{cases}
o_{xw_i''p_i} \in Q \Rightarrow \langle p_i, t_i'' \rangle = \omega_i''p_i \\
o_{xw_i''p_i} \notin Q \Rightarrow \langle p_i, t_i'' \rangle = \langle p_i, t_i \rangle
\end{cases}
$$

where

$$x \in \{s, s'\}$$

$$Q = c2_{s'} \bigcup \{o_{sw_ip_i} | o_{s'\omega_i'p_i} \notin c2_{s'} \wedge o_{swp_i} \in c1_s\}$$

$$w_i'' = \begin{cases} w_i' \ if \ o_{sw_i'p_i} \in Q \\ w_i \ if \ o_{sw_i p_i} \in Q \end{cases}$$

which can be rewritten as:

$$\forall \langle p_i, t_i'' \rangle \in \sigma'' : \begin{cases} o_{xw_i''p_i} \in Q \Rightarrow \langle p_i, t_i'' \rangle = w_i''p_i \\ o_{x,w_i''p_i} \notin Q \Rightarrow \langle p_i, t_i'' \rangle = \langle p_i, t_i \rangle \end{cases}$$

where

$$Q = c2_{s'} \bigcup \{o_{sw_i p_i} \in cl_s | o_{s'w_i'p_i} \notin c2_{s'}\}$$

using (18) it is clear that $Q = cl_s \to c2_{s'}$:

$$\forall \langle p_i, t_i'' \rangle \in \sigma'' : \begin{cases} o_{xw_i''p_i} \in cl_s \to c2_{s'} \Rightarrow \langle p_i, t_i'' \rangle = w_i''p_i \vee \\ o_{xw_i''p_i} \notin cl_s \to c2_{s'} \Rightarrow \langle p_i, t_i'' \rangle = \langle p_i, t_i \rangle \end{cases}$$

which is the definition for states that are target of $(c_{1s} \to c_{2s'})(\sigma)$ *by using (14).*
□

Using operations a definition of an *action* is proposed based on three important aspects of an action:

- In which states it applies
- Its label
- The operations (+ or -) it applies on different propositions

Definition 9. *Action Descriptions are a mapping of a state description, a label and a set of operations over some propositions to a set of possible states. Action descriptions must follow a principle of effectiveness, therefore the set of targeted states cannot be the same as the starting state description. The set of all actions is called A:*

$$\Delta : S \times V \times C \times S$$

$$A = \{\langle s, v, c, s' \rangle \in \Delta | s \neq s'\} \tag{20}$$

Moreover, the specific state targeted by an action starting from a specific state σ *is obtained by using the corresponding* $c(\sigma)$ *operator :*

$$a_{s,c}(\sigma) = c_s(\sigma) \tag{21}$$

2.3   State-Action Model Extension to Include Roles

A conversation involves always at least two participants. In an abstract description of a conversation like the one proposed here, these participants are represented as *roles* (r) members of a set called $r \in R$. With the intention of modeling conversations using the state-action model, the concept of roles is integrated in this section.

Every action in our model is always performed by a role and is targeted at another role. In the present model, actions represented as operations over propositions mean that an agent is performing an action of communicating information to another agent, in other words, sending a message. Therefore the definition of action will be enhanced with the sender and receiver roles of the actions:

Definition 10. *A speech act a_r is an association of a role, an action as defined in Definition 9 and a different second role, they are all members of the set A_R:*

$$A_R : R \times A \times R \tag{22}$$

where

$$a_i = \langle r_{xi}, \langle s_i, l_i, c_i \rangle, r_{yi} \rangle$$

$$\forall a_i \in A_R : r_{xi} \neq r_{yi}$$

For instance, the speech act

$$a_r = \langle r_1, \langle s(p_1), "respond", \{-p_1\} \rangle, r_2 \rangle$$

represents the action labeled as "respond" that can be sent by role r_1 when p_1 is true to the role r_2 and defined as removing the fact p_1.

For simplicity, the term action will be used from here on for both concepts, action description as in Definition 9 and speech act as in Definition 10, whenever there is no chance for confusion.

3   Special Kinds of Propositions

Even though the present model is intended to be of general domain, some particular kinds of propositions are frequently needed when modeling interaction protocols. In the present model three of them will be defined, timeouts, commitments and operational propositions.

3.1   Timeouts

Protocols are mechanisms to rule actions over time. Sequencing and turn taking are problems that are solved with the present model, but there are certain cases where concrete time-windows are to be specified. For this purpose timeouts will be defined.

Definition 11. *A Timeout $T(t_p, a) \in T$, where $a \in A_R$, $T \subseteq P$, is a proposition member of the set of timeout propositions T that states that the action a will be performed after a certain period of time t_p that starts to count after the action that brings about the timeout is performed. Action a in a timeout is not necessarily performed by the sending role mentioned in a, but instead it can be an assumption the receiver of a can make. Also, this action will always have implicitly the operation $-T(t_p, a)$ declared, hence, timeouts are removed automatically after a is performed.*

For instance, the action a says, that after performing call for proposals, M will send the message "*done*" after a period of size t_d, after which *proposition requested (p_r)* will not longer hold:

$$a = \langle M, \langle s, cfp, \{+p\_r, +T(t_d, \langle M, \langle \{p\_r\}, done, \{-p\_r\} \rangle, B \rangle) \} \rangle, B \rangle\},$$

3.2   Commitments

Singh [2] and his group have proposed an algebra for commitments [3] which provides the advantage of allowing better modularity in the design of processes [4]. Taking advantage of the similarities of this algebra and the proposed operations in the previous section, the concept of commitment will be integrated to the state-action model.

Definition 12. *Commitment* $C(a_d, a_c, p, c, t) \in P$ *is defined as the commitment of the debtor agent* a_d *to the creditor agent* a_c *to bring about the proposition* $p \in P$ *under the condition that the proposition* $c \in P$ *becomes true. After the condition c becomes true, agent* a_d *is expected by agent* a_c *to perform some action that produces p to be true. This action is to be performed before timeout t that represents the time limit is enabled. This timeout starts to count as soon as the condition is brought about.*

Definition 13. *Unconditional Commitment* $C(a_c, a_d, p, t)$: *As an abbreviation the following notation will be taken:*

$$C(a_d, a_d, p, true, t) \; = \; C(a_c, a_d, p, t) \tag{23}$$

Meaning simply that agent a_c *expects* a_d *to bring about the proposition p within the time period specified in t.*

Timeouts t in commitments are not restricted to any specific purpose, but the main intention to include them in the definition of commitments is to provide the semantics of what will happen if the commitment is not satisfied.

It is important to note that the commitments are part of the set of propositions P, they are part of the propositions that can also be used for specifying state descriptions and actions. They are also operands for the defined operators + and -. The detailed semantics of these two operators specifically on commitments will be defined next:

Definition 14. *Commitment creation:* $+C(a_c, a_d, p, c, t)$. *Creating a commitment means that after the creation of it, agent* a_d *is committed to agent* a_c *to bring about p under the condition c. An action specifying this operation states that after the action is performed, the specified commitment starts to exist.*

Definition 15. *Commitment canceling:* $-C(a_c, a_d, p, c, t)$. *If the commitment exists, performing the operation - on it cancels it, makes it a false proposition, meaning that it does not longer exist,* a_d *is no longer expected by* a_c *to bring about p. An action specifying this operation states that after the action, the specified commitment, including its timeout, does not exist anymore.*

Definition 16. *Bringing about the condition c enables the commitment. If the condition is true, the commitment is transformed to an unconditional commitment: the conditional commitment is canceled and the unconditional commitment is created enabling the timeout countdown:*

$$\frac{c \wedge C(a_d, a_d, p, c, t)}{c \wedge C(a_c, a_d, p, t) \wedge \neg C(a_d, a_d, p, c, t)} \tag{24}$$

Any state where a conditioned commitment and its condition are at the same time true are automatically transformed to a state where the condition still exists, but the commitment has been replaced by an unconditional commitment.

Definition 17. *Commitment discharge: Bringing about the commitment objective p before the timeout t has been enabled cancels created commitments that have p as objective automatically, including their timeouts.*

$$\frac{p \wedge C(a_d, a_d, p, c, t)}{p \wedge \neg C(a_d, a_d, p, c, t)} \tag{25}$$

Any state where a commitment to bring about a proposition p and at the same time the condition p are true are automatically transformed to a state where the condition p still exists, but the commitment has been canceled and does not exist any more.

In Singh's proposal [2], there are two more operations on commitments that will be included, but integrated as actions part of our model. These are namely, *delegation* and *assignation* of commitments. These will not be extra defined, but instead two examples of how these operations are present in the model are presented:

- Delegation: The action d, labeled *delegates*, changes the debtor of a commitment C from agent a_{d1} to a_{d2}:
  $d = \langle s(C(a_c, a_{d1}, p, c, t)), \text{``delegates''}, \{-C(a_c, a_{d1}, p, c, t), +C(a_c, a_{d2}, p, c, t)\}\rangle$
- Assignation: The action a, labeled *assigns*, changes the creditor of a commitment C from agent a_{c1} to a_{c2}:
  $a = \langle s(C(a_{c1}, a_d, p, c)), \text{``assigns''}, \{-C(a_{c1}, a_d, p, c, t), +C(a_{c2}, a_d, p, c, t)\}\rangle$

Speech acts can also be used with commitments, an example of such an action can be sending the acceptance of a role r_1 to r_2 whenever p_1 is not true (for instance p_1:box 1 is in slot A) to commit doing something to make p_1 to be true if the fact c_1 (for instance c_1: there is nothing on top of box 1) is true:
$a = \langle r_1, \langle s(\neg p_1), \text{''accept''}, \{+C(r_2, r_1, p_1, c_1, t_1)\}, r_2\rangle$

3.3 Operational Propositions

In order to have better control over conversations and to specify specific ways a role is allowed to decide or react, some propositions will have to be more complex than simple statements about the environment. Some of these propositions are arithmetic propositions, like counters or variables holding values, others are conditional logic statements that can produce other propositions given some specific condition. Another kind of operational proposition that will be mentioned specifically is the binding of specific concepts used in the action model to variables.

In the case of variables, the most crucial aspect is to manage their scope. Variables can exist one for each conversation, or one for each instance of a role or even a single global variable that is the same instance in all conversations in the protocol.

The aspect of how to use and define propositions will be discussed in further depth later in this paper, at this point, only these aspects of representing propositions or connecting them to more concrete concepts will be presented.

An example of an action with the three different kinds of propositions is the following, where a bidder B bids to an auction manager M the value bid:

$$\langle B, \langle \{a\_a, v = x, \}, bid, \{bid, bid > v \Rightarrow v = bid,$$
$$-C(M.W, M, pay, win, t_w),$$
$$+C(B, M, pay, win, t_w), M.W = B\}\rangle, M\rangle$$

where:

      a_a: auction active
      v: current winning value in the auction
      $M.W$: Winner role holding variable in M
      bid: the bid given by B

A conditional proposition will tell how the manager is expected to react: if the bid is bigger than the current value v, v will be assigned the new value of bid, any previous commitment to a winner is removed and a new commitment with the sender of the bid B is created, finally this bidder is assigned the role of the winner $M.W$.

4   Definition of a Conversation Protocol

Using the proposed model of a conversation based on actions sent between roles participating in a conversation, the following section will provide the mechanisms to compose these actions in such a way that they describe how complex conversations are to be performed.

Protocols represent specific ways that it allows over the whole state-action space. The different ways a protocols can take are known as a *runs*. In the concrete case of an agent performing a protocol with more than one participants, there will be several instances of the protocol, called *conversations*, each of which will take its own run, some of them will have the same run. Figure 1 illustrates the relation between these 3 concepts. In synthesis a protocol is a specification of a set of runs, each of which represent at the same time a set of conversations. The cardinality of runs is limited by the amount of actions that are enabled for the same state description. The cardinality of conversations, on the other hand is to be ruled by an amount that is associated with each action:

Definition 18. *The set C_A, the set of cardinality constraints for actions and the set C_S, the set of cardinality constraints for states, will represent the minimal and maximal cardinality of conversations associated to each action or state respectively:*

$$C_A : \mathbb{N} \times \mathbb{N} \times A_r \tag{26}$$

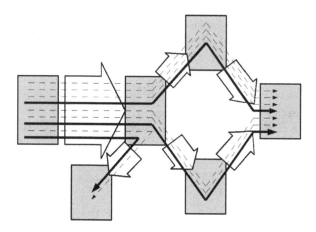

Fig. 1. Protocol (boxes and white arrows) composed of 3 runs (thick lines) and some conversations as instances of runs (dashed thin lines)

where

$$\forall \langle p, q, a \rangle \in C_A : p < q$$

$$\forall a \in A_r : \langle p, q, a \rangle \in C_A$$

$$C_S : \mathbb{N} \times \mathbb{N} \times S \tag{27}$$

where

$$\forall \langle p, q, s \rangle \in C_S : p < q$$

$$\forall s \in S : \langle p, q, a \rangle \in C_S$$

For brevity and agility, the following abbreviated version of a cardinality constraint will be used:

$$\langle p, q, a \rangle =^q_p a \tag{28}$$

Also in cases where the cardinality of actions is free: minimum is 0 and maximum not bound, represented with N, the cardinality constraints can be omitted:

$$\langle 0, N, a \rangle = a \qquad \langle p, N, a \rangle =_p a \qquad \langle 0, q, a \rangle =^q a \tag{29}$$

For instance, the following cardinality association means that the action called "inform" can be sent from the role r_1 to the role r_2 a maximal of 7 times and a minimal of 1 times from states in s.

$$^7_1 \langle r_1, \langle s, \text{``}inform\text{''}, o \rangle, r_2 \rangle$$

Protocols will be specified similarly as in [5], in terms of the propositions required to start it, called preconditions and propositions describing the effects it has in the context of the conversation, called post-conditions. Protocols, like actions, will be also labeled.

Definition 19. *A protocol π is an association of preconditions in the form of one or more state descriptions, a label, post-conditions in the form of one or more state descriptions and a set of speech acts. Pre-, post-conditions and speech acts are associated to cardinality constraints, the set of all protocols is called Π:*

$$\Pi : \mathcal{P}(C_S) \times V_\pi \times \mathcal{P}(C_S) \times \mathcal{P}(C_A) \tag{30}$$

where V_π is the set of labels for protocols.

Protocols have cardinality constraints associated to their starting and ending state descriptions as follows:

$$\forall \pi \in \Pi :$$
$$where$$
$$\pi = \langle \mathcal{S}, l, \mathcal{E}, \mathcal{A} \rangle$$
$$\mathcal{A} = \{^{q_1}_{p_1} \langle r_x, \langle s_1, v_1, c_1 \rangle, r_y \rangle, \ldots, ^{q_h}_{p_h} \langle r_x, \langle s_h, v_h, c_h \rangle, r_y \rangle\}$$

all actions sharing a starting state of the protocol $^{q_a}_{p_a} s_a \in \mathcal{S}$ as precondition must satisfy the cardinality constraints, which are the cardinality constraints associated to the state description s_a: p_a and q_a :

$$\forall (^{q_i}_{p_i} \langle r_x, \langle s_i, v_i, c_i \rangle, r_y \rangle \in \mathcal{A} | s_a = s_i) : p_i \leq p_a \wedge q_i \geq q_a$$
$$where \tag{31}$$
$$i = 1, \ldots, |\mathcal{S}|$$

all actions that result in a state description that matches an end state description of the protocol $^{q_e}_{p_e} s_e \in \mathcal{E}$ must have the same cardinality constraints, which are the cardinality constraints associated to the end state description p_e and q_e:

$$\forall (^{q_i}_{p_i} \langle r_x, \langle s, v, c \rangle, r_y \rangle \in \mathcal{A} | S(c_s) \in \mathcal{E}) : p_i \geq p_e \wedge q_i \leq q_e$$
$$where \tag{32}$$
$$j = 1, \ldots, |\mathcal{E}|$$

A protocol cannot have disconnected actions in its definition:

$$\forall r \in R \, \exists s_s \in \mathcal{S} \wedge R' \subset R : s_i = s_{i-1}(c_i) \; for \; 0 < i \leq k \tag{33}$$

where:

$$r = \langle r_x, \langle s, v, c \rangle, r_y \rangle$$
$$R' = \{r_0, r_1, \ldots, r_k\}$$
$$r \notin R'$$
$$r_i = \langle r_{xi}, \langle s_i, v_i, c_i \rangle, r_{yi} \rangle \; for \; 1 \leq i \leq k$$
$$r_0 = \langle r_{x0}, \langle s_s, v_0, c_0 \rangle, r_{y0} \rangle$$

This more relaxed approach facilitates different composition mechanisms for protocols and reflects the multi-directional nature of conversations. The set of actions of the protocol are also called *rules* as used in dialogue games [6].

Protocols that have the same pre- and post- conditions are not necessarily the same, but are expected to fit in a protocol composition well according to the semantics treated in the present work.

The nature of conversations makes the task of modeling and structuring them very hard. It is the intention of this work to provide mechanisms of organization and modularization of complex conversations without restricting them unnecessarily or in such a manner that ends up being unnatural for practical purposes. Therefore a technique for composing protocols using rigid structures that not always fit the nature of conversations will not be pursued here. Such structures found commonly in similar approaches are probably inherited from other programming structures, like *if... then... else...*, *while loops* and specially strict *joining* associated to a previous *split* in the transition system. Even though this approach allows such structures, it is by far not restricted to them. Even so, some basic structures that appear in conversation models will be described next using the model for protocols:

4.1 Atomic Protocol

An atomic protocol is the most basic protocol possible, in essence a speech act. Its preconditions is the state description and its post-conditions is the composed operation of the action. The cardinality constraints associated to the starting and ending state description is the same as the ones for the action.

Definition 20. *The atomic protocol for the* roled action $_p^q a =_p^q \langle r_s, \langle s, v, c \rangle, r_r \rangle$ *is:*

$$\pi = \langle \{_p^q s\}, l, \{_p^q s(c)\}, \{_p^q \langle r_s, \langle s, v, c \rangle, r_r \rangle\} \rangle \tag{34}$$

4.2 Protocol Sequence

A protocol sequence is a protocol which seen from the outside will have only one possible run, which means it has only one starting and one ending state description with identical cardinality constraints.

Definition 21. *Protocol sequence is a protocol π such that:*

$$\pi = \langle \{_p^q s\}, l, \{_p^q e\}, R \rangle \tag{35}$$

All atomic protocols are hence protocol sequences.

4.3 Protocol Splits

Protocols splits represent the most common situations found when modeling conversations. These are the situations in which a protocol has a set of rules, all of them sharing the same starting state description.

Splits are the situations in which different *runs* are created, therefore a very relevant aspect of splits in a protocol is the definition of cardinality constraints for each run. This same procedure is also used in several previous approaches, for instance in Agent UML [7].

Definition 22. *A protocol split π is composed of more than one rule, all of which share the same starting state description.*

$$\pi = \langle \{_{p_s}^{q_s} s\}, l, \{_{p_1}^{q_1} s(c_{s1}),_{p_2}^{q_2} s(c_{s2}), \ldots,_{p_n}^{q_n} s(c_{sn})\}, \{a_1, a_2, \ldots, a_n\}\rangle \qquad (36)$$

where

$$n > 1$$

$$a_i =_{p_i}^{q_i} \langle r_{xi}, \langle s, l_i, c_{s_i}\rangle, r_{yi}\rangle$$

Protocol splits can be, in principle, of two kinds: a choice or a parallel split.

Choice: These are situations in which choosing one action, where all the actions have the same sending role, will disable the other ones, making it impossible to perform other actions that start at the splitting state description. This is a situation where the role in turn is expected to decide which of the options it will take, choosing this way the path in the protocols to be taken. π is a choice split if

$$\forall a_i : s(c_{si}) \bigcap s = \emptyset \wedge r_{xi} = r_x \qquad (37)$$

In a choice, different runs are created, but each conversation can follow only one of them.

Parallel: These are situations in which actions belonging to the split do not disable themselves reciprocally or have different senders, making it possible to perform one or more of these actions. In the present model only one action is possible to be performed at the same time, but the enabling conditions for other actions in a parallel split are still valid after an actions is performed, making it still possible to perform the other ones. π is a parallel split if

$$\forall a_i, j \leq n \wedge j \neq i : s(c_{si}) \subset s \vee r_{xi} \neq r_{xj} \qquad (38)$$

In a parallel, different runs are created as well, but a conversation can follow one or more paths.

Protocol Merges. In opposite to protocol splits, where new runs are created, there are also situations where different runs merge into the same path.

Definition 23. *A protocol merge π is composed of more than one rule all of which share the same ending state description.*

$$\pi = \langle \{_{p_{s1}}^{q_{s1}} s_1,_{p_{s2}}^{q_{s2}} s_2, \ldots,_{p_{sn}}^{q_{sn}} s_n\}, l, \{s_f\}, \{a_1, a_2, \ldots, a_n\}\rangle \qquad (39)$$

where

$$n > 1$$

$$a_i =_{p_{si}}^{q_{si}} \langle r_x, \langle s_i, l_i, c_{si}\rangle, r_y\rangle$$

$$s(c_{si}) = s_f$$

5   Protocol Composition

Protocol composition is the creation of new conversation protocols by connecting other protocols together.

Definition 24. *Two protocols π_1 and π_2 can be composed to a new protocol π_3, if there is at least one ending state description s_1 in π_1 that is subset of a starting state s_2 in π_2 and at the same time, cardinality constraints in s_1 are equal or more restrictive than in s_2. Propositions and roles have to be* bound *together to establish the semantic connection between the two protocols π_1 and π_2, by specifying which roles and propositions in the first protocol will take the roles and replace the propositions in the second protocols respectively:*

$$\pi_1 = \langle S_1,'' \pi_1'', E_1, A_1\rangle$$
$$A_1 = \{\langle x1_1, a1_1, y1_1\rangle, \langle x1_2, a1_2, y1_2\rangle, \ldots, \langle x1_n, a1_n, y1_n\rangle\}$$
$${}^{cq_1}_{cp_1} s_1 \in E_1; s_1 = \{p1_1, p1_2, \ldots, p1_f\}$$
$$\pi_2 = \langle S_2,'' \pi_2'', E_2, A_2\rangle$$
$$A_2 = \{\langle x2_1, a2_1, y2_1\rangle, \langle x2_2, a2_2, y2_2\rangle, \ldots, \langle x2_m, a2_m, y2_m\rangle\}$$
$${}^{cq_2}_{cp_2} s_2 \in S_1; s_2 = \{p2_1, p2_2, \ldots, p2_g\}$$

where

$$g < f$$
$$cp_1 \geq cp_2$$
$$cq_1 \leq cq_2$$

a specific binding of roles is specified:

$$x1_i = x2_j$$
$$y1_i = y2_j$$
$$1 \leq i \leq n; 1 \leq j \leq m$$

and a specific binding of propositions:

$$\left.\begin{array}{c} p1_k = p2_l \\ 1 \leq k \leq g \\ 1 \leq l \leq g \end{array}\right\} \Rightarrow s_1 \subseteq s_2$$

$$\pi_3 = \langle S_1 \bigcup S_2,'' \pi_3'', E_1 \bigcup E_2, A_1 \bigcup A_2\rangle \qquad (40)$$

5.1   Protocol Example

As an example, the case of a specific kind of auction will be observed. Figure 2 shows a graph representing the protocol. A manager M can send any time a message called *cfp1* to a set of bidders represented by the role B, which can be 0 to the maximum possible (N). *cfp1* creates the conversations making some propositions valid: that the auction is active (*auc_act*), a timer is created that after a period *ta* will enable the action *done*. The value v is created with the starting

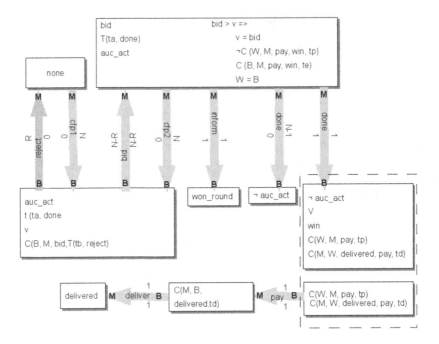

Fig. 2. Example of a protocol modeling a composition of an auction and a simple commitment resolution

value of the auction, say 0 and finally a commitment is created $C(B,M,bid,T(tb, reject))$ that states that the bidder B will be committed to the manager M to bid within a period tb, after which, if no replies are received, it will be assumed that the Bidder has performed the action *reject*. B has to decide to send either a reject message, which practically takes him out of the auction, removing all propositions including *auc_act* or to bid, providing a bid value called *bid* which in case it is greater than v will have further effects: v will have the value of *bid*, a commitment to a previous winner of a auction round M.W will be removed (has no effect in the first iteration) and a commitment with the same terms is created for the bidder of *bid* in which it is committed to pay an amount *pay* in case it wins the auction: *win*. This leading bidder is then bound to the winning role. Notice that after each iteration, M *informs* M.W that it won the round. Finally the timeout for *done* is enabled finishing the auction: M sends *done* to all participants which removes the fact *auc_act* finishing the auction and to the winner M.W it sends a different kind of done which also brings about the final value of the auction v, the fact that the receiver won: *win* which automatically transforms the the conditional commitment created with the winner *bid* to an unconditional commitment of the bidder to the manager to pay within the timeout tp. Also the commitment of M to B to make *delivered* true within the timeout td in case *pay* is brought about is created. This would be the ending state of the auction, with another ending state for the rejected bidders and non winner bidders.

As an example of protocol composition, a very simple protocol π_2 is defined which has a starting state matching the end state of the auction. The first an only possible action is *pay* which automatically discharges the commitment from B to M and frees the commitment of M to B of its condition. After that, the only possible action is *deliver* which discharges the last commitment ending the protocol in a state where *delivered* is true. This example has the same propositions and roles which makes the binding explicit. The states are connected and a new protocol π_3 is created that resolves the commitments.

The protocols π_1 and π_2 look like this:

$$\pi_1 = \langle \{\}, \pi_1, \{ \quad s(\neg auc\_act), s(\neg auc\_act, v, win,$$
$$C(M.B, pay, tp), C(M, B, delivered, pay, td))\},$$
$$\{\langle M, \langle \quad \{s(tb < ta)\}, cfp1, \{+auc\_act, +T(ta, done), +v,$$
$$+C(B, M, bid, T(tb, reject))\}\rangle, B\rangle,$$
$${}_0^R\langle B, \langle \quad \{s(auc\_act, C(B, M, bid, T(tb, reject)))\}, reject,$$
$$\{-C(B, M, bid, T(tb, reject), -auc\_act,$$
$$-T(ta, done))\}\rangle, M\rangle,$$
$${}_{N-R}^{N-R}\langle B, \langle \quad \{s(auc\_act, C(B, M, bid, T(tb, reject)), v\}, bid,$$
$$\{+bid, bid > v \Rightarrow v = bid, -C(M.W, M, pay, win, tp)),$$
$$+C(B, M, pay, win, tp), +(M.W = B)\}\rangle, M\rangle,$$
$$\langle M, \langle \quad \{s(auc\_act, T(ta, done), tb < ta)\}, cfp2,$$
$$\{+C(B, M, bid, T(tb, reject)), \}$$
$$-won\_round, +v\}\rangle, B\rangle,$$
$${}_1^1\langle M, \langle \quad \{s(M.W = B), inform, \{+won_round\}\rangle, B\rangle$$
$${}_0^{N-1}\langle M, \langle \quad \{s(auc\_act), \neg M.W = B\}, done, \{-auc\_act\}\rangle, B\rangle,$$
$${}_1^1\langle M, \langle \quad \{s(auc\_act), M.W = B\}, done, \{-auc\_act,$$
$$+v, +win, +C(B, M, pay, tp),$$
$$+C(M, B, delivered, pay, td)\}\rangle, B\rangle\}\rangle$$

$$\pi_2 = \langle\{ \quad s(C(B, M, pay, tp), C(M, B, delivered, pay, td))\}, \pi_2,$$
$$\{s(delivered)\}\},$$
$$\{\langle B, \langle \; s(C(B, M, pay, tp), C(M, B, delivered, pay, td)), pay,$$
$$\{+pay, +C(M, B, delivered, td)\}\rangle, M\rangle,$$
$$\langle M, \langle \; \{s(pay, C(M, B, delivered, td), deliver,$$
$$\{+delivered\}\rangle, B\rangle,$$

6   Discussion

The usage of propositions in this approach is crucial, since it decouples the actions of their effects, allowing other actions or protocols that can have the same effects to be used instead, making the approach modular and protocols that have been predefined reusable. How successful a model is, will depend significantly on how the scenario being approached is modeled using propositions. In Section 3.3 some basic connections between the domain and this propositions was proposed, still how the effects of the actions are modeled is left free to the protocol designer. The options are between, on one side, the most trivial approach: making a proposition for each action that simply states that the specific action was performed, working similarly to not declarative approaches like [8] and, on the other side, very accurately selected proposition that are based on the effects several actions or protocols have in common. In the first case, the development will be very simple, but the protocols might end up rigid or difficult to recombine. The more flexible approach will take advantage of modularity, but at the same time, participating roles might be demanded to cope with very complex reasoning. A well balanced model would be the most suitable solution in most of the cases. It is clear that the minimum requirement to take advantage of this approach for modularity is to choose propositions that represent the effects of the actions, using them in all actions that semantically have the same effect.

The first part models the exhaustive state space, solving the *Frame Problem* [9] with a model of state descriptions and actions based on these descriptions and operations, to focus only on the relevant facts. Then actions are defined based on state descriptions and using composed operations that specify effects relative to their current state. This model helps to consolidate various contributions of the multiagent community using very heterogeneous models in a single comprehensive model.

6.1   Related Work

A survey of current approaches to interaction protocol models is provided by [10]. The reader is referred to it to get more insight on proposals in the community.

The present work has as main objective to allow for formal modularity of protocols as was initially intended in FIPA [11]. The FIPA approach was not successful due to various issues, but one of the main causes was that the FIPA speech acts were defined always from the perspective of the sending agent, which contrasts with the global perspective required for conversation protocols of this kind. This objective was, in principle, only tried by Singh et. al. [12]. As mentioned in Section 3.2, the same technique has been used here to model commitments, making some adaptations and modifications to integrate it concretely with the state-space model.

Timeouts are used by [13] as a "system" event. In the present approach timeouts are declared as propositions representing some facts about the environment. The concept of a global system [14] has been completely avoided, since it would not fit in an open system, as it is intended here. Timeouts have to be interpreted in the realization of roles, they are to be managed normally by the creating roles and simply represent facts about the conversation and things expected from roles.

This approach focuses only on the scope of a conversation, what is allowed, expected and demanded from participants in the conversation, it goes a bit beyond simple dialogue games [15] focusing not only in the actions that can be performed but also in their consequences. General norms and commitments of a scope outside the conversation are not treated in this model.

The present model is another alternative to give semantics to modeling techniques like in UML. For instance [16] proposes a Petri-Net for this purpose. Our approach has strong similarities, but has enabled the possibility to integrate critical concepts like commitments and the usage of propositions to connect better actions between each other and to the domain.

The way composition is approached, based on the state-action space model allows a more detailed specification of how composition can be done, compared to [17,18] and some similar approaches, having the state-action space model serves better to achieve more detailed specifications, like propositions and cardinality constraints that give deeper insight about the conditions of the conversation.

7 Conclusion

A comprehensive and consolidating model for interaction protocols has been proposed. It provides a solution for modularity and composition of protocols for complex conversations. It involves many ideas proposed by the multi-agent community. The model discusses many issues about interaction protocols, the most important one is how to achieve modularity. Decoupling of actions and their effects is a fundamental advantage for this purpose. By separating this two concepts, it is possible to formalize a model that enables modularity, based on the simple fact that actions (an protocols) that share the same effect can replace, or at least be considered to replace each other. The model goes further and specifies, what has to be taken into account and how does a composition of protocols have to be.

Future work will be to extract out of a conversation protocol as presented here the set of rules and expectations for each participating role, also known as the projection of the protocol. This model has been proposed in an abstract level and shows how complex it can be to model protocols. It will be important to produce modeling tools that follow the concepts shown here in order to tame complexity and take advantage of reuse and composition.

The model proposed here can be used at different levels of abstraction, depending on how the propositions the model is based on are defined. This model can also be used to reason about the different concepts in the protocol, to help systems make decisions during conversations. They are modeled as first class objects, they can be used by designers but also by software agents to reason about them and first choose which protocol to use and second which path in the conversation to take.

References

1. Singh, M.P., Chopra, A.K., Desai, N.V., Mallya, A.U.: Protocols for Processes: Programming in the Large for Open Systems. In: OOPSLA Companion. ACM SIGPLAN Notices, vol. 39, pp. 73–83. ACM, New York (2004)
2. Singh, M.P.: An Ontoloy for Commitments in Multiagent Systems. Artificial Intelligence and Law 7(1), 97–113 (1999)
3. Yolum, P., Singh, M.P.: Commitment machines. In: Meyer, J.-J.C., Tambe, M. (eds.) ATAL 2001. LNCS, vol. 2333, pp. 235–247. Springer, Heidelberg (2002)

4. Mallya, A.U., Singh, M.P.: A Semantic Approach for Designing Commitment Protocols. In: van Eijk, R.M., Huget, M.-P., Dignum, F.P.M. (eds.) AC 2004. LNCS, vol. 3396, pp. 33–49. Springer, Heidelberg (2005)

5. Eijk, R.M.V., Boer, F.S.D., Hoek, W.V.D., Meyer, J.J.C.: A verification framework for agent communication. Autonomous Agents and Multi-Agent Systems 6(2), 185–219 (2003)

6. McBurney, P., Parsons, S.: Dialogue game protocols. In: Huget, M.-P. (ed.) Communication in Multiagent Systems. LNCS, vol. 2650, pp. 269–283. Springer, Heidelberg (2003)

7. Bauer, B., Müller, J.P., Odell, J.: Agent UML: A Formalism for Specifying Multiagent Software Systems. In: Ciancarini, P., Wooldridge, M.J. (eds.) AOSE 2000. LNCS, vol. 1957, pp. 91–103. Springer, Heidelberg (2001)

8. Alberti, M., Daolio, D., Torroni, P., Gavanelli, M., Lamma, E., Mello, P.: Specification and verification of agent interaction protocols in a logic-based system. In: SAC 2004: Proceedings of the, ACM symposium on Applied computing, pp. 72–78. ACM, New York (2004)

9. McCarthy, J., Hayes, P.J.: Some philosophical problems from the standpoint of artificial intelligence. Readings in nonmonotonic reasoning, 26–45 (1987)

10. Miller, T., Mcginnis, J.: Amongst first-class protocols. In: Artikis, A., O'Hare, G.M.P., Stathis, K., Vouros, G. (eds.) ESAW 2007. LNCS, vol. 4995, pp. 208–223. Springer, Heidelberg (2008)

11. FIPA: Foundation for Intelligent Physical Agents (2002), http://www.fipa.org

12. Desai, N., Mallya, A.U., Chopra, A.K., Singh, M.P.: Interaction Protocols as Design Abstractions for Business Processes. Transactions on Software Engineering 31(12), 1015–1027 (2005)

13. Artikis, A., Sergot, M., Pitt, J.: Specifying Electronic Societies with the Causal Calculator. In: Giunchiglia, F., Odell, J.J., Weiss, G. (eds.) AOSE 2002. LNCS, vol. 2585, pp. 1–15. Springer, Heidelberg (2003)

14. Robertson, D.: Multi-agent Coordination as Distributed Logic Programming. In: Demoen, B., Lifschitz, V. (eds.) ICLP 2004. LNCS, vol. 3132, pp. 416–430. Springer, Heidelberg (2004)

15. McBurney, P., Parsons, S.: Games that agents play: A formal framework for dialogues between autonomous agents. J. of Logic, Lang. and Inf. 11(3), 315–334 (2002)

16. Cabac, L., Moldt, D.: Formal semantics for auml agent interaction protocol diagrams. In: Odell, J.J., Giorgini, P., Müller, J.P. (eds.) AOSE 2004. LNCS, vol. 3382, pp. 47–61. Springer, Heidelberg (2005)

17. Miller, T., McBurney, P.: Using constraints and process algebra for specification of first-class agent interaction protocols. In: O'Hare, G.M.P., Ricci, A., O'Grady, M.J., Dikenelli, O. (eds.) ESAW 2006. LNCS (LNAI), vol. 4457, pp. 245–264. Springer, Heidelberg (2007)

18. Miller, T., McBurney, P.: Annotation and matching of first-class agent interaction protocols. In: AAMAS 2008: Proceedings of the 7th international joint conference on Autonomous agents and multiagent systems, pp. 805–812 (2008)

Agent Interaction Modeling Based on Product-Centric Data: A Formal Method to Improve Enterprise Interoperability

Marco Stuit and Gerben G. Meyer

Department of Business & ICT, Faculty of Economics and Business
University of Groningen, Landleven 5, P.O. Box 800,
9700 AV Groningen, The Netherlands, +31 50 363 {7083 / 7194}
{m.stuit,g.g.meyer}@rug.nl

Abstract. This paper shows how companies can use product-centric data to locally represent the interactions with and between their partners. An agent-based
interaction modeling language is used to capture these interactions graphically
and formally. Moreover, a formal method is introduced that enables partners to
automatically construct a global interaction diagram from their local interaction
representations. This global interaction diagram improves enterprise interoperability, since it increases overall process visibility. A simple process example is
used to illustrate the approach.

Keywords: Agents, interaction structuring, global and local process representations, product-centric data, enterprise interoperability, business process modeling.

1 Introduction

Nowadays, there is an ongoing trend towards collaborative business processes that are
provided by autonomous partners, which together deliver complex products and/or
services in a collaborative network. This is explicitly shown by the emergence of new
organizational forms like the networked or virtual enterprise [18]. The decentralized
nature of cross-organizational business settings is a good match for agent technology
[28, 35]. The autonomous partners in a collaborative business process can be seen as
agents that execute certain tasks locally, while the interactions between the partners
can be seen as interactions in a multi-agent system. To capture these interactions, the
TALL modeling language has been developed [32, 33] (see Section 2). As TALL is
interaction-based, it is suitable for creating a description of the multiple interactions
that occur in cross-organizational business environments. In this paper, it is shown
how these descriptions are built using TALL Interaction Structure (IS) diagrams.

The manufacturing industry is increasingly moving from a supplier-driven to a cus-
tomer-driven market. This transition is a great challenge to the manufacturing process
itself since it must be more flexible and robust as well as demonstrate enhanced scalability [4]. Supply chains are evolving in order to keep in line with these developments. This is particularly shown by the move from conventional location-centric

K. Fischer et al. (Eds.): ATOP 2005 and ATOP 2008, LNBIP 25, pp. 197–219, 2009.

Location based materials management   Item-centric materials management
(products anonymous)   (Identified products)

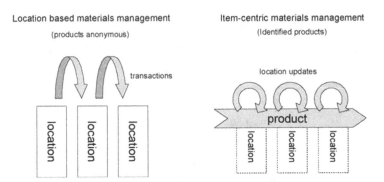

Fig. 1. Location-centric (left) and product-centric supply chains (right). Source [16].

supply chains to product-centric supply chains [15], as shown in Figure 1. A conventional supply chain is based on a systems design that is focused on location-specific material accounts and transactions between locations. A solution-design that tracks and controls individual products independently of the location and the ownership of the product individual characterizes a product-centric supply chain. In [6], it is mentioned that product-centric integration makes explicit the role of the product as the coordinating entity in the delivery of customized products and services.

Product-centric control is the focus of the TraSer project[1], in which control efforts are directed at individual products of the value-adding network. The idea behind product-centric control is that individual products and components are the basic entities in the information system rather than orders, production orders, or shipment batches. In the TraSer approach, each product is labeled with an RFID or barcode, containing an ID@URI code [17]. With this ID@URI, each product carries a unique identification number (ID), as well as a reference (Uniform Resource Identifier) to the location of the database where the product-centric data is stored. In this way, each partner in the supply chain can access this data, which results in product visibility throughout the supply chain. A recent survey about product-centric control and product visibility, as well as their enabling technologies can be found in [24].

The product visibility offered by the use of product-centric control does not imply process visibility. In this paper, it is proposed to use product-centric data to identify the multiple interactions between the different partners in the supply network, which form the collaborative business process. Currently, none of the partners has a global view of the entire collaborative business process in the supply chain, as each partner only has data about the interactions with direct partners. To increase interoperability between the partners, it is considered beneficial to build a global process definition. By using the product-centric data available in the network, each partner is enabled to identify the local interactions of and between all the partners in the supply chain. The identified local interactions can be merged to create a global process definition. This global process definition increases the understandability and visibility of the supply chain for this partner. In this paper, an algorithm is presented that enables partners to automatically create a global process definition from identified local interactions of partners. The goal of the algorithm is to build a minimal global interaction representation where the

---

[1] http://www.traser-project.eu

local interactions are merged when there is no conflict. A conflict indicates the existence of alternative local views on the same interaction. In the remainder of this paper, this algorithm is called the global construction algorithm. The approach presented in this paper assumes a common shared ontology in the business domain under consideration. Ontology matching is outside the scope of this paper.

The paper is structured as follows. Section 2 introduces the TALL modeling language and covers related work. The language is applied to a case example in Section 3. Next, Section 4 presents the global construction algorithm that enables partners to merge different local interaction representations. Section 5 applies this algorithm to the case example. After, Section 6 addresses public and private process representations in the context of TALL. A discussion is presented in Section 7 along with directions for future research. The paper ends with conclusions in Section 8.

2 Agent Interaction Modeling

This section discusses agent interaction modeling. Section 2.1 introduces the TALL modeling language. Afterwards, Section 2.2 motivates and evaluates TALL against related modeling languages.

2.1 The TALL Modeling Language

A network of organizations (e.g. a supply chain) can be viewed as a multi-agent system consisting of autonomous agents that are involved in the provision of a collaborative business process. Therefore, all the partners in a supply chain can be viewed as agents. In order to capture the interactions between these agents, a new graphical modeling language named TALL (The Agent Lab Language) has been developed [32, 33]. In the language, collaborative business processes are conceived as a structure of role-based interactions through which agents cooperate and coordinate their work. Similarly, related research considers business processes as a special kind of social interaction process [36] or as social constructs [21].

The top part of Figure 2 shows the abstract symbols that represent the essential components of the language. Rounded rectangles represent *agents*, ellipses represent *roles*, and hexagons represent *interactions*. From a modeling perspective, TALL distinguishes between atomic agents (human and software agents) and composite agents (synthetic agent). Graphically, icons that appear in the top left corner of the agent symbol distinguish between the different types of agents. Circle icons represent human agents, square icons represent existing software agents, and triangle icons represent synthetic agents. By playing roles, agents interact with other agents. Moreover, Figure 2 demonstrates how the symbols are connected to denote that agents play the roles that are attached to an interaction. The fact that an agent is playing a role means that the agent has the necessary skills and responsibilities to perform the required activities.

The different agents interact autonomously in order to complete their individual and joint goals. Autonomy means here that the participants act in empowered roles in which they can make decisions and take actions on their own. Interactions are related to other interactions through composition (one interaction being part of another) and-dependency (one interaction must be completed before the other can start). The Interaction Structure (IS) diagram depicts interactions and their relations in a tree structure.

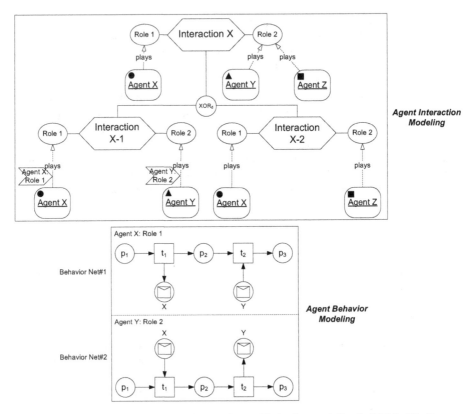

Fig. 2. The separation between agent interaction and behavior modeling in TALL. The Interaction Structure (IS) diagram shows how a collaborative business process is represented as an interaction tree with agents playing the roles attached to the interactions. Agents bring explicit behaviors in the form of Agent Behavior (AB) diagrams to perform interactions.

The sub-interactions or direct child interactions are linked to their parent interaction by a routing symbol that indicates the process flow of the children. The parent interaction completes if all sub-interactions have completed taking into account the specified routing.

In Figure 2, the XOR_d label indicates an exclusive deterministic OR-split, that is, only one of the two sub-interactions is executed. If either interaction *X-1* or interaction *X-2* completes, interaction *X* completes. Thus, completion is a bottom-up process in the IS diagram. Besides XOR, also sequential (SEQ) and parallel (PAR) routing is supported by the language. Graphically, the (sequential) order of a set of children under a common parent is read from left to right. A decision rule set is assigned to the three routing types to enable condition-based execution of a set of direct child interactions. Graphically, a (non-empty) decision rule set is depicted by attaching a subscripted letter *d* to the routing type (as in Figure 2). Decision rule sets can for instance be used to achieve an exclusive deterministic choice (XOR_d), or to make an inclusive choice for N-out-of-M direct children. In the latter case, when $N \geq 2$, the children are executed in sequence (SEQ_d) or in parallel (PAR_d).

With TALL, collaborative business processes are addressed in two ways. A clear separation exists between (1) the composite interaction specification in the IS diagram and (2) the specification of the agent's behaviors. The IS diagram introduces a higher-level notion of process that focuses on inter-agent interactions whereas behavioral models focus on individual agent behaviors. The agents' behaviors are modeled using swimlaned process diagrams named TALL Agent Behavior (AB) diagrams. AB diagrams are based on the Behavior net formalism [22], which is an extension of the colored Petri net formalism with the message place type. An agent that is assigned to a specific role in the IS diagram owns an AB diagram that is used to perform the specific interaction. The bottom part of Figure 2 shows an example in which *Agent X* and *Agent Y* own an AB diagram that is used to perform interaction *X-1*. Each AB diagram represents the internal states of the agent and the activities/events that cause the agent to change states. Message places enable the flow of tokens between different agent behaviors in an interaction.

In the IS diagram, AB diagrams appear on a higher level of abstraction in the form of chevron symbols. A chevron symbol carries an agent-role label and is connected to the tail of the agent-role connector (as in Figure 2). In this way, a chevron symbol appears adjacent to its owner agent. Each chevron symbol serves as an abstract representation of the agent's local behavior in the form of an AB diagram. References [22] and [23] discuss in more detail the agent behaviors and how nonaligned behaviors are dealt with. In nonaligned behaviors, the message places are not necessarily matched by type name and number like in Figure 2.

The IS diagram is mainly used to increase process understandability and visibility for analysis and/or redesign purposes. However, it can also support the execution of the process by acting as a coordination structure for an (agent-based) execution environment [29]. Such an environment performs the collaborative business process by coordinating the distributed agent behaviors. In this paper, the focus is on the IS diagram as a tool for supply chain partners to automatically build a global interaction representation from local interaction representations.

2.2 Related Work and Motivation

In this section, TALL is compared to existing agent-based modeling techniques and traditional process modeling languages.

Traditional process modeling languages like BPMN [37], UML [12], EPCs [30], IDEF0 [20], and Petri nets [11] create structured well-defined process models. In these languages, the collection of tasks or activities in a business process is ordered in a prescriptive process model that is performed in an imperative way [27]. Such languages are appropriate for modeling business processes that display complex flows, but are less appropriate for modeling business processes that involve the co-operation of several entities [21].

Contemporary organizations are complex collaborative networks [7]. The business processes of such organizations involve more people that collaborate both within and across organizations. In such business processes, collaboration instead of task sequence determines the nature of the working activity. According to [14], collaborative activity simply does not match in any way the underlying "parallel flowchart" paradigm of current mainstream process notations and languages. The development of TALL is motivated by the need for new methods and languages to model collaborative work practice.

TALL is inspired by the agent paradigm to model collaborative work practice. Existing agent-based languages include (amongst others) stand-alone languages like AUML [2], AORML [36], AML [8], and OPM/MAS [34]. Moreover, agent-based languages are at the centre of well-known agent-oriented software engineering methodologies like MASE [10], Prometheus [26], TROPOS [3], GAIA [38], and MESSAGE [5]. Although many of these languages incorporate the same basic agent-oriented constructs, they are mainly focused on the software development process for agent systems. These languages are software design techniques that are mainly used by software architects. Hence, they do not focus on business process specification.

The main contribution TALL makes as a modeling language is that it presents a process-oriented approach, based on agent-oriented concepts and notations, which is more useful for business architects and analysts. The language focuses on process modeling, and can be used outside a software development or system implementation context. TALL should be seen as a complement to the existing agent-based languages and frameworks that have proven to be useful for agent-based software development activities. The main strength of the language is the strong conceptual separation between global agent interaction specification and local agent behavior specification. The language is based on the premise that human collaborative work is not about carrying out steps in a pre-defined sequence, but instead requires a higher-level notion of process. Therefore, the IS diagram allows general constraints to be put on the overall process independently of the agent behaviors. In other words, process-wide behavior can be partially defined at design time and used at run-time independently of the autonomous behaviors of the agents.

The agent behavior specification is done from a local viewpoint using explicit process models in the form of AB diagrams. The use of explicit process models is in line with a process-based approach. In comparison, in traditional process modeling languages the concept of locality does not exist. Local process variation is lost at the whim of the business analyst who creates a centralistic high-level model of the process in order to increase process standardization. TALL models the operational flow of the process from the local perspectives or beliefs of the agents [31]. In this way, TALL is also in line with an agent-based approach. For a more elaborate discussion on TALL's modeling concepts and notations, and an explicit comparison with the related modeling languages above and several others the reader is referred to [32, 33].

3   Product-Centric Case Example

This section presents a typical tracking and tracing case from the perspective of one agent in a supply chain. This scenario is used to illustrate how this one agent can build a global process definition of the supply chain using local process information (i.e. interactions this agent has with its direct partner agents) and product-centric data, which is linked to individual products. The scenario is a simplified supply chain, based on [9], in which agents have the shared goal of delivering Personal Computers (PCs) to end customers. The scenario is shown in Figure 3.

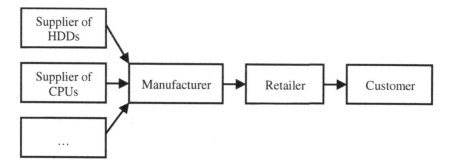

Fig. 3. The simplified supply chain

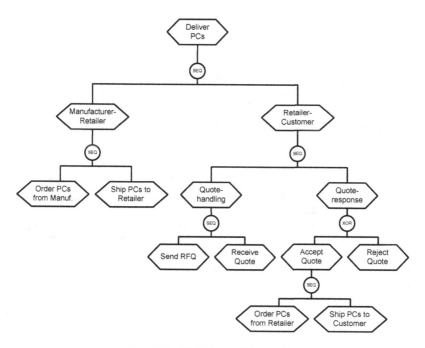

Fig. 4. The IS diagram of the retailer

In this supply chain, several supplier agents deliver computer parts to a manufacturer agent, who assembles the computer(s), and ships them to a retailer agent. The retailer agent sells the assembled computer(s) to a customer. This scenario is focused on the view of the retailer. The retailer can build an IS diagram of the interactions he has with his direct partner agents. This diagram is shown in Figure 4. The roles are omitted in this diagram for clarity reasons. However, the agents are playing their specific roles as supplier, manufacturer, retailer, or customer. As can be seen in the diagram, the root interaction of the retailer agent is "Deliver PCs", which is also the common shared goal of the whole supply chain. For this purpose, the retailer interacts with the manufacturer (called "Manufacturer-Retailer") and with the customer (called

"Retailer-Customer"). In case of the interaction with the manufacturer, the retailer agent interacts with him to order PCs, and later on to receive the shipments of PCs. The interaction with the customer is a bit more complex, it consists of a partially ordered set of interactions, in which a quote is requested, a quote is send to the customer, and if the customer accepts the quote, an order and shipment of the PCs follows.

To improve the insight of the retailer agent in the whole supply chain, the retailer agent can build IS diagrams from the perspective of the other agents in the supply chain by generalizing over available product-centric data. Table 1 shows an example of product-centric data of an individual product. However, the product-centric data only reveals a part of the interactions in which the other agents are involved, as the product-centric data per product individual only contains information about location and shape changes including the time when these changes happened. Based on this, the proposed approach assumes incomplete interaction models.

Table 1. Example of product-centric data

Product-ID	Time	Type	Location
123456	10.01.2008 12:34	Shipment	Manufacturer X
123456	15.01.2008 13:35	Assemble	Manufacturer X
123456	20.01.2008 14:36	Shipment	Retailer Y
123456	25.01.2008 15:37	Shipment	Customer Z

The behaviors used by the partners within the interactions remain private knowledge, as this approach only reveals interactions with and between partners, which are extending the product-centric data. Furthermore, confidentiality is provided to partners as they can decide to either share or withhold certain product-centric data. The benefits of the proposed approach are maximized in situations where the trust between partners is high. In such situations, partners feel less inhibition to share product-centric data (or any other information) throughout the supply chain. Trust between partners is usually built up in long-term supplier-customer relationships. In case of complex products, product-centric data of the components of the product can also be retrieved, at least if the data of the components is stored with or linked to the product data.

As mentioned before, a partial IS diagram of the manufacturer agent can be built by the retailer agent, based on the available product-centric data. Figure 5 illustrates this diagram for the described scenario. Such a diagram can be built by using a set of simple rules, based on the location changes of the product, as well as the physical changes made to the product. A physical change is modeled as an interaction, as it can be considered an interaction between the manufacturer and the product. An example is the "Assemble PCs"- interaction in Figure 5.

This diagram only reveals when products are shipped between agents, when products are changed, and in which order this occurs. Therefore, an interaction is allowed to only have one child, since the interactions identified by using the product-centric data can be incomplete like for instance the "Manufacturer-Retailer"-interaction in Figure 5. The "Customer-Manufacturer"-interaction does not always occur, but only when one or more of the delivered computers need to be repaired by the manufacturer agent. Thus, a decision rule set that can check this condition is attached to the SEQ routing type that graphically appears below the "Deliver PCs"-interaction. If one or

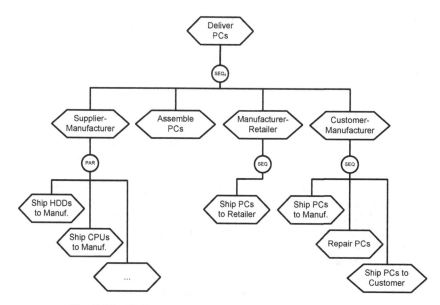

Fig. 5. The IS diagram of the manufacturer from the retailer's viewpoint

more of the computers needs to be repaired, all interactions occur in sequence. If not, N-out-of-M children occur in sequence. In this specific example, three out of four children occur in sequence in the latter case.

In a similar way, an IS diagram from the perspective of the customer agent can be created by the retailer agent. This diagram is shown in Figure 6. Again, by using the product-centric data, only the shipments of and physical changes to the product are revealed.

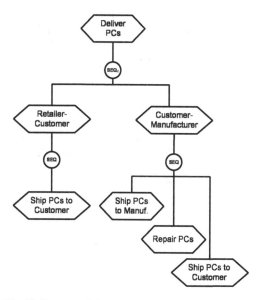

Fig. 6. The IS diagram of the customer from the retailer's viewpoint

4 Building the Global Interaction Diagram

This section presents the method for building a global IS diagram from a set of local IS diagrams. Section 4.1 introduces the global construction algorithm. After, Section 4.2 discusses tool support.

4.1 Global Construction Algorithm

As explained, each agent involved in a collaborative business process can use product-centric data to identify agent-to-agent interactions. Each agent builds a set of local IS diagrams (in which each set can be different), representing its own interactions, as well as interactions other agents are performing. This is considered necessary, as agents (in a supply chain) are not always willing to exchange their process definitions. The global construction algorithm is listed in Table 2. The algorithm is expressed in pseudo-code, which uses set-theoretic notation mixed with the control structures of conventional high-level programming languages. Below Table 2, the different parts of the algorithm are explained.

Table 2. Global Construction Algorithm

```
 1: function CONSTRUCT (GI,LI)
 2: begin
 3:        GO := GI
 4:        for each li∈ LI do
 5:              for each i∈ IH^li do
 6:                    if i∉ subtree(parent(i)^li)^GO then
 7:                          i_new := clone(i)^li
 8:                          GO := GO ∪ {comp(i_new)}
 9:                          <_I^GO := <_I^GO ∪ {(parent(i)^li, i_new)}
10:                    else if conflict(subtree(i)^GO, subtree(i)^li) then
11:                          i_dum := j: j∈ I^GO ∧ i = j ∧ dum(j)
12:                          if ¬∃ i_dum then
13:                                i_dum := clone(i)^GO
14:                                DR(i_dum) := ∅
15:                                dum(i_dum) := TRUE
16:                                GO := GO ∪ {comp(i_dum)}
17:                                <_I^GO := <_I^GO ∪ {(parent(i)^GO, i_dum)}
18:                                <_I^GO := <_I^GO \ {(parent(i)^GO, i^GO)}
19:                                <_I^GO := <_I^GO ∪ {(i_dum, i^GO)}
20:                                i_conflict := clone(i)^li
21:                                comp(i_dum)^GO := comp(i_dum)^GO ∪ comp(i_conflict)^GO
22:                                RT(i_dum) := XOR
23:                                GO := GO ∪ {comp(i_conflict)}
24:                                <_I^GO := <_I^GO ∪ {(i_dum, i_conflict)}
25:                          else
26:                                comp(i)^GO := comp(i)^GO ∪ comp(i)^li
27:        return GO
28: end
```

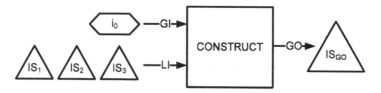

Fig. 7. Illustration of the global construction algorithm, as executed by every agent

Figure 7 shows the input and output of the algorithm graphically. The algorithm expects a global IS diagram *GI* (Global Input) which only contains the root interaction i_0. The root interaction represents the common shared goal of the collaborative business process under consideration. Furthermore, the algorithm expects a set of local IS diagrams *LI* (Local Input) that are to be merged. Each local diagram is based on the same root interaction i_0. The algorithm returns a new global diagram *GO* (Global Output). As mentioned before, the goal of the global construction algorithm is to build a minimal interaction representation *GO* where the interactions, from the diagrams that are being compared, are merged when there is no conflict. Conflicts are detected by the function **CONFLICT** (see Table 3 and the explanation below it).

The global construction algorithm uses some notations from the formal definition of the TALL interaction diagrams [33]. Here, these notations are explained informally:

- *I* is the set of interactions that form an IS diagram;
- $L_I(i)$ is a function that assigns a label to each interaction from the set *I*. Although interactions can share labels in the same diagram, each interaction is unique. Thus, interactions with identical labels are completely unrelated when executed;
- *RT* is the routing type function that assigns a routing type to each interaction from the set *I*. The function *RT* indicates how the direct child interactions are routed in order to complete their parent interaction. As indicated above, the supported routing types are SEQ, PAR, and XOR;
- The partial ordering relation $<_i \subseteq I \times I$ connects parent interactions to their child interactions. Graphically, a line is drawn between a parent and each direct child. These lines converge in the routing type symbol that graphically appears below each parent;
- *DR(i)* is a function that assigns a decision rule set to each interaction. As mentioned above, graphically the routing type is augmented with a subscripted letter *d* if the decision rule set is non-empty;
- The set *R* contains all roles that are relevant to the set of interactions *I*;
- *RI* is a function that assigns roles to interactions. Graphically, this is depicted by a connector line between a role and an interaction (as in Figure 2);
- $L_R(r)$ is a function that assigns a label to each role from the set *R*;
- i_0 denotes the root interaction;
- *children(i)* is a function that returns the set of direct child interactions of the parent interaction *i*;
- *parent(i)* is a function that returns the parent of the interaction *i*;
- *ht(i)* is a function that returns the height of interaction *i*.

In addition, some new operators and notations are used in the global construction algorithm, as an extension of the formal definition in [33]:

1. an operator for the union of two IS diagrams is needed. If IS_1 and IS_2 are two IS diagrams, then the union of IS_1 and IS_2 is an IS diagram $IS_{IS1 \cup IS2} = IS_1 \cup IS_2$ such that: $I_{I1 \cup I2} = I_1 \cup I_2$, $<_{I \lhd I1} \cup_{\lhd I2} = <_{I1} \cup <_{I2}$, $R_{RI \cup R2} = R_1 \cup R_2$, $RI_{RI1 \cup RI2} = R_{I1} \cup R_{I2}$. The union of the set of interactions and the set of roles includes the union of the interaction attributes (label, routing type and decision rule set) and role attributes (label). Hence, if I_1 and I_2 are two sets of interactions then the union of I_1 and I_2 is an interaction set $I_{I1 \cup I2} = I_1 \cup I_2$ such that: $L_{I1 \cup I2} = L_{I1} \cup L_{I2}$, $RT_{RT1 \cup RT2} = RT_1 \cup RT_2$, $DR_{DR1 \cup DR2} = DR_1 \cup DR_2$. Similarly, if R_1 and R_2 are two sets of roles then the union of R_1 and R_2 is a role set $R_{R1 \cup R2} = R_1 \cup R_2$ such that: $L_{R1 \cup R2} = L_{R1} \cup L_{R2}$;
2. *subtree(i)* is a function that returns a segment or subtree of the IS diagram with root i. Thus, $subtree(i) \subseteq IS$ (see Figure 8);

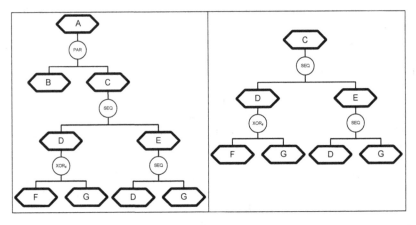

Fig. 8. Illustration of the input (left) and output (right) of the *subtree* function applied to interaction C

3. *comp(i)* is a function that returns a single component of the IS diagram. In other words, it returns a subtree (read: diagram) with the single interaction i. In this regard, a component comprises an interaction, and all its attributes and roles;
4. *clone(i)* is a function that returns a new interaction with all attributes and roles of i. In other words, it creates a copy of the component i;
5. *dum:* $I \rightarrow \{TRUE, FALSE\}$ is a function that is used to differentiate between 'normal' interactions and dummy interactions. Dummy interactions are introduced during execution of the global construction algorithm to act as the parent of identically labeled interactions, which the algorithm cannot merge because of a conflict. Such interactions are alternative views on the same interaction. This means all children of a dummy interaction have identical labels. Initially, the default setting for all interactions is FALSE: $\forall i \in I$: $\neg dum(i)$;
6. *IH* is an ordered set in which all interactions $i \in I$ are ordered according to the binary relationship $R = \{(i_1, i_2) \mid i_1 \in I \land i_2 \in I \land ht(i_1) \leq ht(i_2)\}$;

7. elements are augmented with an index *GI, GO,* or *li* indicating that the element appears in the global input diagram, the global output diagram or in the local diagram under consideration. For instance, interaction $i_0{}^{GO}$ is the root interaction that appears in the global output diagram.

The global construction algorithm is contained into a main **for each**-loop (Lines 4-27) that for each iteration compares *GO* to a local IS diagram $li \in LI$. During the comparison, the algorithm searches for commonalities and/or differences between *GO* and *li* by comparing (labels of) the interactions in both diagrams. If possible, interactions in both diagrams are merged and a new global IS diagram is produced that serves as input for the next iteration. This global IS diagram is compared with the next local diagram from *LI*, until all the local IS diagrams have been processed. In the end, the global construction algorithm produces a global IS diagram *GO* that takes into account all the local IS diagrams of the agents involved.

The global construction algorithm first assigns *GI* to *GO* (Line 3). Inside the main **for each**-loop, an inner **for-each** loop (Lines 5-26) processes one by one all the interactions from the local diagram *li* under consideration according to the ordering in the set *IH*. This means the algorithm starts with the root interaction from the local diagram *li* that has height zero. Next, the algorithm continues with the interactions that have height one (i.e. the direct child interactions of the root interaction), and so until all the interactions in the local diagram *li* have been processed. In general, three cases can apply to the interaction i^{li} that is being processed.

Case 1: Interaction i^{li} does not exist in the same segment of GO (Line 6)
The **if** statement in Line 6 of the algorithm tests whether interaction i^{li} should be added to *GO*. Interaction i^{li} is added to *GO* when i^{li} is does not exist in the subtree of its parent in *GO*. When the condition in Line 6 is true, a clone of i^{li} is created (Line 7), this clone is added to *GO* (Line 8) and connected to the correct parent in *GO* (Line 9).

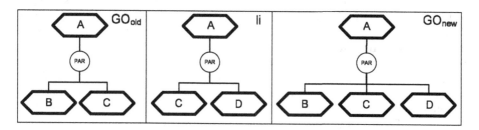

Fig. 9. A generic example of a Global Input diagram (GO_old), a local input diagram (li), and a Global Output diagram (GO_new) that illustrates the case in which interaction D^{li} is added to GO_new since it does not exist in GO_old

Figure 9 shows a generic example (without roles) in which the condition in the **if** statement is true for interaction D^{li}. In the specific example, interaction D^{li} does not exist in the subtree of its parent in *GO*, that is, the subtree of A^{GO}. Therefore, interaction D^{li} including its attributes and roles are added to *GO*. Each IS diagram shows a local process view, from one agent's perspective, that is build based on product-centric data. In this regard, each IS diagram represents a specific incomplete part of the overall collaborative business process in the supply chain. Thus, the local IS diagrams, which are input to the algorithm are assumed to be incomplete.

In Figure 9, GO_{old} and li are the two IS diagrams being compared. Both diagrams show the incomplete local process perspective or view of an agent. The local IS diagram of the first agent shows that interactions B and C occur in parallel as part of interaction A. The local IS diagram of the second agent shows that interactions C and D occur in parallel as part of interaction A. The two agents provide complementary views that are merged in the output in order to create a more complete representation. Based on this, it is sufficient to perform interaction A once in GO_{new}. However, merging only occurs when the views of agents are not conflicting. Case 2 discusses how the algorithm deals with a conflict situation.

Case 2: Interaction i^{li} exists in the same segment of GO and generates a conflict situation (Line 10)

If the condition in Line 6 is false, which means i^{li} has a counterpart i^{GO} in the same segment, the algorithm continues with the **else if** statement in Line 10. The **else if** statement tests whether there is a conflict between the interactions i^{GO} and i^{li}. A conflict is detected by the function **CONFLICT** that is listed in Table 3 and explained below Table 3. In general, a conflict means that the interactions being compared cannot be merged since they are alternative views on the same interaction. Hence, the global construction algorithm keeps both interactions (i^{GO} and i^{li}) in the global output diagram. A new interaction i_{dum} (dummy interaction) is introduced (Line 13) to act as the parent of i^{GO} and i^{li}. Since i_{dum} carries the decision rule set of i^{GO} (assigned by the clone function in Line 13), Line 14 empties the decision rule set of i_{dum}. Next, Line 16 adds i_{dum} including all its attributes and roles to GO. The algorithm then assigns i_{dum} as parent interaction of i^{GO} (Line 19). In the scenario in which i^{GO} already has a parent, Lines 17 and 18 make sure that this parent is detached as parent of i^{GO} and instead is assigned as parent of i_{dum}. Any newly introduced dummy interaction is assigned TRUE by the function $dum(i)$ (Line 15). Together with Lines 11 and 12 this prevents that in a future iteration another dummy interaction is introduced in GO for the same i^{GO} and i^{li}. Since i_{dum} acts as parent of i^{GO} and i^{li}, the next step is to add i^{li} to GO. To this end, Line 20 first creates a clone of i^{li} named $i_{conflict}$. Line 23 adds the clone of i^{li} to GO and Line 24 assigns this clone as a child of i_{dum}. Line 21 assigns the union of the components of i_{dum} and $i_{conflict}$ to the dummy interaction. In this way, the combined roles of its child interactions are attached to i_{dum}. Since the direct child interactions of i_{dum} are different views on the same interaction, i_{dum} is assigned the routing type XOR by Line 22. The use of a different routing type than XOR would imply that the interaction is executed more than once.

The function **CONFLICT** receives as input, from the global construction algorithm, the subtrees of i^{GO} and i^{li} (see Table 3). This means that the root interactions in the function **CONFLICT** are (the currently being processed) interaction i^{li} in the global construction algorithm and its counterpart i^{GO}. A conflict arises in two situations. First, when the routing types of i^{GO} and i^{li} are different (Line 3 in Table 3) they are considered alternative views on the same interaction. In this case, the function returns TRUE (Line 4 in Table 3). Next, the function builds a set X that contains all children of i_0^{li} (Line 6 in Table 3) and builds a set Y that contains all interactions that are members of both X and the set of interactions in sGO (Line 7 in Table 3). For all

Table 3. The function **CONFLICT**

```
1: function CONFLICT (sGO,sli)
2: begin
3:        if RT(i₀GO)GO ≠ RT(i₀li)li then
4:            return TRUE
5:        else
6:            X := children(i₀li)li
7:            Y := X ∩ GO
8:            for each j∈ Y do
9:                if ht(j)GO ≠ ht(j)li then
10:                    return TRUE
11:        return FALSE
12: end
```

the interactions in the set Y, the function then tests whether these interactions occur on the same level (i.e. height) in sGO and sli. In other words, the function checks whether the children of i_0^{li} have counterparts in sGO that occur another level. If this is not true, there is no conflict and the function returns FALSE (Line 11 in Table 3). However, if this is true (Line 9 in Table 3) then i_0^{GO} and i_0^{li} are considered alternative views on the same interaction and the function returns TRUE (Line 10 in Table 3). The latter forms the second conflict situation.

Figure 10 shows a generic example in which the interactions A^{GO} and A^{li} are in conflict because they have different routing types, that is, they are alternative views of the same interaction. A new (dummy) interaction with routing type XOR and the same label is introduced in GO to act as the parent of A^{GO} and A^{li}.

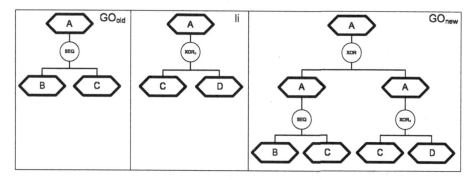

Fig. 10. A generic example of a Global Input diagram (GO_{old}), a local input diagram (li), and a Global Output diagram (GO_{new}). The example illustrates the case in which A^{li} generates a conflict because a counterpart A^{GO} exists that has a different routing type.

Figure 11 depicts a generic example of the second conflict situation. In this specific example, interactions A^{GO} and A^{li} are in conflict because parent interaction A^{li} has a child D^{li} with a counterpart D^{GO} that exists in the subtree of A^{GO} on a different level. Therefore, the same dummy interaction A with routing type XOR is added to GO in this situation.

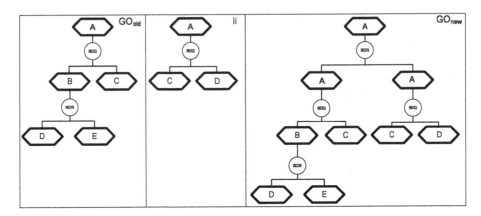

Fig. 11. A generic example of a Global Input diagram (GO_{old}), a local input diagram (li), and a Global Output diagram (GO_{new}). The example illustrates the case in which A^{li} generates a conflict because it has a child that occurs in the subtree of its counterpart A^{GO}.

Case 3: Interaction i^{li} exists in the same segment of GO and there is no conflict situation (Line 25)

From here, any line numbers refer to Table 2 again. If i^{li} exists in the same segment of GO but there is no conflict, the statement in Line 26 is executed. In this case, the components of i^{GO} and i^{li} are simply merged since it is possible for them to have different roles, decision rules etc. Figure 9 provides an example of this case. In Figure 9, parent interaction A^{li} has a child C^{li} with a counterpart C^{GO} in the subtree A^{GO}. However, in this case there is no conflict between A^{GO} and A^{li} because C^{li} and C^{GO} occur on the same level in GO_{old} and li. Thus, in Figure 9 it is unnecessary to keep both A^{GO} and A^{li} in the output by introducing a dummy interaction.

4.2 Tool Support

A software toolset is available to create and modify TALL diagrams, diagram elements, and properties of these elements using a graphical interface[2]. All diagrams, elements, and their properties are stored in an associated database. The current release of the software tool contains an implementation of the global construction algorithm. The user can create multiple IS diagrams and merge these into a global IS diagram.

5 Applying the Global Construction Algorithm

This section applies the global construction algorithm to the example case described in Section 3 in order to illustrate the workings of the algorithm. The retailer agent in the supply chain can run the algorithm, using the different IS diagrams it has generated (as shown in Figures 4, 5, and 6) as inputs. Figure 12 shows the generated output of the global construction algorithm. This global IS diagram shows the process starting from

---

[2] The latest release of the software tool can be downloaded from the software section on http://www.agentlab.nl/

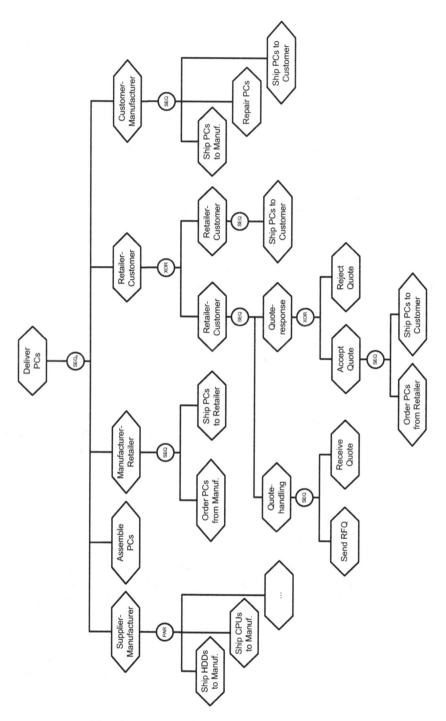

Fig. 12. The generated global IS diagram by the retailer

the supplier, until the product reaches the customer, and afterwards, when optionally a product is returned by the customer to be repaired by the manufacturer. Despite its simplicity, this example demonstrates several important features of the global construction algorithm.

First, this example shows how different views on an interaction are merged when an interaction i^{li} appears in the local diagram li under consideration but does not appear in the global diagram GO. This reflects the first case in the global construction algorithm. An example of such an interaction is the "Assemble PCs"-interaction from the manufacturer diagram (see Figure 5), which does not appear in the retailer diagram (see Figure 4). A clone of this interaction is created, the clone is added to GO, and connected to the same parent in GO (see Figure 12).

Second, this example shows how the algorithm deals with a conflict situation, that is, the second case in the algorithm. In the example, the retailer and the customer diagrams both include the "Retailer-Customer"-interaction. The "Ship PCs to Customer"-interaction, which is a child of the "Retailer-Customer"-interaction in the manufacturer diagram, exists also, on a different level, in the subtree of the "Retailer-Customer"-interaction in the retailer diagram. Because of this, the function **CONFLICT** returns TRUE since the two "Retailer-Customer"-interactions are considered alternative views on the same interaction. In this case, the global construction algorithm keeps both views in the output, and adds a new parent interaction for both views (see Figure 12). In this way, the ordering constraints of both views are preserved. Since both views are alternative descriptions on the same interaction, the new parent interaction is assigned the XOR routing type.

The third feature shown is how the algorithm deals with the third case in the algorithm. For instance, when the root interactions in the retailer and manufacturer diagrams are being compared, a conflict does not arise. These interactions have similar routing types and the children of the "Deliver PCs"-interaction in the manufacturer diagram do not occur on a different height in the retailer diagram. Thus, the **CONFLICT** function returns FALSE and the algorithm executes the statement in Line 26. This statement merges the attributes and roles of both interactions. This merging includes the decision rule sets of both interactions, which explains the SEQ_d routing type of the "Deliver PCs"-interaction in the global output diagram (see Figure 12).

6 Public and Private Process Representations

In a business domain where no product-centric data is available, the global construction algorithm can be used by several partners to build a shared global interaction model that coordinates (and possibly enacts) the overall collaborative business process. Each partner can represent its own local interactions that are part of the collaborative business process in an IS diagram. All local IS diagrams can then be used as input for the algorithm. In such a business setting, one of the issues is how much each organization (with its own legal and business boundaries) is willing to share with its partners. In the design of inter-organizational workflows, 'local' modelers strive to keep details opaque as much as possible. This attitude is based on the argument that organizations in general tend to keep their internal workings (i.e. process models) hidden. Though, a certain degree of disclosure is inevitable, especially in collaborative domains, in order to achieve good cross-organizational business process alignment and interoperability.

In TALL, a separation between public and private process views can be made on the same lines as the separation between interaction descriptions and agent behavior descriptions as discussed in Section 2. The agents are involved in interactions that have shared names, routing types, decision rules and roles, and exhibit behaviors that show their internal workings. All partners (and their internal agents) can hide their behaviors and expose only their local interaction structures (i.e. local IS diagrams) to their partners as input for the global construction algorithm. In this approach, the agent behaviors constitute private business process descriptions. Interoperability is achieved by the global IS diagram that is built, using the global construction algorithm, from the local IS diagrams.

This separation between public and private models only works if the private process descriptions of all the participants are aligned. Otherwise, a minimal disclosure of the behavioral touch points (i.e. the messages send and received) and their sequence is necessary in order to achieve simple alignment [22]. One agent has to inform the other agent what and when it is expected to send and receive a message during an interaction. Still, this level of disclosure does not reveal the exact activities in the private descriptions since only the message exchange points are made public. In conclusion, the following two views on public and private process representations apply to TALL:

- if the goal is to have minimal process disclosure, then only the local IS diagrams are made public for coordination of the overall collaborative business process using a shared global IS diagram. The agent behaviors are kept completely private;
- if the goal is to have more alignment, the agent behaviors can be made partially public by sharing the behavioral touch points.

Related work, like [1], separates between private and public process levels and recognizes the need for an organization to hide parts of its private process implementation. However, it is also mentioned that too much hiding can be counter-productive. In [19], the need for a process abstraction concept is stressed in the design and analysis of collaborative business processes. Such a concept must be able to represent internal or private processes and at the same time provide a process-oriented interface to the outside world, facilitating interweaving into partner processes. The merging of local IS diagrams, using the global construction algorithm, into a global IS diagram provides such a feature. Other works show how public representations can be (formally) translated from internal representations [13]. Moreover, modeling languages like WS-BPEL [25] and BPMN [37] distinguish between public and private process representations. However, the public (named also abstract) process is a mere non-deterministic protocol that describes possible message exchanges. TALL brings an interaction structure that can and should be made public, and has an option to decide on the degree of exposure of the agent behaviors.

7 Discussion and Future Work

All agents involved in a collaborative business process have their own local, distributed views. Typically, no agent will have a complete view of all the interactions that occur in the process. In other words, each agent owns one or more local IS diagrams. Since interactions may influence each other, it makes sense to build an IS diagram that shows a global picture of the entire process. This global IS diagram increases process visibility and the understandability of the agent with regard to the supply chain. In the presented supply chain scenario, this is the retailer agent. The global IS diagram provides a more complete description of the entire supply chain, that is, it serves as a presentation of the multiple interactions that occur in the supply chain.

Such global models are especially useful when a set of parties interact in such a way that none of them sees all messages being exchanged, yet interactions taking place between some parties have an impact on the way other parties interact [39]. The presented approach only reveals the interactions with and between partners based on the available product-centric data. Partners do not have to share their behaviors, that is, their private business processes. In this way, interoperability can be achieved in situations where the (complete) models of behavior are not shared. Moreover, the global IS diagram could be used for analysis purposes. This potentially enables the retailer agent to better align its processes with the processes of its partner agents.

The presented example of product-centric data for the supply chain scenario contains data about one product individual. Future research intends to investigate how interaction diagrams can be build using product-centric data that contains data about multiple products or components with slightly different lifecycles.

The global construction algorithm can be improved by enhancing the **CONFLICT** function. First, an enhanced version of the **CONFLICT** function should, in some cases, return FALSE even if the interactions have different routing types in the global and local IS diagram. For instance, the PAR routing type is quite weak in the sense that it allows interactions to be executed in parallel or in any order. Therefore, it could be possible to merge two interactions with similar labels but with routing types PAR and SEQ. Second, the function should, in some cases, be able to merge alternative views with the same interactions occurring on different heights in the tree. In the current version of the **CONFLICT** function, the "Retailer-Customer"-interactions in the retailer and customer diagram are considered alternative views because the "Ship PCs to Customer" interaction appears on a different height in the retailer diagram. It is for instance possible that the "Ship PCs to Customer"-interaction in the customer diagram is a secondary shipment. Thus, in the output the "Ship PCs to Customer"-interaction appears twice in the subtree of the highest level "Retailer-Customer"-interaction. Although it is possible that both "Ship PCs to Customer"-interactions are the same (i.e. the customer diagram may be based on incomplete product-centric data), it is considered more important to represent the views of all the agents even though this can lead to redundant interactions in the output. In line with the goal to create a minimal interaction representation, future research will investigate an improved version of the algorithm that reduces the number of (redundant) interactions in the output. Based on this, a third possible enhancement to the algorithm would be a "pruning"-feature, which compresses the global output diagram, by removing redundant interactions. Besides possible redundant views like the "Ship PCs to Customer"-interaction above, interactions can also be redundant when they have the same routing type as their parents. Often, the children of a redundant interaction can be directly connected to the parent of the redundant interaction. Together with these improvements, a mathematical evaluation of the algorithm in terms of formally specified properties like termination, correctness, complexity etc. is planned for the future.

As mentioned in Section 6, the global construction algorithm can also be used in cross-organizational environments where no product-centric data is available. In this case, the global construction algorithm can be used to build a shared global interaction diagram that manages the (distributed) behaviors of all the partners. Such a global interaction structure could be implemented on a collaborative IT platform and act as a coordination framework. This line of research is to be explored in more detail.

8 Conclusion

In product-centric supply chains, coordination and control efforts are aimed at individual products instead of orders, production orders or shipment batches like in conventional supply chains. The TraSer project is concerned with research into product-centric supply chains. In the TraSer approach, product-centric data is stored in a database that is associated to each product individual. Each product contains a label in the form of an RFID or barcode, which contains an ID@URI code. Besides the unique product identification number, this code contains an URI (Uniform Resource Identifier) that refers to the location of the associated database. Product visibility is achieved in the supply chain when each partner can access the available product-centric data.

This paper uses an illustrative example to show how a partner can use product-centric data to build a set of local interaction diagrams in which each diagram models the perspective of one partner in the supply chain. The interaction diagrams are part of a novel graphical modeling language named TALL, developed and adopted by the authors, which models collaborative business processes as a structure of role-based interactions in which agents play the roles. A formal method is introduced to enable the partner to automatically construct a global interaction diagram from the set of local interaction diagrams. In this way, the partner obtains a global view of the supply chain. The formal method comprises an algorithm that processes and compares all local diagrams, detects any conflicts, and outputs a global interaction diagram. The global interaction diagram depicts a minimal representation where the interactions from the local diagrams are merged when there is no conflict.

By representing all views of the agents involved, the global interaction diagram increases process visibility and understandability in the supply chain for the partners that use the presented approach. This benefits process alignment and enterprise operability in the supply chain.

References

1. van der Aalst, W.M.P., Weske, M.: The P2P Approach to Interorganizational Workflows. In: Dittrich, K.R., Geppert, A., Norrie, M.C. (eds.) CAiSE 2001. LNCS, vol. 2068, pp. 140–156. Springer, Heidelberg (2001)
2. Bauer, B., Müller, J.P., Odell, J.: Agent UML: A Formalism for Specifying Multiagent Software Systems. The Int. J. of Software Engineering and Knowledge Engineering 11(3), 207–230 (2001)
3. Bresciani, P., Perini, A., Giorgini, P., Giunchiglia, F., Mylopoulos, L.: Tropos: An Agent-Oriented Software Development Methodology. Autonomous Agents and Multi-Agent Systems 8(3), 203–236 (2004)

4. Bussmann, S., Schild, K.: Self-organizing Manufacturing Control: An Industrial Application of Agent Technology. In: 4th International Conference on Multi-Agent Systems, pp. 87–94. IEEE Computer Society, Washington (2000)
5. Caire, G., Coulier, W., Garijo, F., Gomez, J., Pavon, J., Leal, F., Chainho, P., Kearney, P., Stark, J., Evans, R., Massonet, P.: Agent Oriented Analysis using Message/UML. In: Wooldridge, M.J., Weiß, G., Ciancarini, P. (eds.) AOSE 2001. LNCS, vol. 2222, pp. 119–135. Springer, Heidelberg (2002)
6. Callon, M., Méadel, C., Rabeharisoa, V.: The Economy of Qualities. Economy and Society 31(2), 194–217 (2002)
7. Camarinha-Matos, L.M., Afsarmanesh, H.: Collaborative Networks: A New Scientific Discipline. Journal of Intelligent Manufacturing 16(4/5), 439–452 (2005)
8. Cervenka, R., Trenanský, I.: The Agent Modeling Language – AML: A Comprehensive Approach to Modeling Multi-Agent Systems. Birkhäuser, Basel (2007)
9. Collins, J., Aruachalam, R., Sadeh, N., Eriksson, J., Finne, N., Janson, S.: The Supply Chain Management Game for the 2007 Trading Agent Competition. Technical report, Carnegie Mellon University, Pittsburgh, PA, USA (2006)
10. DeLoach, S.A., Wood, M.F., Sparkman, C.H.: Multiagent Systems Engineering. The Int. J. of Software Engineering and Knowledge Engineering 11(3), 231–258 (2001)
11. Desel, J.: Process Modeling using Petri Nets. In: Dumas, M., van der Aalst, W.M.P., ter Hofstede, A.H.M. (eds.) Process-Aware Information Systems: Bridging People and Software through Process Technology, pp. 147–177. John Wiley & Sons, Hoboken (2005)
12. Dumas, M., ter Hofstede, A.H.M.: UML Activity Diagrams as a Workflow Specification Language. In: Martin, G., Kobryn, C. (eds.) UML 2001. LNCS, vol. 2185, pp. 76–90. Springer, Heidelberg (2001)
13. Eshuis, R., Grefen, P.: Constructing Customized Process Views. Data & Knowledge Engineering 64(2), 419–438 (2008)
14. Harrison-Broninski, K.: Human Interactions: The Heart and Soul of Business Process Management. Meghan-Kiffer Press, Tampa (2005)
15. Holmström, J., Främling, K.: Product Centric Integration: Exploring the Impact of RFID and Agent Technology on Supply Chain Management. In: Camarinha-Matos, L.M., Afsarmanesh, H., Ollus, M. (eds.) PRO-VE 2006. IFIP, vol. 224, pp. 565–572. Springer, Heidelberg (2006)
16. Holmström, J., Kajosaari, R., Främling, K., Langius, E.: Roadmap to Tracking Based Business and Intelligent Products. Computers in Industry 60(3), 229–233 (2009)
17. Huvio, E., Grönvall, J., Främling, K.: Tracking and Tracing Parcels using a Distributed Computing Approach. In: Solen, O. (ed.) 14th Annual Conference for Nordic Researchers in Logistics, pp. 12–14. Norwegian University of Science and Technology, Trondheim (2002)
18. Jagdev, H.S., Thoben, K.D.: Anatomy of Enterprise Collaboration. Production Planning & Control 12(5), 437–451 (2001)
19. Lippe, S., Greiner, U., Barros, A.: A Survey on State of the Art to Facilitate Modelling of Cross-Organisational Business Processes. In: Nüttgens, M., Mendling, J. (eds.) 2nd German Informatics Society Workshop on XML Interchange Formats for Business Process Management, pp. 7–22. Gesellschaft für Informatik, Karlsruhe (2005)
20. Mayer, R.J., Painter, M.K., deWitte P.S.: IDEF Family of Methods for Concurrent Engineering and Business Reengineering Applications. Technical Report, Knowledge Based Systems, Inc. (1992), http://www.idef.com/pdf/IDEFFAMI.pdf
21. Melao, N., Pidd, M.: A Conceptual Framework for Understanding Business Processes and Business Process Modelling. Information Systems Journal 10(2), 105–129 (2000)

22. Meyer, G.G., Szirbik, N.B.: Anticipatory Alignment Mechanisms for Behavioral Learning in Multi Agent Systems. In: Butz, M.V., Sigaud, O., Pezzulo, G., Baldassarre, G. (eds.) ABiALS 2006. LNCS, vol. 4520, pp. 325–344. Springer, Heidelberg (2007)
23. Meyer, G.G., Szirbik, N.B.: Agent Behavior Alignment: A Mechanism to Overcome Problems in Agent Interactions During Runtime. In: Klusch, M., Hindriks, K.V., Papazoglou, M.P., Sterling, L. (eds.) CIA 2007. LNCS, vol. 4676, pp. 270–284. Springer, Heidelberg (2007)
24. Meyer, G.G., Främling, K., Holmström, J.: Intelligent Products: A Survey. Computers in Industry 60(3), 137–148 (2009)
25. Organization for the Advancement of Structured Information Standards (OASIS): Web Services Business Process Execution Language Version 2.0. OASIS Standard (2007), http://docs.oasis-open.org/wsbpel/2.0/OS/wsbpel-v2.0-OS.pdf
26. Padgham, L., Winikoff, M.: Developing Intelligent Agent Systems: A Practical Guide. John Wiley & Sons, Chichester (2004)
27. Pesic, M., van der Aalst, W.M.P.: A declarative approach for flexible business processes management. In: Eder, J., Dustdar, S. (eds.) BPM Workshops 2006. LNCS, vol. 4103, pp. 169–180. Springer, Heidelberg (2006)
28. Presley, A.R., Liles, D.H.: A Holon-Based Process Modeling Methodology. Int. J. of Operations & Production Management. 21(5/6), 565–581 (2001)
29. Roest, G.B., Szirbik, N.B.: Escape and Intervention in Multi-Agent Systems. AI & Society 24(1), 25–34 (2009)
30. Scheer, A.W., Thomas, O., Adam, O.: Process Modeling using Event-Driven Process Chains. In: Dumas, M., van der Aalst, W.M.P., ter Hofstede, A.H.M. (eds.) Process-Aware Information Systems: Bridging People and Software through Process Technology, pp. 119–145. John Wiley & Sons, Hoboken (2005)
31. Stuit, M., Szirbik, N.B., de Snoo, C.: Interaction Beliefs: A Way to Understand Emergent Organizational Behaviour. In: 9th International Conference on Enterprise Information Systems, pp. 241–248. INSTICC, Funchal (2007)
32. Stuit, M., Szirbik, N.B.: Modelling and Executing Complex and Dynamic Business Processes by Reification of Agent Interactions. In: O'Hare, G.M.P., Ricci, A., O'Grady, M.J., Dikenelli, O. (eds.) ESAW 2006. LNCS, vol. 4457, pp. 106–125. Springer, Heidelberg (2007)
33. Stuit, M., Szirbik, N.B.: Towards Agent-based Modelling and Verification of Collaborative Business Processes. Int. J. of Cooperative Information Systems. Under Review (2009)
34. Sturm, A., Dori, D., Shehory, O.: Single-Model Method for Specifying Multi-Agent Systems. In: 2nd International Conference on Autonomous Agents and Multiagent Systems, pp. 121–128. ACM, New York (2003)
35. Taveter, K., Wagner, G.: A Multi-Perspective Methodology for Modelling Inter-Enterprise Business Processes. In: Arisawa, H., Kambayashi, Y., Kumar, V., Mayr, H.C., Hunt, I. (eds.) ER Workshops 2001. LNCS, vol. 2465, pp. 403–416. Springer, Heidelberg (2002)
36. Wagner, G.: The Agent-Object-Relationship Metamodel: Towards a Unified View of State and Behaviour. Information Systems 28(5), 475–504 (2003)
37. White, S.A.: Introduction to BPMN. BPTrends White Papers & Technical Briefs (2004), http://www.bptrends.com/publicationfiles/07-04%20WP%20Intro%20to%20BPMN%20-%20White.pdf
38. Wooldridge, M., Jennings, N.R., Kinny, D.: The GAIA Methodology for Agent-Oriented Analysis and Design. Autonomous Agents and Multi-Agent Systems 3(3), 285–312 (2000)
39. Zaha, J.M., Dumas, M., ter Hofstede, A., Barros, A., Decker, G.: Service Interaction Modeling: Bridging Global and Local Views. In: 10th IEEE International Enterprise Distributed Object Computing Conference, pp. 45–55. IEEE Computer Society, Washington (2006)

Security Aspects on Inter-organizational Cooperation Using Wrapper Agents

Bengt Carlsson[1], Paul Davidsson[1], Andreas Jacobsson[2], Stefan J. Johansson[1], and Jan A. Persson[1]

[1] School of Information and Communication Technology, Blekinge Institute of Technology, Box 520, 372 25 Ronneby, Sweden
{bca,pdv,sja,jps}@bth.se
[2] Malmö University, School of Technology, 205 06 Malmö, Sweden
andreas.jacobsson@mah.se

Abstract. The significance of electronic information exchange in inter-organizational cooperation is well-known. We will here focus on the particular requirements of SMEs. We describe a general *wrapper agent* solution based on open source freeware that makes it possible (in principle) for any business system to exchange information with any other business system. It has been successfully applied in a pilot study involving two companies in a transport chain using different business systems. We also suggest further improvements by addressing security issues as well as an extended, possibly dynamic, set of involved companies and higher levels of cooperation.

Keywords: Security, Inter-organizational cooperation, wrapper agents, SME.

1 Introduction

Most organizations recognize the critical role that information and communication technology (ICT) plays in supporting their business objectives as well as fueling profitability and growth. As more and more small and medium sized enterprises (SME) adjust their businesses to the increasing demands for ICT solutions, there is a set of criteria that should be met. Some of these are; interoperability (both within the enterprise and with other enterprises), scalability, adaptability (handling shifting customer needs), independence (avoiding technological lock-in[1] and high entry-costs), cost-effectiveness, simplicity and usability, as well as security (preventing unintended exposure of sensitive information). We will here focus on inter-organizational cooperation and we discriminate between three dimensions of such cooperation:

---

[1] Technological lock-in occurs when old and subordinate technologies become entrenched in the market, i.e. they become locked into new products despite the fact that better and more efficient technologies are available [13]. Getting *locked-in* means having to accept inferior standards or products, even though superior alternatives exist, even though it is known that superior alternatives exist, and even though the costs of switching may not be high.

K. Fischer et al. (Eds.): ATOP 2005 and ATOP 2008, LNBIP 25, pp. 220–233, 2009.

1. *The level of cooperation:* This is related to the content and purpose of the exchanged information with tasks ranging from administrative information exchange to complex operation planning. An example of a simple task is ordering and invoicing, whereas a more complex task may concern making critical information available to the cooperating partners, in order to improve operations by more efficient planning and scheduling.

2. *The number of involved enterprises:* The more parties involved in the cooperation, the more complex solutions are needed. The simplest case concerns cooperation between only two enterprises (one-to-one cooperation), whereas the general case involves a large number of enterprises cooperating with each other in different ways (many-to-many cooperation).

3. *The dynamics of the cooperation community:* In the simple static case, the parties involved are known from the start and will not change. In a truly dynamic cooperation, on the other hand, participants may join and leave the cooperation at any time with little time left to build trustful relationships.

Previous work by Davidsson et al. describes a decentralized solution that meets most of the requirements listed above by using wrapper agents [4]. In principle it can be used for all types of inter-organizational cooperation, but has currently been applied only to the simplest case (according to the three dimensions identified above), i.e., information exchange between two enterprises in a static environment. The wrapper agent solution increases productivity by enabling simplified administrative tasks, and by improving business operations. It was originally tested in a transport chain setting; however, we believe that the wrapper agent approach is of a general nature. Here, we will analyze the *security* aspects of this approach. This will be done by applying a modified version of the information security risk analysis matrix [11] in order to investigate vulnerabilities with the wrapper agent system. This work can be seen as one step in giving a concrete form to the vision of Virtual Enterprises [12].

The next section describes central concepts and related work and in Section 3 we present the wrapper agent solution that was developed to support and facilitate information exchange. Section 4 describes one simple and one complex case of cooperation, which in Section 5 are discussed from a security point of view. Finally, some conclusions are drawn and suggestions are made for future work.

2 Concepts and Related Work

The review includes existing software solutions available on the market, a conceptual overview of the security aspects addressed within the wrapper agent solution, and a short characterization of transport chains.

2.1 Existing Technology

Support for electronic information exchange is often found in large business systems, e.g., ERP (Enterprise Resource Planning) systems. Such systems often focus on a specific type of company, e.g., a producer in the process industry or a transport operator. The systems do often have some ability to exchange information with other types of business systems, but this is often limited to a standard set of formats and systems. There exist several off-the-shelf TA (Transport Administrative) systems for storage, synthesis and communication of data, such as Movex [10], Hogia MobiLast [8] and many more. These systems and the other systems that support electronic data interchange have varying characteristics, but all of them require substantial investments by the user. As a consequence, SMEs are able only to invest in one system, if any at all. This, in turn, makes it impossible to carry out electronic business activities with several companies using different business systems due to system interoperability problems. Also, security-enhancing mechanisms are not very prominent features of these systems.

One existing solution that meets some of the interoperability requirements is Microsoft BizTalk [2]. The main purpose with BizTalk is to facilitate system communication independently of the individual communication formats in the systems by acting as an interpreter between the systems. It is based upon a central server through which all exchanged information passes. According to Microsoft, BizTalk includes "services that support seamless configuration of security credentials across heterogeneous enterprise domains". BizTalk uses XML and supports the main protocols for email and http. However, being a proprietary client-server solution it has several disadvantages, such as, making the actors dependent of third party, being expensive and possibly having communication bottlenecks.

2.2   Security

Today's highly connected ICT infrastructures exist in an environment which is increasingly hostile—attacks are being mounted with growing frequency and are demanding shorter reaction times. Due to an increase in the amount of information that is being made openly available, the risks of unsolicited, unintended or malicious use have augmented. Often, organizations are unable to react to new security threats before their businesses are impacted, let alone recover from any damage. In a setting where more and more aspects of organizations are being adjusted for IT, it is seemingly problematic to keep the overall related risks in control. Managing security of ICT infrastructures, and the business value that those infrastructures deliver, has become a primary concern for most ICT departments.

Violations on ICT infrastructures occur in numerous ways throughout the Internet and both small and large organizations need to consider internal (e.g. insiders) and external threats (e.g. hackers, rival competitors, etc.). A large supply of security-intrusive and malicious software is already available. Malware, that is malicious code planted on computers, gives attackers a truly alarming degree of control over systems, networks and data. For instance, when spyware programs are involved, the loss in control of sensitive corporate information, pose a threat to distributed (or shared) information resources. The unauthorized user gets confidential information either directly or indirectly by utilizing an infiltrated system for additional attacks. Letting go of control increases the risk for security violations.

The EU-FP6 project TrustCom [16] dealt with security aspects in business applications by tackling trust and contract management frameworks, and offer services above individual enterprise level. Ecolead [5] was another EU-FP6 project focusing on dynamic virtual organizations with a breeding environment including an invisible, secure, plug and play infrastructure for collaboration.

Information security is about preventing adverse consequences from the intentional and unwarranted actions of others [12]. Typically, information security services ensure *confidentiality, integrity* and *availability*.[2] Although information security is by no means strictly a technical topic, its technical aspects (firewalls, authentication mechanisms, encryption techniques, etc.) are important. However, we do not focus this work on the technicalities of access control systems, such as Shibboleth [14], although we see the potential of using such technologies in combination with our wrapper agents. Managing information security is an increasingly high-profile problem, as hackers, malicious actors and rival competitors may take advantage of the fact that organizations are opening up parts of their systems to employees, customers and other businesses via the Internet. This is very much the case with SMEs when they go digital.

Within the wrapper agent solution presented Section 3, two technical measures are used in order to enable security, namely (identification and) authentication and encryption. Authentication is used to confidently associate an identity with a wrapper agent, person or entity in an organization [15]. A well-designed authentication system allows agents, users or organizations to prove their identities conveniently and to gain access to a network without threatening the safety of the organization. Encryption is the process of scrambling a message so that it can only be read by the party it is intended for [1]. Typically, business transactions on the web and email messages are encrypted, for security or privacy reasons. This is also the case for the messages sent or received by the wrapper agents. Authentication in combination with encryption mechanisms enables availability and addresses three aspects of information security: confidentiality, integrity and non-repudiation [15].

2.3   Characteristics of Inter-organizational Transport Chains

A transport chain usually involves a large number of actors, and in order to reach an acceptable level of efficiency it is important to synchronize these actors and their activities. For example, information concerning the status of the cargo needs to be available to the right person, at the right place, and at the right time. Although this is obvious for everyone involved and that advanced technology to collect and distribute information exists, this information is sometimes not fully utilized, particularly in cases when things go wrong. We argue that the an important reasons are not due to lack of solutions, but rather due to difficulties in integrating existing software systems and the high costs associated

---

[2] However, other services like, e.g. non-repudiation (which is a method by which the sender of data is provided with proof of delivery and the recipient is assured of the sender's identity, so neither can later deny having processed the data), could also be included.

with this task. Instead, a large amount of transport-related information, such as bookings and cargo specification, is exchanged manually via fax machines and phones. Problems that arise due to the manual work required are for instance that information may not be accessible at a certain place when needed and also information duplication is complicated. Further, due to the complexity and the cost of (current) systems of collecting information and making it available to relevant actors, a number of opportunities for improving efficiency and service is left out. The question that remains to be answered then is: are advanced and expensive systems required to solve these problems, or are there other, simpler and less expensive, solutions?

In the project "Transport informatics for increased cooperation between the parts in a logistic chain", the overall aim was to develop and demonstrate the use of a common platform where the companies are able to exchange the necessary information between themselves as well as their other customers and suppliers [4]. The platform and its functionalities were later demonstrated in one of the transport chain case studies and evaluated. Besides the software platform, the project also generated insights in the problems related to technological aspects as well as organizational issues within the freight transportation industry.

3   The Wrapper Agent Solution

As mentioned in the introduction, some of the most important needs for improvements were simplifications of administrative activities, such as, transport booking, tracing of goods and carriers, deviation detection, and calculations of environmental load. Many of these require a complete unbroken process of gathering data, data processing and information distribution. In a pilot study we decided to focus on the reduction of usage of fax machines and other manual ways of information exchange (reducing the administrative costs as well as the number of errors caused by the human factor) and increase the accessibility of information by making electronic information exchange possible [4].

A software prototype was built using only freeware with open source code such as, Java, MySQL, J2EE, JBoss, etc., and state-of-the-art technologies like XML and web services. The prototype provides the possibility for different business systems to communicate and support information exchange via web portals, email, fax and SMS. The prototype is an information carrying system meaning that the system acts independently of what type of data that is transferred through it.

The basic idea can be seen as a generalization of the well-known *Adapter design pattern* [7] used within object-oriented software engineering, corresponding to the concept of *wrapper agents* [9]. It is also similar to the concept of connectors [3]. To each (legacy) business system a wrapper agent is built that enables the system to interact with the other business systems in the transport chain. Such a wrapper agent is mainly composed by three parts; *a bridge, an interpreter,* and *a message handler* (see Figure 1). The bridge handles the interaction with the business system, and the interpreter translates the data from

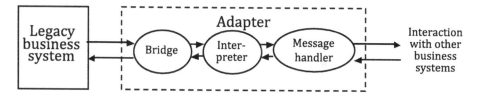

Fig. 1. The structure of the wrapper software

the format that the sending business system is using to the format which the receiving business system is using (and vice versa). The message handler takes care of the communication with the adapters of the other business systems. The bridge typically makes use of the functions for exporting and importing information that most business systems are equipped with. If this is not the case, more sophisticated methods must be used.

Many legacy business systems only have primitive import/export functionality, and in such cases the adapter needs to be proactive, giving the wrapper software a distinct agent character. For instance, we have encountered several systems where there is only an *In* and an *Out* folder. We have then implemented the Bridge as three separate threads. *Import*, which receives XML messages from the Message handler via a web service client, and saves them as files in the *In* folder. *Export*, which regularly checks the *Out* folder (the time interval should be chosen based on the response time requirements for the particular application) and when a new file is detected, it is sent via a web service client to the Interpreter for further processing. When it gets an acknowledgement from the Message handler that the message was successfully sent, the file is moved from the Out folder to a *Sent Orders* folder. The third thread, *Status monitor*, monitors changes regarding the orders that are currently active, by making requests concerning the status of these orders regularly and saves them as XML-requests to the In folder. It then reads the reply from the Out folder and sends it to Interpreter for further processing.

The wrapper prototype software is available as freeware and is relatively easy to install. It includes general message handling components and shells for the interpreter and the bridge. Much effort was spent on reusability making it easy to adapt the software to arbitrary business systems (at least those that have basic data import and export functionalities). Also modifiability was considered and since the software is module-based, extensions of the system are facilitated. The system requires an authentication mechanism (*log in*) for usage, and encryption of data as well as digital labeling to increase the degree of security.

4   Case Studies

Below we present two case studies. The simpler case (case A) involves information exchange in a static environment containing two enterprises whereas a more complex case (case B) uses an, at least partly dynamic, environment with several enterprises, making activities such as planning and scheduling more efficient.

4.1 The Study of Case A

The transport chain that was selected for the case study was not very complicated. It consisted of just two main actors and little or no cross-border traffic. The focus was on SMEs based in the region of Blekinge, Sweden, with partly very limited resources for investments in ICT but they still needed the functionalities to stay competitive. Many of the needs for improvements and opportunities identified in the specific case studies were also found in other companies in the transportation sector with a variety in size, nationality and resources. An extended description of the participating actors and their identified motives is found in [4].

The prototype platform was tested by having two different major business systems; Hogia Mobilast and Movex, in two different companies, Karlshamns Expressbyrå (KE) and Karlshamns AB (KAB), interacting via the platform. In the demonstration the actual business systems (together with the associated adapters) were executing at the two companies. A number of functionalities were tested. For instance, KAB was able to make transport requests from Movex directly into the Hogia Mobilast system at KE. Similarly, KE was able to confirm the request from inside its system directly to Movex at KAB. Further functionalities include monitoring active requests. The tests indicated that the wrapper agent solution can successfully provide the functionality strived for in Case A.

4.2 The Study of Case B

In the research project "Integrated production and transportation planning within the food industry", a transport chain consisting of one producer, one transport operator, and a number of customers is studied [6]. The project aims at achieving improved performance (cost reduction) through the development and usage of advanced planning tools. A system perspective is taken which requires a higher level of cooperation and information exchange between the actors than in the first case study. The studied chain consists of the producer KAB, the transport operator FoodTankers, and typical customers to KAB. In the studied transport chain, it is customer orders that drive the transportation and production planning. Currently, the first planning step is to decide whether a new order can be accepted or not. The subsequent production planning is about deciding when and in which order the products should be produced; and about planning the inventory storage. The transport planning concerns meeting the transport requirements specified by customer orders obtained via the producer. When transport orders appear which require high cost solutions (or the planner can deliver significant cost savings by replanning), the transport planner may suggest changes to the producer which in turn checks for such changes with the customer. This implies that there are tentative plans and cost implications shared between the partners.

Currently, it is hard to alter the delivery times and quantities of transport orders. One reason for this is the lack of information about the *true demand* of the customer, e.g. safety stock levels and consequences of delivering earlier or later than requested. Another reason is the lack of decision support tools for capitalizing on this potential additional information. In the studied transport chain it has been observed that the level of information sharing/exchange is different between different customers and the producer and between different customers and the transport operator. Moreover, now and then some new customers join the transport chain and others leave it. It is believed that in order to significantly improve the performance at least some of the customers need to exchange more information with the producer and the transport operator. In particular an introduction of Vendor Managed Inventory (VMI) could potentially improve the utilization of the transport resources. This would, however, require the customers to share information, for instance, about the inventory levels, inventory restrictions, anticipated consumptions of the products.

Our preliminary analysis suggests that using wrapper agents for connecting producer, transport operator, and customers is possible also in Case B. However, a number of aspects of the system become more important compared to Case A, e.g.: efficient administration of multiple users/agents, easy adoption to different legacy business systems and having a communication language suitable for the various needs of the actors in a transport chain. Further, security aspects are certainly affected, which we discuss in the next section. Note that customers in this case may very well be competitors and may be unwilling to reveal their production plans to competitors (but probably to their suppliers if it implies reduced cost).

5   Wrapper Agent Solution: Security Analysis and Discussion

We explore the effects on security caused by the wrapper agent solution to inter-organizational cooperation. The fact that the system is computerized implies that there is, at least, just as large a threat to information security for SMEs that adapt to the system as there are for SMEs using alternatives such as web services, email, etc. Security risks within the wrapper agent system can be managed (though not necessarily eliminated) by utilizing authentication and encryption mechanisms since they are designed to protect security (confidentiality, integrity and non-repudiation). However, interoperability-based decentralized solutions convey numerous security threats, which are difficult to neutralize using only authentication and encryption. Among many things, SMEs must also configure other security mechanisms. The SME holding the poorest security settings constitutes a great threat to other parties in the cooperation alliance. Such threats could be the use of firewalls not investigating both incoming and outgoing traffic, poor virus detection software, and the lack of intrusion detection systems (IDS) and anti-spyware tools. In general, the consequences of being exposed to intrusions, attacks, deception and infiltration may be loss and/or tampering of data and/or system resources, as well as unnecessary costs for network and system maintenance. Another aspect concerns data access. For instance, a result of users interacting with other business systems of the cooperating parties may be that they gain a non-intentional all-or-nothing access to other available databases, which may contain sensitive data.

While the wrapper agent system has some clear advantages in that it supports scalability, adaptability, independence, cost-effectiveness, usability and interoperability, we must also carefully consider what specific risks that are conveyed by this particular system.

5.1   Security Aspects

Based on the two case studies (one simple, case A, and one complex, case B), we analyze how security is affected given the three dimensions of cooperation mentioned in the introduction. We base our analysis of inter-organizational cooperation on the, so called information security risk analysis (ISRA) matrix (although modified to suit the purpose of the analysis[3]) [11]. The purpose is to illuminate desired system properties with respect to confidentiality, integrity and availability (of functionality). Further, the purpose is to find out whether the suggested system supports these desired properties, or if additional development is required. Also, we want to pinpoint-areas where it is an open question if, and in such case how, the wrapper agent solution can provide the desired properties (see Table 1).

It can be observed that the confidentiality and the integrity aspects are closely related and that the availability aspects impose a trade-off in relation to the other two concepts. It can be seen in Table 1, that many of the desired measures are implemented by the wrapper agent solution *(included),* which is mainly achieved by its authentication and encryption mechanisms. Properties desired for the one-to-one cooperation is of course also relevant when the setting becomes more complex in any of the dimensions, but has not been repeated in the table. In the next sections, the analysis is focused on the areas for which the solution needs development. We also address the open issues to explore whether is possible that the wrapper agent solution can achieve improvements of the desired property.

For a scenario of one-to-one party cooperation (illustrated in Case A), the wrapper agent solution provides an adequate solution in general. However, since we exclude this case from the ISRA matrix, general security configurations, e.g. upgrade to a business version of the anti-virus software and include an IDS-tool should be handled by each SME involved in the cooperation.

Increased Level of Cooperation. In the wrapper agent solution, partners might gain unintentional access to other available databases, which may contain sensitive data. The risk of unintentional revealing of information is accentuated when shifting from solely information exchange functions into information

---

[3] We have excluded the *accidental* and *deliberate* acts from the ISRA matrix.

Table 1. Desired measures given the security services and the environment aspects of the wrapper agent solution in the one-to-one party cooperation. The measures are graded as *incorporated* (already implemented), *minor/major development* (need to be achieved) or *open* (if the question of achievement is open).

Env. aspects	Security services		
	Confidentiality	Integrity	Availability
Increased level of cooperation	- Increased control of read and write access (Incorporated) - Increased control of indirect information disclosure (Open)	- Increased control of read and write access (Incorporated)	- Increased possibilities to exchange large quantities of data (Incorporated) - Shorter response time (Minor development)
Increased number of involved enterprises	- Better differentiated access control (Minor development) - Increased control of (unauthorized) third-party access (Major development)	- Better differentiated access control (Minor development) - More appropriate administrative routines (Minor development) - Increased control of (unauthorized) third-party access (Major development)	- Higher level of robustness through avoiding single points of failure (Incorporated) - More appropriate administrative routines (Minor development)
Increased dynamics of the cooperation community	- More dynamic access control (Open) - Harder time limits on information (Open)	- More dynamic access control (Open)	- Make participation and defection easier (Minor development)

sharing for operations planning with other parties (more information is shared in this way). Further, since for instance cost implications on tentative plans might be revealed, other partners can build up information profiles about its partners which are critical for the business (e.g. a transport operator's exact costs of operations might be revealed). Information might be analyzed for purposes not anticipated by the other partners, i.e. indirect disclosure of information. It may be difficult to control what information is actually obtained by the other parties, as well as how and to what extent it is used. This may create an imbalance in the business relationship between the SME and other companies, since the information can be used in, for example business negotiations about terms of contracts. We believe tools can be developed for analyzing information revealed directly and possibly indirectly by the participants in the cooperation.

Increased Number of Involved Enterprises. When there is a shift from a one-to-one to a many-to-many relationship between the interacting parties, there is an exponential growth of confidentiality related conflict of interest. Problems arise in that the difficulties for guaranteeing that information, which may be sensitive to one party, is not being misused by rival competitors or malicious actors. As a counter-measure, certified third-party coordinators may make it more difficult for the agents to extract information about the other participants. Also, when many companies are involved in the wrapper agent system, access to available data is more difficult to restrict than if there is a one-to-one relationship, since the access control needs to be differentiated between different organizations. The weakest link in a scenario involving wrapper agents is the SME that holds the poorest general security settings, i.e. lacking a sufficient firewall and a business edition of the anti-virus software, and having weak authentication mechanisms among many things.

Here, in particular, security mechanisms must protect against attacks, deception, intrusions, and insiders so that confidentiality and integrity can be ensured. If security solutions are proven efficient over time, trust between the different parties is enabled, which is necessary for the prosperity of a wrapper agent network. One aspect of achieving system efficiency, as well as of building trust, is the administrative processes (e.g. setting access levels) and responsibility/ownership of the system. A distributed ownership, which is the effect of a solution based on wrapper agents, might facilitate the building of trust in that respect.

Increased Dynamics of Cooperation Community. A generalization of the many-to-many scenario is when the case changes from static to dynamic and when the relations change over time, i.e. participants may join or leave the setting. This shift creates similar but not identical security problems as above, although the consequences here are a bit more problematic to analyze.

Complexity in terms of security is increasing due to that the number of participating parties changes dynamically. The level of cooperation between the involved entities may be fluctuating, resulting in problems with the restrictions of data access over time in a dynamic environment of companies. This implies that the participants may have access to information exchanged, even though cooperation with the wrapper agent system is terminated. This may affect the other parties within the system in that sensitive business information may be distributed or used by unauthorized companies for their own purposes. Hence, dynamic cooperation increases the difficulties in ensuring confidentiality.

A desired property is to have a suitable dynamic access control. However, there are a number of issues to be resolved in order to achieve this: efficient propagation of changes in the system, community membership control, etc. Besides keeping track of authorized users and of the data in use, the wrapper agent system grows and diminishes as the number of entities changes, which among many things makes it hard to build trustful relationships. At the same time, threats of deception, infiltration and attacks get accentuated, implying that general security configurations of involved parties are crucial for enabling trust. Malicious actors may otherwise gain access to or attack the wrapper agent system by launching, e.g. malware via an SME holding poor security configurations. In particular, confidentiality and integrity are difficult to enhance when cooperation parties changes dynamically.

One aspect that is not covered in the wrapper agent system is the time limit for data. If we could terminate data which was accessed within the system when an SME ends it cooperation with the system, the long-term and negative consequences to confidentiality could be mitigated. Perhaps, this would also lead to a better platform for enabling trust, since SMEs do not risk letting go of the control of their most precious information resources. It is a generic problem that confidentiality and privacy commissioners have debated and researched for some time now and is hence specified as an open issue.

5.2 Wrapper Agent Solution and Centralized Solution

The suggested wrapper agent solution has some different characteristics compared to a centralized server solution such as BizTalk [2]. With respect to the security problems outlined above, there appear to be no imperative problems with the wrapper agent solution (compared to a centralized server solution). If no automated solution is used, the control of the information to be exchanged is typically handled by the actors directly and locally when for instance sending faxes and email messages, as well as doing phone calls. A wrapper agent solution might change this situation less with respect to the level of control experienced by the actor than a centralized server solution controlled by another actor (or controlled by a third-party). Some security aspects might be easier to ensure using the wrapper agent solution than using a centralized server since such a solution is probably closer to the ways many SMEs currently manage their business (e.g. individually for each actor it is exchanging information with). Another great benefit is that there is no risk of a single point of failure with a decentralized system, as there is with a centralized one.

6   Conclusions and Future Work

An evaluation of the practical relevance and economic gain of the prototype was made based on interviews of the participating companies. The prototype provides a direct use since it offers cost-effective (due to the use of freeware and easiness of adaptation) and platform-independent communication. Thus, the prototype seems to perform well with respect to attributes such as interoperability and undependability with several interfaces. These benefits make the prototype useful in numerous contexts and this not only for the project participants. In addition, a cost-effective communication solution generates several implicit benefits such as a possible reduction of error in documents that are exchanged (due to minimization of manual duplication work) and increased information accessibility which have costs in terms of loss in control of sensitive data.

Our solution includes basic security settings by means of authentication of the user and encryption of transmitted data for Case A. Case B uses operations planning where partners join or leave in a many to many coalition. We discuss both internal and external security issues when handling such a complex environment.

Compared to existing centralized solutions, such as BizTalk, the proposed solution has a number of advantages, e.g., being independent of third parties, avoiding central communication bottlenecks and avoiding single point of failure.

We have demonstrated the possibility to achieve basic and sufficient communication functionalities like the large-scale TA systems offer, but to a considerably lower cost with no apparent loss in security. This is something that is of significant importance to the survival of smaller actors with same needs as the larger ones but with a much more limited investment possibility.

The wrapper agent solution, as described in Section 5, focuses on the tasks directly connected to achieve interoperability, but nothing restricts it from having additional tasks to fulfill. For instance, by extending the number of threads in the bridge (Figure 1), we may include security checking of the XML messages sent to the bridge. Similarly, the message handler may place restrictions on the communication with the wrapper agents of the other business systems.

We have been investigating the possibilities of developing an (or using an existing one, such as the one suggested by [17]) ontology so that a common communication language can be used between the wrapper agents. This would significantly reduce the need of developing interpreters. In addition, it is our ambition to explore some of the properties as graded as Development and Open in Table 1.

References

1. Anderson, R.: Security Engineering—A Guide to Building Dependable Distributed Systems. John Wiley & Sons, New York (2001)
2. Biztalk home page (2009), http://www.microsoft.com/biztalk/
3. Bures, T., Plasil, F.: Communication style driven connector configurations. In: Ramamoorthy, C.V., Lee, R., Lee, K.W. (eds.) SERA 2003. LNCS, vol. 3026, pp. 102–116. Springer, Heidelberg (2004)
4. Davidsson, P., Ramstedt, L., Törnquist, J.: Interoperability in transport chains using adapters based on open source freeware. In: Interoperability of Enterprise Software and Applications. Springer, Heidelberg (2005)
5. Ecolead home page (2009), http://ecolead.vtt.fi/
6. Integrated production and transportation planning within the food industry home page (2009), http://www.ipd.bth.se/fatplan/
7. Gamma, E., Helm, R., Johnsson, R., Vlissides, J.: Design Patterns: Elements of Reusable Object-Oriented Software. Addison-Wesley, Reading (1994)
8. Hogia mobilast home page (2009), http://www2.hogia.se/website3/1.0.3.0/64/1/index.php
9. Kolp, M., Do, T.T., Faulkner, S.: Introspecting agent-oriented design patterns. In: Chang, S.K. (ed.) Advances in Software Engineering and Knowledge Engineering, vol. III. World Publishing (2004)
10. Movex project home page (2009), http://www.lawson.com/wcw.nsf/pub/App_E76358

11. Persson, R.S.: Information Security Risk Analysis. CRC Press, Boca Raton (2001)
12. Petrie, C.J., Bussler, C.: Service agents and virtual enterprises: A survey. IEEE Internet Computing 7(4), 68–78 (2003)
13. Shapiro, C., Varian, H.R.: Information Rules: A Strategic Guide to the Network Economy. HBS Press, Boston (1999)
14. Shibboleth home page (2009), `http://shibboleth.internet2.edu/`
15. Smith, R.: Authentication: From Password to Public Keys. Addison Wesley Professional, Boston (2002)
16. Trustcom home page (2009), `http://www.eu-trustcom.com`
17. Zimmermann, R., Butscher, R., Bodendorf, F.: An ontology for agent-based supply chain monitoring, ECAI 2002 workshop. In: Agent Technologies in Logistics, France (2002)

Agent-Community-Network-Based Secure Collaboration Support System

Tsunenori Mine[1], Kosaku Kimura[2], Satoshi Amamiya[2], Ken'ichi Takahashi[3], and Makoto Amamiya[4]

[1] Faculty of Information Science and Electrical Engineering, Kyushu University
744 Motooka, Nishi-ku, Fukuoka 819-0395, Japan
mine@is.kyushu-u.ac.jp
[2] Graduate School of Information Science and Electrical Engineering, Kyushu University
744 Motooka, Nishi-ku, Fukuoka 819-0395, Japan
{kimura,roger}@al.is.kyushu-u.ac.jp
[3] Institute of Systems & Information Technologies/KYUSHU, 2-1-22 Momochihama, Sawara-ku, Fukuoka 814-0001, Japan
takahashi@isit.or.jp
[4] Faculty of Information Science and Technology, Osaka Institute of Technology
1-79-1, Kitayama, Maikata, Osaka 573-0196, Japan

Abstract. Community-based collaboration support systems are useful for exchanging information on topics that community members are interested in. Most of them developed so far are based on server-client architecture and provide their services on Web servers. They require special administrative facilities, and ask users to upload their data on the systems. Furthermore, security mechanisms are not often provided for the communities. Considering these problems, we have been developing an Agent-Community-Network-based collaboration support system: in particular, a business-matching support system. Our system requires neither any special administrative facilities nor the need to upload user data to a special server. Furthermore, it supports secure peer-to-peer communication between users. It is implemented with a multi-agent Kodama framework.

Keywords: Multi-agents, peer-to-peer, community, agent community network, business matching and collaboration, security.

1 Introduction

Community-based collaboration support systems such as mailing lists, electronic bulletin board services, social networking services (SNS) or Weblog services have been attractive and actively used for facilitating user communication. Since they have usually been developed as Web-server-based systems, flexible access and useful interfaces are available. However, they have the following problems:

K. Fischer et al. (Eds.): ATOP 2005 and ATOP 2008, LNBIP 25, pp. 234–255, 2009.

(1) Special administrative facilities are required for the system administrators.
(2) The users have to upload their data when updating it. The upload costs are negligible.
(3) As the number of users accessing a system increase, the load borne by the system becomes heavier.
(4) Administrators of the system can easily eavesdrop on the data stored or information exchanged on it.

Considering these problems, we believe that community-based collaboration support systems should be managed by a user exclusively so that the information used for communication can be exchanged only with the user's communication partners. The systems should accordingly be constructed as distributed ones and support one-to-one and one-to-many communication with each other. These problems are wedded to security issues. When making one-to-one or one-to-many communication by e-mail, we face lots of problems such as SPAM, phishing mail attacks on the general public, or targeted phishing mail attacks, the last of which have been growing up since June 2005[1]. In addition, since current e-mail systems are based on server-client architecture, a server administrator can easily eavesdrop upon e-mail messages on the server[2]. The appearance of these kind of problems makes necessary secure systems that support secure peer-to-peer communication between users.

Another crucial issue is to create a community where users with the common interests or aims stay together and efficiently communicate on topics related to the community. The community can facilitate the secure exchange of privacy-related information by restricting communication within a community. For instance, almost all community-based systems create their community by requesting users to subscribe as members for secure interaction. Since most of the community-based systems are, however, constructed on different Web servers, they have the problems of server-based systems as mentioned above. In addition, each community of systems is itself closed, and users in the communities between different Web servers can hardly communicate with one another by way of their communities. Therefore, community-based collaboration support systems should be constructed as a community-based distributed system and be able to support secure peer-to-peer communication in and between communities. Such communities should have a hierarchical structure so that they can represent real societies. Such communities may have community manager agents that help community member agents search for other agents giving information the member agents want, and can facilitate communication between the member agents. Such manager agents are called middle agents[1,2].

According to the roles of middle agents classified by Decker et al.[1], we will basically adopt such a middle agent that is initially a broadcaster who does not know any preference information of requesters or capability information of

---

[1] http://www.niscc.gov.uk/niscc/docs/ttea.pdf

[2] Although everyone can encrypt his/her mail with encryption software such as PGP, most users do not do that because both a sender and a receiver have to use the encryption software, and most mailers do not support encryption features.

providers, but will gradually become an anonymizer who knows preference information of requesters, or a broker who knows both preference information of requesters and capability information of providers. This is based on the knowledge of the agent-community-based peer-to-peer information retrieval (ACP2P) method[3].

Ferreira and Ferreira[4] discusses a method of constructing an e-market place based on a peer-to-peer network by combining some existing technologies and methods: in particular, a method for realizing peer-to-peer communication based on the technologies of JXTA Project[3]. However, it still has an issue to realize one-to-many communication and does not discuss the problems for constructing a practical system, which are the main subjects of this paper.

This paper presents an Agent-Community-Network-based Secure Collaboration Support System. We aim to develop an agent-oriented technique that is useful to realize an ubiquitous computing environment at a low cost. We have been developing a business matching and collaboration support system for small and medium-sized companies and a secure social networking service collaboration support system as case studies.

Our target users are those who do not have enough knowledge on a mechanism of information exchanging between computer systems. We would like our system to enable users to get information they need without being aware of security mechanisms, places of information providers, or mechanisms of exchanging information, and enable users to enjoy various services that are helpful for their business and everyday activities. Although there are several choices to meet these requirements, we chose a multi-agent-based system, Multi-agent Kodama framework[5], because it originally supports a hierarchical community structure and has flexible characteristics and configuration options. Moreover, Kodama separates agent name retrieval and agent physical address retrieval, which suggests the availability of an efficient retrieval technique for former retrieval, according to an application of the system, and an efficient node-lookup or message delivering technique for the latter retrieval.

We adopted the ACP2P method [3] for the former retrieval method and the node lookup and routing method based on the Ordered-Tree-with-Tuft (OTT) shaped overlay network as the latter one[6].

The rest of the paper is organized as follows: Section 2 shows related work; Section 3 describes the functions of Agent-Community-Network-based system; Section 4 shows a case study of the system; Section 5 discusses an experimental system; and Section 6 concludes and describes our future work.

2   Related Work

Although there is lots of work related to the topics touched on in this paper, we here focus on community-based systems[7]. The community-based systems, such as SNS systems[4], provide various functions useful for creating communities

---

[3] http://www.jxta.org/
[4] Friendster http://www.friendster.com/, MySpace http://www.myspace.com

where users with the common interests or aims stay together, supporting their communications, and searching for the information that they want. Most of the systems are based on server-client architecture.

Tamura et al.[8] proposed a framework for online communities called a Transparent Community, which facilitate silent users[5] to turn into active information providers. The framework is based on a peer-to-peer technology called SIONet[9] and proposes a method of automatically creating users' communities by using their metadata or attributes. However, it consider neither the node churn nor security mechanisms. It is also uncertain if this method can construct hierarchical communities.

When creating a community on a peer-to-peer network, we pay attention to maintaining the community. Each community contains at least one member as a known member who is the representative of that community. In [10], a fellow for the representative is statically determined. However, it does not discuss the case that both the fellow and the representative peer simultaneously leave the network. On the other hand, our method can dynamically determine a fellow for the representative of the community, the method can maintain the community until the last peer leaves.[11] Round robin DNS[6] was introduced for load balancing of DNS. However, it is difficult to apply this method to dynamically determine the representative and its fellows because the method does not distinguish any servers in a group.

3   Agent-Community-Network-Based System

3.1   Agent Community Network

An agent community is a community in which agents (whose users have common interests or aims) stay together and which facilitates efficient communication on the topics related to their interests. Such communication gradually creates a network between agents. We call the network an agent community network, or ACN. In the ACN, agents freely make one-to-one or one-to-many communication in and between communities. Such ACN often depends on a community structure, especially a hierarchical one that represents real and practical societies. Fig. 1 depicts an image of the agent community network.

Every agent joining the ACN belongs to one or more communities and is assigned a logical address that directly represents the hierarchical structure of communities. The relationship between hierarchical communities is represented by connecting them with a dot (.). The topmost community name comes to the leftmost place in the address, and the name of the next lower level community is placed to its immediate right by connecting with a dot. A nick name of the agent is placed at the rightmost place in the address. For example, in Fig.1,

---

[5] Silent users are a user group who regularly collect information in particular online communities and utilize such information for developing their own knowledge, but they rarely provide information for online communities[8].

[6] RFC1794: http://tools.ietf.org/html/rfc1794

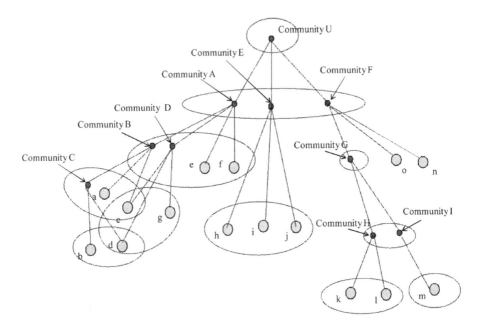

Fig. 1. An Image of an Agent Community Network

the logical address of agent h is $U.E.h$. The logical address also represents the role of an agent. Each agent is accordingly in charge of one or more roles. The representative roles of agents are as a portal and as a member in a community. An agent with a portal role is called a portal agent and an agent with a member role is a member agent. A portal agent of a community manages the addresses of all member agents in the community and accepts a request of multicasting a message to them in the community. The portal agent also has a member role of the community, i.e., it is a member agent, too. At least one portal agent should exist in a community. This portal role model is useful both for making a system robust and distributing the system's load. As the number of portal agents in a community increases, the system becomes more robust and the number of member agents that a portal agent is in charge of decreases. Accordingly, using the ACN, we can make a practical distributed system that represents a real society. We call the development method based on the ACN model an ACN-based system development.

On the other hand, since agents freely join and leave communities, a synchronization mechanism should be introduced to the data that portal agents in a community are responsible for, such as the member list in the community and the symmetric-key or private-public key for encrypted communication there. In addition, an exclusive control mechanism is also required for key sharing.

We employ a multi-agent Kodama (Kyushu university Open & Distributed Autonomous Multi-Agent) framework [5] for this development and have already implemented both mechanisms[11].

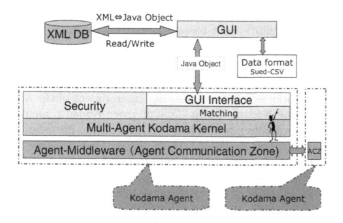

Fig. 2. Kodama Agent and System Modules

3.2 Multi-agent Kodama

Kodama comprises hierarchical structured agent communities based on a portal-agent model. A portal agent (PA) is the representative of all member agents in a community and allows the community to be treated as one normal agent outside the community. A PA has its role limited in a community, and the PA itself may be managed as an agent by another higher-level portal agent. A PA manages all member agents in a community and can multicast a message to them. Any member agent in a community can ask the PA to multicast its message. All the agents form a logical world which is completely separated from the physical world consisting of agent host machines. That means agents are not network-aware, but are organized and located by their places in the logical world. This model is realized with the agent middle-ware called Agent Communication Zone, or ACZ. ACZ is primarily designed to act as a bridge between distributed physical networks, creating an agent-friendly communication infrastructure on which agents can easily and freely be organized in a hierarchical fashion. One or more Kodama agents can act on one ACZ. ACZ is also designed to realize a peer-to-peer communication between agents.

A Kodama agent consists of a kernel unit and an application unit. The kernel unit comprises the common basic modules shared by all Kodama agents. The application unit comprises a set of plug-in modules, each of which is used for describing and realizing a specialized or original function of agents.

All the applications of this system such as a GUI module, a security module, and a matching module are plugged in as application units. They are completely separated from the Kodama kernel unit. The relationship between Kodama agent and other system modules is shown in Fig. 2.

Since the system is composed of several modules that are completely separated and independent, we can individually develop each module. That means all we need is to be aware of the interface between the modules. This is one of the most important benefits of multi-agent-based software engineering.

3.3   ACZ: Agent Communication Zone

The ACZ, which works as a message routing environment of the Kodama agent, is separated from the Kodama agent. One or more Kodama agents can act on one ACZ. The ACZ adopts a robust and efficient routing protocol with a simple and stable network topology. We call the topology Ordered Tree with Tuft, or OTT[6]. The OTT is an ordered tree whose node has substitute nodes that construct a ring, which we call a tuft.

Fig.3 shows an example of the OTT, where N bit is assigned to each OTT node. The node is located by top M bit. In this case, u is the top M bit value and v is the $N - M$ bit value. The value u is used for constructing an ordered tree and presents the address of a node of the tree. The value v is used for constructing a ring attached to a node and presents the address of a node on a ring. We call a node of the ordered tree of the OTT a tree node, and a node on a ring of the OTT a ring node. When we call a node an OTT node, the node presents either a tree node or a ring node. The ring node is introduced considering the maintenance costs of join and leaving of nodes from a network. A ring node can replace a tree node even if the tree node leaves from a network. Accordingly, reconstruction of a tree will not occur as long as the ring nodes remain.

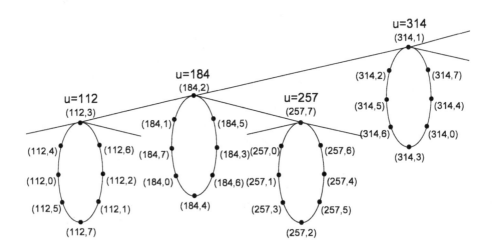

Fig. 3. An example of Ordered Tree with Tuft (OTT)

The OTT is constructed as follows:

1. An ordered tree of ACZs is created using a hash value transformed from an ACZ address (IP address + port number).

- the hash value is a tuple (u, v). Both u and v are created by two hash functions H_1, H_2, respectively.
- a different ACZ address is transformed into a different hash value (u, v) by H_1 and H_2.

2. Constructing Ordered Tree with Tuft(OTT)
   - an ACZ is placed onto each OTT node.
   - Assume the hash value of the address of ACZ_0 is (u_0, v_0) and that of ACZ_1, ACZ_2 are (u_1, v_1), (u_2, v_2), respectively.
   - When $u_1 < u_0 < u_2$ then ACZ_1 is the left node of ACZ_0 and ACZ_2 is the right node of ACZ_0.
   - If $u_1 = u_0$, then both ACZ_1 and ACZ_0 are placed onto the same OTT node and connected with a ring of the node, where v_1 should not be equal to v_0.
   - There is no order of placement on the ring.

Furthermore, each node on the OTT sets up a bypassing route by caching its neighbor node on the bypassing route that has been used in the previous communication. Each node of the OTT maintains its neighbor nodes, and if one of the neighbor nodes is lost, it searches other paths and updates its neighbor nodes on the paths. The OTT method is effective in performance-by-cost of the route maintenance, because each node can maintain in $O(1)$ with high probability as long as tufts (rings) remain and can find paths to a destination node, whose length is much less than $\log N$ for OTT with N nodes in practical use[6].

Compared with conventional Distributed Hash Table (DHT)(e.g. [12],[13]), the OTT has an advantage of maintenance cost because the maintenance cost of DHT is not cheap when the network will often change.

3.4 Security Functions

Even in a community, secure communication is indispensable because the community often consists of other companies. The security functions of the system are defined as a set of Java classes so that they can flexibly be updated. As the right of utilization of the system, a combination of login ID and password that allows an agent to join the community, is given to an applicant whose qualification is examined by a representative of an organization running the community[7].

The main characteristics of security functions of the system are as follows:

1. **Join a community:** Both the login ID and the password are issued to an authority agent of the community, which is called a portal agent. The portal agent authenticates them and permits the enrolment to the community. At that time, the portal agent gives the authenticated agent both a unique name of the community and a group key, which is one based on the Symmetric-Key Cryptosystem (SKC). The authentication is performed according to the Public-Key Cryptosystem (PKC).

---

[7] A hierarchy of communities can be set up by the organization or created by users of the communities. It depends on an application.

2. **Encrypted communication in a community:** In the community, two
   ways of communication, which are one-to-one (or peer-to-peer) and one-to-
   many communication, are available. For peer-to-peer communication, a peer-
   to-peer (P2P) key, which is a session key based on SKC, is used. The key is
   generated by exchanging random numbers between two agents. Exchanging
   the random numbers is done based on PKC. For one-to-many communication, a group key given by a portal agent is used. The group key is updated
   when any agent joins or leaves the community. Fig. 4 depicts one-to-many
   communication with the group key in the left-hand side, and peer-to-peer
   communication with the P2P key in the right-hand side.

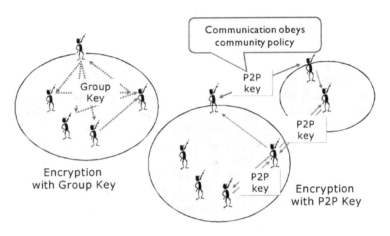

Fig. 4. Communication with Group Key (left) and P2P Key (right)

Although a community is a closed environment, all the members do not always have collaborative relationships with one another; rather, they might have
competitive relationships. Even if all the community members belong to a common group sharing the benefits such as the same company, there would be a
distinction between information according to the organization hierarchy of the
group[8]. Encrypted communication is consequently indispensable.

The system does not employ anonymity of users because a target of the system
is a community where all the members have a qualification to join or know each
other such as a business market, an alumni association, or just a party of friends.
Therefore the company names or user names are attached on the query and
responses; however, users can keep other information private if they want.

Each of the characteristics may not be new; however their combination is
important for secure peer-to-peer collaboration systems. The detailed discussion
of the basic security mechanisms adopted by the systems is described in [14].

---

[8] This would strongly depend on a community structure.

4   Case Study: Business Matching Support System

4.1   Scenario of Business Transaction

Starting to illustrate our system, we will describe a scenario of business transactions between six semiconductor development companies [9]. An example of a semiconductor development community is shown in Fig. 5.

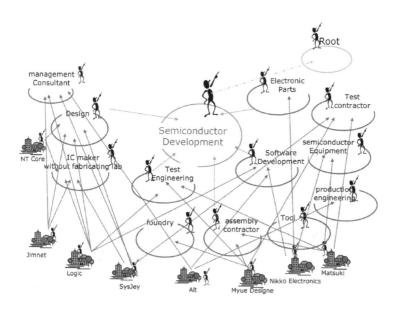

Fig. 5. Examples of Semiconductor Development Industry Communities

The community consists of 12 smaller categories of business communities, which are management consultant, design, IC maker without fabricating lab, test engineering, wafer production, assembly contractor, tool, software development, semiconductor equipment, production engineering, test contractor and electronic parts. This hierarchical community is constructed according to interviews with several people working for semiconductor companies. Another category of business community such as software development could join as the coordinate community.

The scenario says that a person who works for Logic Corp., an IC-maker without fabricating lab, is asked to do a trial production of LSI chips by a university professor. Since the specialty of Logic Corp. is LSI design and Logic Corp. does not have a fabricating lab, he wants to look for business partners: a foundry and test contractors suited to this requirement. Logic Corp. creates a business query and asks his agent to issue it so that the agent finds business

---

[9] We have agreements of cooperation with our project from an association related to semiconductors.

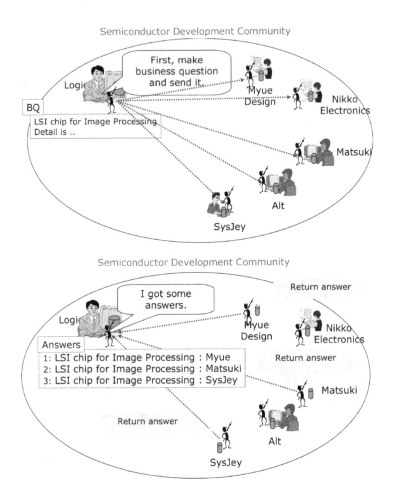

Fig. 6. Issuing Business Question (top) and Receiving Answers (bottom)

partners of Logic Corp. After receiving the query, the agent delivers it to all the other agents in the communities relevant to it (Fig.6, top). Agents of Myue-design, Matsuki, and SysJey return their answers according to their acceptance conditions (Fig.6, bottom). The agents return an answer when there exists one or more items matched between the query and the condition. Each answer has a score calculated by the matched degree. The GUI module will sort the answers by the decreasing order of their score and display them. Since the Logic Corp. representative felt good about the answers of Myue-design and Matsuki, he asks a new question to them (Fig.7, top). After receiving the answer to the question, the Logic Corp. representative selects the most important negotiating partner from the two and gets started a negotiation (Fig.7, bottom).

Considering the scenario mentioned above, the business matching and collaboration support system should take a distributed community structure and be managed solely by a user so that the user's information used for matching and negotiation can be exchanged only with the user's negotiation partners. The systems should accordingly be constructed as distributed ones and support one-to-one and one-to-many communication with one another. In addition, since a user of the system will often power the user's computer on and off, the system should be able to make a robust communication.

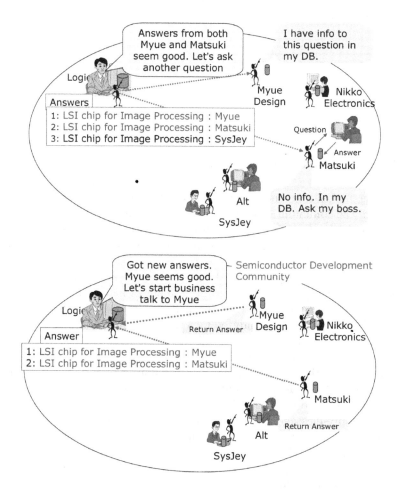

Fig. 7. Issuing Another Question before Negotiation by Face to Face (top) and Starting Negotiation (bottom)

To meet these requirements, we choose a multi-agent Kodama framework[5] because it originally supports hierarchical community structure, and has flexible characteristics and configuration options. Security and matching mechanisms are also introduced as plug-in modules of Kodama.

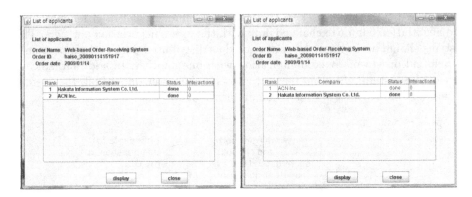

Fig. 8. Rank Varied through Operations Exchanging Messages: before (left) and after (right)

4.2   Matching Function

When a user makes a business question (Q), the user's agent will deliver it to the agents in the communities specified in the question. The agent that received the question checks it up with its acceptance condition (C) created by its user. If there is one or more matched items in it, the agent creates and returns an answer to the query-sender agent.

When making matching between Q and C, the system calculates a similarity score between them by summing the total number of matched choices in all the items considering the weight of each item. If the item gives a free descriptive sentence field, the sentence is analyzed by a morphological analyzer[10]. Then, the average number of matched terms of all the items in Q and C are calculated where all the combination of the items, including a descriptive sentence field in Q and C, are tried for matching as corresponding ones. Let t to be the average number of matched terms of all the items tried in Q and C. $2t/(t + 1)$ is empirically added to the similarity score[11].

To rank a reply-message received, an agent should consider not only the similarity score, but also the frequency exchanged with the agent returning the message. In particular, the messages returned by whom the user continues talking with should be way up on the high level so that they can be easily looked up (Fig.8). We are also considering a new way to introduce reputation mechanisms in the matching function because the reputation mechanisms help to increase retrieval accuracy of a community as a whole[15].

With this matching, even though a user does not know the addresses of agents related to the user's query, the user can, by this matching, get a list of their

---

[10] The morphological analyzer is indispensable especially for the Japanese language because words in a Japanese sentence are not separated by a space. In the case of the English language, we just use a stemmer.

[11] This equation of calculating the similarity score will be modified in the future.

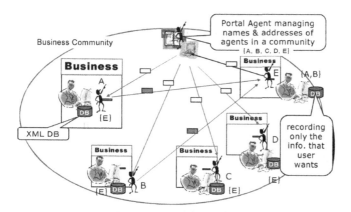

Fig. 9. Matching between a query and an acceptance condition in a business community

addresses in the communities specified in the query. This would be considered as a kind of "know-who".

In addition to receiving reply-messages from matched agents, a user can seamlessly continue to send another message to the users of the agents. In Fig. 9, agent E receives reply-messages from agent A and B. So, the user of agent E can continue to send another query to the user of agent A or agent B.

On the other hand, in conventional systems, getting a set of agent addresses and sending messages by e-mail or something are separated. Actually, many people feel self-conscious about sending an e-mail message to a user with whom they have no personal acquaintance.

4.3   Message Routing Between Agents

In our system, each community is managed by the representative member agent of the community. We call the agent a portal agent. When a query is issued to all the members of a community, the query is firstly sent to the portal agent of the community. The portal agent keeps the query during a given time interval so that any member agent can get it even though it is not in the community at that time. This function is also useful for agents that have recently joined the community and want to get such business questions that have already been delivered.

When a message is directly sent to a target agent that is not logged in at that time, the message is kept at the sender agent's database. This is because the message is sent by peer-to-peer communication. Why is this ? If the message is kept by a portal agent as broadcasting the message to all the members, the message will surely reach the target agent because the machine the portal agent resides will not be powered off and the portal agent can know when the target agent logs in[12]. In addition, the message will not be decrypted by the portal

---

[12] If we use our dynamic switching mechanism of the portal agent[11], we do not have to assume that the portal agent's machine will not be powered off.

agent because the message was encrypted by a peer-to-peer key which only the sender agent or the target agent has. However, the message may include a large attached file. As the number of such the messages increases, the load of the portal agent becomes heavier. Consequently it causes the same problem as server-client architecture. On the other hand, it is true that the sender agent can not know when the target agent will log in. In our current solution, the sender agent asks a portal agent to tell when the target agent logs in, although the computer in which the sender agent resides should not be powered off until the target agent logs in. This is a tradeoff.

5   Experimental System

5.1   Overview of Business Matching Support System

Our system is compact, easy to be moved with a USB memory, and works on any computer system with a Java VM environment. Since a lot of USB memories nowadays support an encryption function, any user can use it with ease. The system will get started just by clicking an icon of the system. A portal agent system works the same as a user agent system, provided that the community organizer requires a user registration function, which is currently realized by a Web service.

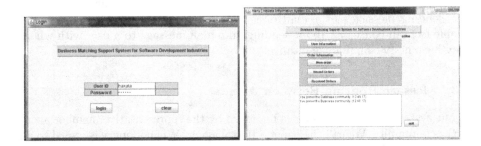

Fig. 10. Login (left) and Menu (right) Window

Fig. 10 depicts the login (left) and menu (right) windows of the user agent system. The menu window has 4 menu buttons: User Information, New Order, Issued Orders, and Received Orders. Those buttons are respectively for making an acceptance condition, making a business question (Fig. 13), showing a list of messages returned to business questions issued by a user (Fig. 11), and showing a list of business questions received.

In order to let a user know whether a message issued by the user has reached a target user (agent) or a message received by the user is matched with the acceptance condition of the user, every action done by an agent is presented on the display of the menu window (Fig. 10, right).

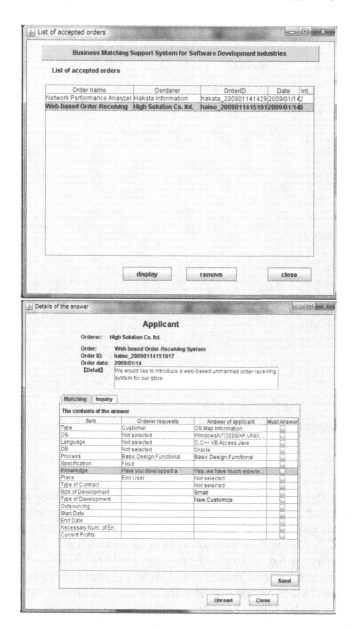

Fig. 11. A list of issued Business Questions (top) and a message matched between Business Question and Acceptance Condition (bottom)

An inquiry window allows a user who issued a business question to make free communication related to the matched condition with the user that returned the message (Fig. 12). Both users can send a message with attached files.

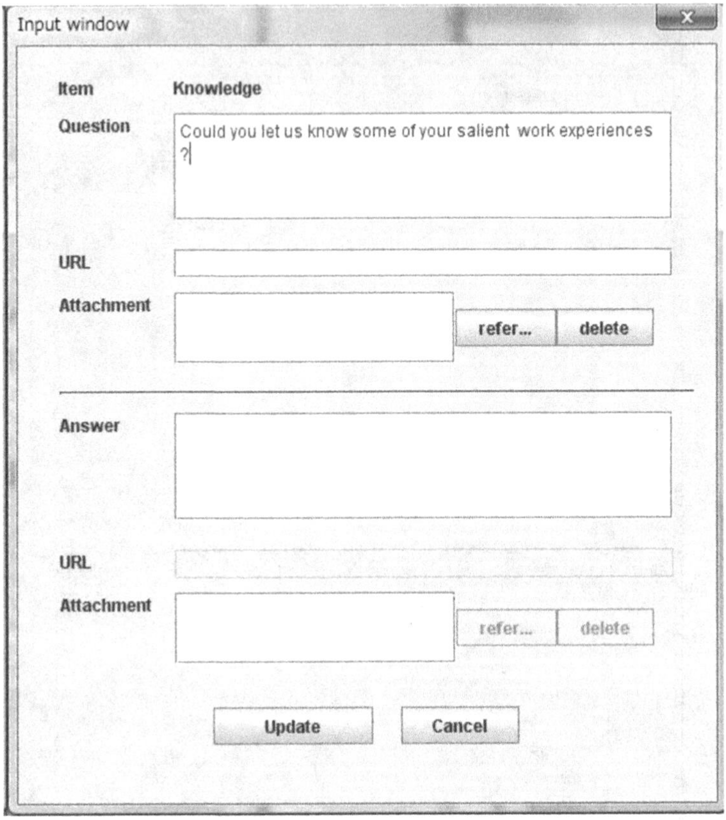

Fig. 12. New Query Window

As well as the packet transmission system, the attached files are split into some numbers of small-sized objects, and issued to a target agent. Thus this does not cause trouble even if we take a simple star-shaped network topology instead of OTT. This will be mentioned later in Section 5.4.

Fig. 11 depicts a list of received business questions (top) and a condition matched between a business question and an acceptance condition (bottom).

When a user wants to issue a new question to an answer by clicking the Inquiry tab or double clicking an item in the matching window. Fig. 12 shows an example when Knowledge item in the window of Matching tab was clicked.

5.2 Look-up of Delivery Address From Business Trading History

Business dealings generally prefer known and reliable clients to new ones. An agent in our system accordingly keeps all its trading records in its XML database so that it can easily search for the clients and the details of their transactions. The information registered in the database is a set of pairs of a business query

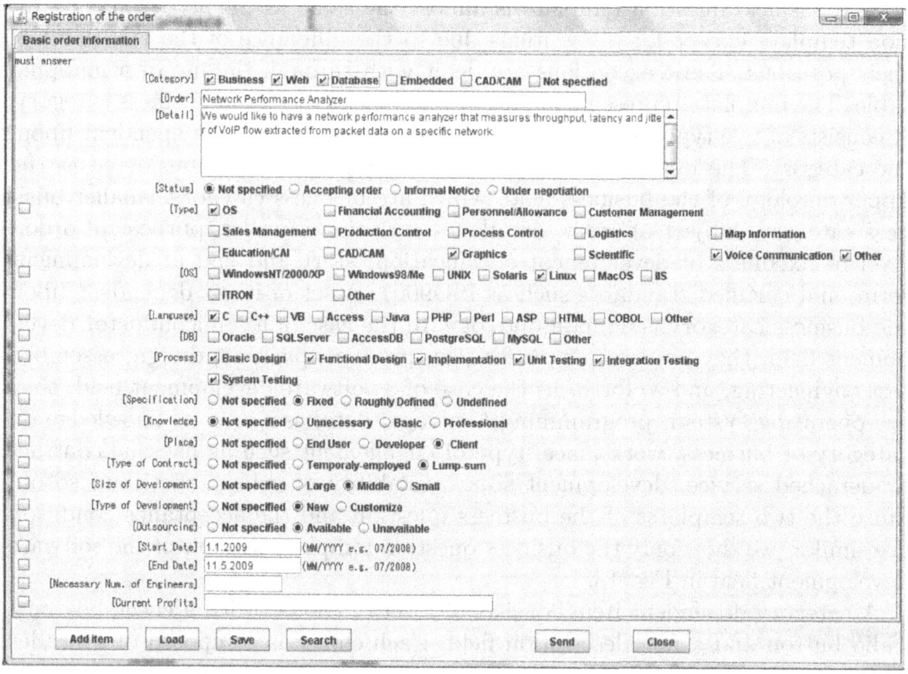

Fig. 13. Demander's Business Question Window, Software Development Field

and its answer. When a business query is created, a business transaction relevant to it will be searched for in the database with XQuery consisting of a business item name and content in the query. The searched results are displayed in a ranking list according to the score calculated for relevancy. Users will choose addresses for delivery in the list and send the query to the addresses. If the users cannot find any address that they want to send, or if they want to find new clients that are not in the history, they will issue the query to all the members of the communities specified in the query. According to the query and answer operations using the trading history, we believe that business-to-business or person-to-person relation networks will gradually be created. This basic idea is based on the knowledge of the ACP2P method [16].

5.3   Template of Business Question and Business Acceptance Condition

A demander's business question and a supplier's acceptance condition are defined as a CSV-like template. They can easily be exchanged according to the business category of a company. The reason why we adopt a template-based query and an acceptance condition is that they would easily be described by anyone who is not good at operating computers. According to our interviews with some company people, our decisions were empirically acceptable.

The business question template is almost the same as the acceptance condition template except for a few items due to the difference of the viewpoint of their positions. These exceptions are dealt with through the use of a mapping table. The template represents a kind of small ontology of the business category. It consists of two types of items: the items independent of, and dependent upon, the category. The items independent to the category can be considered as the upper ontology of the business field, which are business category, smaller business category, subject of order, detailed description of order, purpose of order, level of fixedness of development specification, start and end of development term, and certified standards such as ISO9001. A set of items dependent upon the business category is domain ontology. In the case of a semiconductor development field, they are process, wafer size, product, package, design, assembly, test engineering, and so forth. In the case of a software development field, they are operating system, programming language, database, level of knowledge on category of business, work place, type of engagement such as package contract or detached service, development size, availability of subcontract, and so on. Since the two templates of the business question and the acceptance condition are similar, we show only the business question template window of the software development field in Fig. 13.

A category dependent item consists of a set of choices with a check box or a radio button and a free description field. Each choice is composed of a header and a description field for describing comments. By having question templates selectable, matching between various industries becomes possible.

5.4   Robust Routing on ACZ Network

We assume that a lot of users of our system use their computers on their private network and connect to the Internet via a NAT (Network Address Translation) or NAPT (Network Address Port Translation) system. Since our system provides one-to-one communication, we have to support routing via NAT or NAPT. When an agent is starting to join a community, the ACZ where the portal agent of the community resides keeps the connection with the ACZ where the agent resides. Thus, the ACZ of the community portal agent can make a communication with the ACZs of community member agents. When another agent joins the community, the ACZ of the portal agent also keeps the connection with the ACZ of the agent. This constructs star-shaped connections between the ACZ of the portal agent and the ACZs of other member agents. Although this star-shaped routing may not be scalable, we made sure that it could support more than 1000 agents through our empirical experiments in which 512 pairs of agents sent 1 Gigabyte file with each other without a break just after each agent received the file of the other agent. Supporting 1000 agents is enough for our current objectives because the current targets are closed communities, each of which has less than 1000 members.

In this situation, we conducted the following experiments. First, we added one pair of agents, and made one of them send files to the other. At that time, we measured the relationship between the size of a file and the transfer time of

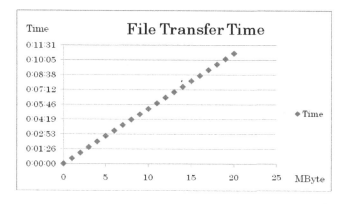

Fig. 14. Relationships between Time and Size of File Transferred

the file. The experiments were conducted on a cluster machine with 32 Personal Computers (PCs) connected on a Giga bit ether network.

Figure 14 depicts the relationship between the transfer time of a file and the size of the file in the experiments. It says that the transfer time was proportional to the size of the transferred file and its transfer rate was 250 kbps. Considering the network with 1 Gpbs was shared by 513 pairs of agents, the value 250 kbps was proper.

We also made sure that our systems are robust when agents of some PCs suddenly join and leave the network by powering on/off, getting started running or falling into sleep mode by opening or shutting the display of a laptop PC, and inserting/pulling the network cables to/from the laptop PC.

6 Conclusion and Future Work

This paper discussed ACN-based system development and described an ACN-based Collaboration Support System, especially a detail of a Business Matching Support System as a case study.

We have just finished developing a beta test version of the system. It suggests that this system is useful for determining business companies to be contacted. Since it is important to meet a contact person of a target business company and to talk to that person by face to face, business people may be reluctant to rely solely on this system. Such a face-to-face meeting is not supported by the system; however after meeting, the system can help to exchange important information that can lead to making a contract.

Our system has many capabilities to be applied to various kinds of fields and languages by changing the matching templates.

In addition, not only business matching, but also a distributed SNS system or a dynamic mailing list service system will be supported by the mechanism described in this paper. Especially, the secure distributed SNS service system is very useful for exchanging secure messages among specific people that consist of a community. A snapshot of the system is shown in Fig.15. It supports some

Fig. 15. An Example of ACN-based SNS System

crucial mechanisms for practical distributed systems such as dynamic portal role assignment service mechanisms, data synchronization mechanisms among portal agents and exclusive access control mechanisms of encryption keys[11]. We will explain more about this system in the near future.

References

1. Decker, K., Sycara, K., Williamson, M.: Middle-agents for the internet. In: Proceedings of the Fifteenth International Joint Conference on Artificial Intelligence (IJCAI 1997), pp. 578–584 (1997)
2. Sycara, K., Lu, J., Klusch, M., Widoff, S.: Matchmaking among heterogeneous agents on the internet. In: Proceedings AAAI Spring Symposium on Intelligent Agents in Cyberspace (1999),
http://www.cs.cmu.edu/~softagents/papers/aaai4.pdf

3. Mine, T., Kogo, A., Amamiya, M.: Agent-community-based peer-to-peer information retrieval and its evaluation. Systems and Computers in Japan 37(13), 1–10 (2006)
4. Ferreira, D.R., Ferreira, J.J.P.: Building an e-marketplace on a peer-to-peer infrastructure. International Journal of Computer Integrated Manufacturing 17(3), 254–264 (2004)
5. Zhong, G., Amamiya, S., Takahashi, K., Mine, T., Amamiya, M.: The design and application of kodama system. IEICE Transactions INF.& SYST. E85-D(04), 637–646 (2002)
6. Kimura, K., Satoshi Amamiya, T.M., Amamiya, M.: A semi-structured overlay network for large-scale peer-to-peer systems. In: The Seventh International Workshop on Agents and Peer-to-Peer Computing (May 2008)
7. Ishida, T.: Towards computation over communities. In: Ishida, T. (ed.) Community Computing and Support Systems. LNCS, vol. 1519, pp. 1–10. Springer, Heidelberg (1998)
8. Tamura, H., Hidaka, T., Oishi, T., Kikuma, K.: Transparent community:creating a novel community framework using p2p technologies. In: The 10th international Conference on Human-Computer Interaction (June 2003)
9. Hoshiai, T., Koyanagi, K., Sukhbaatar, B., Kubota, M., Shibata, H., Sakai, T.: Sion architecture: Semantic information-oriented network architecture (in Japanese). IEICE Trans. Commn. J84-B(3), 411–424 (2001)
10. Modarresi, A., Mamat, A., Ibrahim, H., Mustapha, N.: A community-based peer-to-peer model based on social networks. International Journal of Computer Science and Network Security 8(4), 272–277 (2008)
11. Kimura, K., Mine, T., Amamiya, S., Amamiya, M.: Construction method for robust and secure agent-community network (in Japanese). In: Joint Agent Workshops and Symposium 2008 (October 2008) CD–ROM
12. Ratnasamy, S., Francis, P., Handley, M., Karp, R., Shenker, S.: A scalable content-addressable network. In: SIGCOMM, pp. 161–172 (2001)
13. Stoica, I., Morris, R., Karger, D., Kaashoek, M.F., Balakrishnan, H.: Chord: A scalable peer-to-peer lookup service for internet applications. In: Proceedings of the 2001 conference on applications, technologies, architectures, and protocols for computer communications, pp. 149–160 (2001)
14. Takahashi1, K., Mitsuyuki, Y., Mine, T., Sakurai, K., Amamiya, M.: Design and implementation of security mechanisms for a hierarchical community-based multi-agent system. In: The 10th Pacific Rim International Workshop on Multi-Agents (November 2007)
15. Mine, T., Kogo, A., Amamiya, S., Amamiya, M.: Refinement of the acp2p by sharing user-feedbacks and learning query-responder-age nt-relationships. In: The 8th International Conference on Autonomous Agents and MultiAgent Systems (May 2009) (to appear)
16. Mine, T., Matsuno, D., Kogo, A., Amamiya, M.: Design and implementation of agent community based peer-to-peer information retrieval method. In: Klusch, M., Ossowski, S., Kashyap, V., Unland, R. (eds.) CIA 2004. LNCS (LNAI), vol. 3191, pp. 31–46. Springer, Heidelberg (2004)

Author Index